AF323027

Son of the Cypresses

Son of the Cypresses

*Memories, Reflections, and Regrets
from a Political Life*

Meron Benvenisti

*Translated by Maxine Kaufman-Lacusta in
Consultation with Michael Kaufman-Lacusta*

UNIVERSITY OF CALIFORNIA PRESS
Berkeley • *Los Angeles* • *London*

University of California Press, one of the most
distinguished university presses in the United States,
enriches lives around the world by advancing
scholarship in the humanities, social sciences, and
natural sciences. Its activities are supported by the UC
Press Foundation and by philanthropic contributions
from individuals and institutions. For more
information, visit www.ucpress.edu.

University of California Press
Berkeley and Los Angeles, California

University of California Press, Ltd.
London, England

Library of Congress Cataloging-in-Publication Data
Benvenisti, Meron, 1934–.
    Memories, reflections, and regrets from a political
life / Meron Benvenisti, translated by Maxine
Kaufman-Lacusta in consultation with Michael
Kaufman-Lacusta
        p. cm.
    Includes bibliographical references and index.
    ISBN-13: 978-0-520-23825-1 (cloth : alk. paper)
    1. Israel—Politics and government—20th
century. 2. Arab-Israeli conflict—Influence. 3. Arab-
Israeli conflict—1993—Peace. 4. Israel—Ethnic
relations. 5. Benvenisti, David. 6. Jews—Israel—
Biography. 7. Sephardim—Israel—Biography.
I. Title.
DS126.995.B46   2006
956.9405092—dc22   2006032386

Manufactured in the United States of America
16   15   14   13   12   11   10   09   08   07
10   9   8   7   6   5   4   3   2   1

This book is printed on New Leaf EcoBook 50, a
100% recycled fiber of which 50% is de-inked post-
consumer waste, processed chlorine-free. EcoBook 50
is acid-free and meets the minimum requirements of
ANSI/ASTM D5634-01 (*Permanence of Paper*).

The publisher and the author gratefully
acknowledge the generous contributions
to this book provided by the United States
Institute of Peace and by the Jewish Studies
Endowment Fund of the University of
California Press Foundation.

Contents

A Founding Father

I had long been grappling with the question of where to begin my story. Before even thinking of the story itself, I had pondered where the opening scene should be set. This initial staking out of the narrative territory was important to me, because it would ground events and thoughts in concrete reality. I could begin at a beginning, at my beginning or at my parents' beginnings: in Jerusalem, or in Salonika and Suwalk; in Eretz Israel (Hebrew for "the Land of Israel"), or in the Balkans and the "Pale of Settlement"—but for some reason I was especially drawn to Zichron Ya'akov, where, a few years after his arrival in Palestine, my father had been sent as a teacher, a calling he followed throughout his long life. He was twenty-four when he came to Zichron at the time, an impecunious teacher living "in a room outside the village, whose windows faced the sea and Mount Carmel on one side and the eucalyptuses of the village on the other."

AN IMPECUNIOUS TEACHER

My father was discharged from the British Army late in June 1920, his commander providing him with discharge papers that indicated his "appropriate profession" as "teacher." After a few months substituting at a Sephardic school in Jerusalem, he was sent by the Yishuv's (Jewish community's) education committee to teach at the school in Zichron Ya'akov. He thus began a career that would span more than sixty years.

We shall never know if the decision to send my father to Zichron, "a large, established community boasting a school complete with all grades, wonderful scenery, and a diverse population," was a result of the enthusiastic letter he had written to the education committee: "Send me to some corner of Eretz Israel," he wrote, "give me children, and I shall dedicate myself to them with all my heart. I feel I have sufficient energies to dedicate to the education of children." Writing to a friend a year after his arrival in Zichron, he enthuses: "All my time is spent immersed heart and soul in the world of the children. All my leisure hours . . . are given over to the pupils. I take part in all their games and outings, and in their most trivial interests, etc. Now it is harvest season, and every evening I roll with them from haystack to haystack, as if I had returned to the days of my childhood—as if I wished to collect a debt from my childhood, which passed without harvest and without the fragrance of God's broad fields. My heart is full of love for the pupils."

Years later when I was an adult, it seemed to me that the love he had lavished upon generation after generation of pupils was stolen from his own sons, toward whom he remained remote and detached.

My father had indeed completed his studies at a teachers' seminary in Jerusalem and was a qualified teacher, but his work nonetheless presented numerous difficulties: "It is an unforgivable sin that the Department of Education did not take into account our lack of teaching experience and sent us off to remote areas, without [first providing us with] an opportunity to obtain experience." "The information," he continued, "I draw from French books and unorganized notes that I have acquired in the village." He lacked not only information but also the Hebrew terms for various objects, not to mention concepts in mathematics and the sciences. Only six or seven years had gone by since the "battle of the languages" that had culminated in the gradual replacement of German by Hebrew as the language of instruction at the teachers' seminary and the Technion. "Even today," he wrote, "I am groping in the fog and must "row" and "row" until I reach the shore I seek." For instance, the fourth grade nature studies curriculum included the following subjects: "Lime (chalk, marble, [production of] sulfuric acid), clay, sand (manufacture of glass), shale, salt (crystalline). Onions, bulbs, fava beans, lupine, clover, the rose, the pepper tree, peas, bananas, codfish, the nightingale, the starling, the ant, the fly, the jackal, domestic cattle, ducks and geese, the grapevine, the oleander, the wolf, the scarab beetle, the spider, the gecko, the sprout (dicotyledonous), the structure and function of the root. Zoology: the metamorphosis of insects. . . . I excel in calisthenics as well as in singing. This Sunday I shall begin teaching musical notation, and I have already prepared several lessons. We shall see how I manage."

SALONIKA

No wonder he complained, "When shall I tend to my soul, when shall I get the full measure of mental relaxation I require?" And inevitably there arose feelings of homesickness for the city of his birth, Salonika: "The question of travel to Salonika has been reawakened in me. . . . I know that this is only [self-]deception. . . . It would require crossing the sea, purifying myself, and leaving the limited world I have given myself over to."

The day in the fall of 1913 that my father left Salonika on a Greek vessel, accompanied on the voyage to Palestine by his father, he received a letter in Hebrew, written in the ancient Rashi script used for the Judeo-Spanish (Ladino) language. His close friend Nathan Shalem wrote: "My dear beloved one—My purpose in writing this letter is not to write you a letter on the occasion of your journey, but to bitterly bewail from the depths of my heart your parting from me. . . . I shall find comfort in this, however—that you are walking about in the land of our forefathers, the land we have yearned for, body and soul. I thought I must give you a memento so that you would not forget me; after searching and searching, I could not find a worthy keepsake for you except for a letter bordered with flowers."

My father answered this letter from Jerusalem five weeks later—also in Rashi script—with a fall flower that he had picked and dried affixed to the top: "I read your letter, which, at first sight and without digging too deeply, gladdened my sad soul, without my even endeavoring to see the signature of the writer of those lines, the flowers fastened round about it tell me . . . it is the hand of Nathan Shalem. . . . Your bitter cry at my parting from you and your joy that I journey to Eretz Israel are only two sentences, but I prize them greatly. You are sad that I have parted from you, and my answer is that I, too, am sad. But who is the more bereft? You have been separated from one friend and I from all of them at once. Today I feel the word 'parting' everywhere I go, in every-thing I do, and all thoughts of childhood go straight-straight to this city that I have left . . . to that home, to that Nathan Shalem like unto whom there is no other, and then my tears flow from my eyes and I weep."

Not many months passed before the two friends met again, with the arrival of a group of young Salonikans who had come to study at the Herzliyya Gymnasium in Tel Aviv, but ended up settling in Jerusalem.

Salonika. Perhaps, after all, the story should have begun there.

More than eight years after my father had left his home and "gone up to Jerusalem" (he defined his goal thus, and not as "Eretz Israel"), his longing for his family (who had remained in Salonika) and his city— "which embodies for me the best memories of the happy days of my youth"—was powerful and persistent. On his first visit to Tel Aviv in September 1916, three years after his *aliya* (immigration to the Holy Land), he muses: "It is pleasant with its handsome, tall buildings and with the Jewish atmosphere palpable everywhere. I swam in the waters of the sea, and the sight of the sea awakened many memories of Salonika in me, and I greatly wished to cross this sea. Who knows when this desire of mine will be fulfilled?"

My father's motivations for "going up" to Jerusalem to study there were similar to those impelling Jewish young people in Poland or Russia in those days: a blend of nationalist longings, personal motives, and reaction to external political events such as wars, revolutions, and persecutions. But their experience of the transition from Occident to Orient differed greatly in depth. The *oleh* (immigrant) from eastern Europe was thrown, unprepared, into the colorful, dusty tumult of the port of Jaffa: the physical surroundings—so different from the landscape of his northern homeland—and the unfamiliar human landscape. For my father and grandfather, by contrast, arriving in the land was like returning home: "We were surrounded by tarboosh-wearing Turkish customs officers and clerks. . . . With the aid of the pure Turkish that we spoke and our familiarity with Turkish etiquette, we speedily negotiated the various official procedures as full-fledged Ottoman citizens." One must remember that Jewish Salonika was not a marginal element in the Ottoman city; it was its heart.

The customary Zionist distinction between "exile" and "homeland" was less acute, to my father's way of seeing things. After all, he came from a city the majority of whose residents were Jews, who dominated the realms of finance, commerce, the port and fishing, culture, and education. My father proudly states: "The city of Salonika acquired a worldwide reputation for its Jewish 'color' and for its autonomy in all branches of the economy—a kind of 'state within a state.' During that era, a person did not experience the reality of exile."

His picturesque descriptions of public and private life in Salonika, of his education and Zionist activism, and particularly of his family's lineage, are full of pride in belonging to the Sephardic Jewish tribe that settled in the ancient Macedonian-Byzantine-Ottoman city founded in the fourth century B.C.E. The city was named after a half sister of Alexander the Great, Thessaloníki, whose name commemorated the victory (*niki*) of their father, Philip of Macedon, in Thessaly.

In 1913, the year my father left his hometown, a census showed that the Jewish community of Salonika was the predominant ethnic group. Out of 157,000 residents, the Jewish community numbered 62,000, the Greek, 40,000, and the Muslim (Ottomans), 46,000 souls. My father's renowned teacher, Dr. Yitzhak Epstein, who had come in 1908 from Palestine to minister to the Salonika Jewish community's educational institutions, wrote:

> It is as if this community has given the lie to reality, to exile, to the dominant environment—different from it in religion, language, and way of life— . . . not only in the synagogue, Talmud Torah [Jewish religious elementary school], on the Sabbath and holidays, but on every workday and in the essence of everyday life. In the marketplace and the port, in the artisanship and in manufacturing, Salonika had become a small island where a sort of Jewish autonomy prevailed, spiritual and economic at one and the same time, . . . effacing in great measure, the imprint of exile. Here Jews of stature arose, imposing in appearance and endowed with grandeur, whose faces displayed courage, self-assurance, and self-knowledge.

Father left Salonika in the autumn of 1913. Exactly one year prior to that, in October 1912, the city had been occupied by the Greek army. Thus had commenced an inexorable decline in the fortunes of the Jewish community, which suffered from the measures employed by the Greek government in its efforts to bolster the position of Salonika's Greek inhabitants and to decrease the economic influence of the Jews. My father and those of his friends who immigrated at about the same time to Jerusalem worriedly followed from afar the misfortunes that plagued their birthplace during World War I, especially the great fire of 1917, which destroyed most of the Jewish homes in Salonika (and all our family's ancient archives). But the fate of Jewish autonomy in Salonika was sealed in the aftermath of the war, when hundreds of thousands of Greek refugees expelled from Asia Minor settled there and in the surrounding area. My father's friend Yosef Uziel wrote in 1929: "The hallucination of a Jewish city in the diaspora has evaporated. . . . But even should this nightmare be fully realized, and Salonika sees the back of the last of its Jews, hundreds of years of history will not be erased."

SMOLDERING HEAPS OF ASH

Only fourteen years later, the nightmare had become reality. The entire Jewish community of Salonika, including my father's sister Sara and three brothers: Benvenisti (first name), Abraham, and Jacob, and scores of family members, perished in the Holocaust. Returning to the city of his birth in 1956, after more than forty years, he writes: "You turn this way and that and the streets shun you. Where are the dwellings of your brothers? Where the synagogues of olden days, which preserved the names of glorious communities in magnificent Sepharad? Where is my father's serene and tranquil home? All of this went up in flames in 5677 [the great fire of 1917]." He continues, referring to the more recent catastrophe:

> On the smoldering heaps of ash an alien city was built. . . . But before I could begin to comprehend the Holocaust that befell a city that had been "a mother in Israel," . . . I said to myself that I would go and stretch myself out on my ancestors' graves and bitterly lament what the Nazi foe did to the nation it exterminated. . . . Let your eyes glance here or there, all has been wiped from the face of the earth. "The house of the living" [the cemetery] is a plowed field, and beyond are new houses just recently built, and beyond them a grove of trees in bloom, and in the distance— the halls of higher learning of the youthful inhabitants of Salonika [the University of Salonika]. . . . From amongst the foliage sometimes sprout fragments of gravestones . . . upon which sacred [i.e., Hebrew] letters stand out. And it is as if they are crying out for retribution from us all. As for the dead, so for the living, one fate for both together.

Only a fraction of the gravestones in Salonika's Jewish cemetery (2,500) have been studied and their inscriptions recorded and published. From the data on these gravestones, my father was able to reconstruct his family history, and this constituted his final piece of research in the year of his death, 1993. The records of these inscriptions in old and new books, along with stories handed down from his ancestors, enabled him to trace his family's genealogy for almost five hundred years, from 1500 to the present. According to his findings, the family had its beginnings in three branches, two of which originated in southern Italy, whereas the third arose in Spain. With undisguised pride my father quotes the chronicles and the lives of his distant forebears: rabbis, judges (in religious courts), and community leaders.

Take, for example, Rabbi Chaim Shabtai (1551–1647):

> Foremost of the sages and teachers of teaching, who by virtue of his wisdom enhanced the reputation of the rabbis of Salonika in the world. . . . A distinguished and greatly respected rabbi, who inspired many disciples. . . . He permitted forty prosperous conversos [Sephardic Jews coerced into converting to Christianity] who had returned to Judaism to settle in Salonika. . . . He suffered greatly from ailments of the stomach and kidneys.

Rabbi Shabtai died at the age of ninety-two.

And here is Rabbi Yosef David (1660–1736), who was called Tsemach David (Branch of David) after his most famous book:

> He inspired many disciples, and they too were great Torah scholars. He lived to a ripe old age, leaving his mark on the lives of two generations of Salonika's Jews. . . . His posthumously published book of responsa on the four sections of the *Shulhan Aruch* [*Beit David* (Salonika, 1740–46)] is among the most famous such works. . . . Rabbi Yosef David's piety and holiness were celebrated even beyond the borders of his country. He revered Nathan of Gaza, the prophet of the false messiah Shabtai Zvi. Most of his writings were published after his death. On his gravestone is inscribed: "Called to the heavens above: a light in Israel, the right-hand pillar, the glory of his generation, his magnificence, the great rabbi, fortress and bastion, our teacher and rabbi, Yosef David. Blessed be his memory."

The presence of the Benvenisti family in Spain is noted first in Catalonia in the early eleventh century and subsequently in Castile. Don Yehudah and his son Don Avraham Benvenisti were leaders of those Spanish Jews expelled in 1492 who settled in Salonika. Yehudah's father Avraham had been treasury minister to Juan II, king of Castile, and was the author of the Valladolid Statute, which regulated the lives of the pre-expulsion Jewish communities of Spain. Accounts of the Spanish patriarchs of his family and their descendents fill the pages of various encyclopedias and were a source of pride for my father, even as he stressed that the family had two other, Italian branches, which had perhaps arrived in Italy even before the destruction of the Second Temple, and thus "had not gone into exile in the accepted sense of the word." One way or the other, my father could claim that his family had never left the shores of the Mediterranean Sea, but had only circled it until they returned to their homeland, Eretz Israel.

ELDER RABBI

The last rabbi in the line was my great-grandfather Elder Rabbi Benvenisti—Shmuel Yosef (1833–1912). In his last days, my father penned these lines about his grandfather:

> I was privileged to grow up in close proximity to my grandfather and my grandmother. The loss of my mother when I was three brought about a change in my status among the members of the family; my grandfather and grandmother set me apart from my father's household in order to bestow upon me the love and mothering that I had been robbed of. The intent of this care and nurture was to groom one of his grandsons to be his "heir" in continuing, from this generation to the next, the family tradition of serving the community in religious/public office. He called me David in honor of Rabbi Yosef David (Tsemach David).
>
> I used to accompany Grandfather to the religious courts in the offices of the Jewish community, and on Friday mornings I went with him when he set out for Jarashi, the street of the great houses of commerce, to meet there with the most prosperous merchants and be apprised of current goings-on in the mercantile world. People passing by, especially on the streets near the *mahala* [quarter], where we lived, would greet him with great respect, and some even approached and kissed his hands, while he smilingly inclined his head toward them; women peeping from windows would send their sons to kiss his hands, and grandfather would stand still for a short while, rest his hand on their heads, and bless them: "May the Lord bless you and keep you." In the synagogue, the worshippers rose to their feet upon his entry and remained standing until he had walked to his permanent place beside the *halachah* [the holy ark]. More than once, these expressions of respect seemed to him to inconvenience the congregation, and he would keep out of sight of those entering the synagogue and would go in through a side gate and straight to his place. Whenever he arrived at the rooms where the religious court sat, the square in front of the building would be thronged with widows and other unfortunates. My grandfather's calming and comforting words could be heard amid the cacophony of crying widows with their orphaned children in tow.

The larger Jewish community of Salonika was subdivided into autonomous communities according to the countries, cities, or regions from which their members had come, with each community having its own synagogue and religious and welfare institutions. Every household belonged to one of these communities, thus facilitating the tracing of family origins. Our family, for example, was affiliated with two communities, New Italy (which had split off from the original Italian community early in the eighteenth century) and the Castilian community. Among the city's numerous Jewish congregations, which included those identified with Lisbon, Catalonia, Portugal, southern Italy, Aragon, the Maghreb, new and old Sicily, and Provence—there was also the community of "Ashkenaz." These were descendents of Ashkenazi Jews who over the years had intermarried with Sephardi families; their Ashkenazi character was now recognizable only in their prayer service.

SEPHARDIM AND ASHKENAZIM

This subdivision according to ethnic group, however, did not prepare my father for the yawning chasm between Sephardim and Ashkenazim in Jerusalem: "In the Salonika community, I did not know the Ashkenazim at all. On coming to Eretz Israel, I sensed that a great abyss lay between these two elements of the community. The simple masses of Ashkenazim despised the Sephardim and saw the Sephardi as an inferior being, like 'an Arab,'" he writes in 1917. "The hatred is passed on from father to son, and even the intelligentsia is not unsullied by this sin— perhaps out of lack of familiarity." He describes a "distressing incident" on a seminary outing to the Ayalon Valley: "Our Ashkenazi brothers sang songs in Russian and 'jargon' (i.e., Yiddish) the whole time and peppered their conversation with Yiddish jokes and words. This, of course, greatly upset us and provoked a raging argument between us. Here we see the effect of the diaspora, which has divided brothers."

The affront was at times unbearable, and the resultant anger sometimes triggered fistfights. But my father concludes by exhorting his fellows, "not to be drawn into the negative phenomena of factionalism and feelings of discrimination, but to delve more deeply into the literature of the Jews of Spain and the study of the history of the Salonika Jewish community down through the generations, that we may become worthy of the name 'Sephardi' with which we were labeled upon our arrival in Eretz Israel." My father persisted in this approach all his life and was greatly angered by those of his friends who expressed their frustration and outrage at the ethnic discrimination they experienced with verbal outbursts and belligerent articles in the Sephardi press. He also decried those who would exploit Ashkenazi guilt feelings over discrimination against Sephardim for their own personal gain. In spite of this, his sense of Sephardi *grandessa* (pride) gave him an attitude of superiority and arrogance toward other Mizrahi (oriental) communities. When a man of Kurdish Jewish origin was chosen to be chair of the Council of the Sephardi and Oriental Communities, my father stopped attending, saying, "If I cannot enjoy a joke in *Judeo-Espagnole* [Ladino], why go to the meetings?" My mother also told me that he treated every setback in his professional advancement as evidence of ethnic discrimination, and that his anxiety and feelings of outrage actually made him physically ill.

Interethnic tensions also affected relations between men and women. My father writes in his journal that he had overheard "few kindergarten teachers speaking about Sephardi youngsters, saying that all the Sephardim were hated because of their base characters, and only because there are no Ashkenazi boys were the girls forced to go with Sephardim (i.e., with us) against their will." He continues: "Their attitude greatly disturbed us. . . . I spoke with my friends about this matter, saying that we have no way to respond except by dissociating ourselves from these spoilt girls and renewing the activities of our group so we might more effectively make our case against all who offended the honor of the tribe of our origins."

MY MOTHER

How did it happen, then, that my father, unlike his friends, chose an Ashkenazi woman as his wife? His journals and letters provide neither answer nor clue. He apparently hid or destroyed his letters to my mother and hers to him, despite the fact that he retained personal letters to other women and theirs to him from the years preceding his marriage. At the age of nineteen, he penned the following lines to his lady friend Ts: "Ho! Innocent heart and innocent soul! From me you have concealed your heart! And you have not given me the opportunity to share the burdens of your soul. The truth is that we were both distant and close. . . . Arouser of emotions, you aroused my heart and gave me a fever of ardor, a fever to worship you; and do not think that these emotions are the fleeting feelings that a young woman might arouse in a young man. . . . You have stirred up in me a storm wind, but have not granted me comfort and pleasure. . . . Perhaps you will laugh at my words. . . . It is a pity that we have remained both distant and close as we have."

He conducted intimate correspondence with other women, and there is no doubt at all that he did so with my mother as well, especially since it is known that they lived in separate cities for an extended period, when my mother worked in Tiberias and my father taught in Jerusalem. Father had met Mother's sister and brother-in-law, Gila and Eliezer Beloch, back in 1922 when they were living in Zichron Ya'akov, but when Mother immigrated in 1924 and lived with her sister in Zichron, Father had gone to teach at an educational institution for girls in Shfeiya (near Zichron) and then to a *kfar yeladim* ("children's village") near Afula, in the Jezreel Valley. My father and mother finally met on one of the outings of the Ramblers' Society (about which more later), apparently in 1927. By that time, Father's personal wanderings had come to an end, and he had settled down in Jerusalem. There he taught at the Beit Hakerem School, where he was to work for more than forty years. Mother, meanwhile, had completed her studies at the Hadassah Nursing School and had begun to work as a school and public health nurse, a career she pursued until close to her death at the age of ninety-six.

This is a fitting place to weave the figure of my mother, Leah, into the story. When she arrived in Palestine, she was twenty-four years old, the third of six children of Chaim (Menachem) Mendel Friedman and his wife, Marie, née Mevzos, to immigrate. The seventh, Kopl, remained in their hometown of Suwalk, on the Lithuanian-Polish-Prussian border, having taken it upon himself to continue to assist his aging parents in their diverse business endeavors. Kopl and his wife and daughter perished in the Holocaust.

HOVEVEI ZION

It was no coincidence that almost all the Friedman children made *aliya*. Their father, Chaim (Menachem) Mendel Friedman, was an ardent Zionist, a founding member of the Hovevei Zion, who owned a citrus grove in Hadera and sent his children to be educated at Hebrew day schools. He himself spoke Hebrew fluently, with Sephardi pronunciation, as favored by many proponents of the revival of the ancient tongue. Chaim Mendel Friedman was, in the words of one of his eulogizers, "a very learned man, philanthropic merchant, and dedicated businessman." He was a graduate of the Volozhyn Yeshiva in Lithuania in the days of its glory, when it produced many of the country's great rabbis, as well as the famed poet Chaim Nachman Bialik. Friedman was a wholesaler, an importer of coffee, tea, and tobacco, a lumber merchant, and owner of a soap factory. He also served for many years as head of the Community Council, the self-governing body of the city's Jews, which had been set up under Polish law in 1919, on the basis of the minorities' treaties imposed upon Poland and other countries by the Versailles Peace Conference. The council had the authority to provide services of a religious nature, maintain cemeteries and schools, and dispense welfare. To finance its operations, it was empowered to levy taxes on all the Jews in its jurisdiction.

All of the Jewish political factions took part in the council elections, including the Zionist parties. Chaim Mendel Friedman, who represented the Mizrachi religious Zionist movement, was elected chair, "because he was acceptable to all the religious groups in the city and even to many who defined themselves as non-religious, such as those affiliated with the Zionist Left and members of the Jewish intelligentsia whose opinion carried considerable weight in the city's Jewish community."[1] It was a great honor to serve as a leader of this community, which included rabbis, educators, and such personalities as the deputy finance minister in the first Bolshevik government, Aharon Scheinman (uncle of the wife of Ch. M. Friedman's son Zorah), and the man who was to become the third finance minister of the state of Israel, Pinchas Sapir, as well as Avraham Stern (whose nom de guerre was Yair), future commander of LEHI (widely referred to by English speakers as the Stern Gang).

SUWALK

The Jewish community of Suwalk could not boast of origins as ancient as those of many in the Pale of Settlement. The first Jews had settled there only at the beginning of the nineteenth century, but by mid-century the proportion of Jews in the city already exceeded 60 percent. It was a well-established community that knew how to take advantage of Suwalk's status as the commercial and administrative center of a large district, as well as of its location on the route of the Saint Petersburg–Warsaw Railroad, whose construction had been completed in 1899. The demarcation of the Polish-Lithuanian border following World War I brought Suwalk under Polish sovereignty, along with only a quarter of the surrounding district; the remaining three-quarters of the district was granted to Lithuania. The city was thus stripped of its economic hinterland, as well as of its position as a commercial and transportation crossroads. This precipitated an acceleration in the rate of emigration from the city, partly to Eretz Israel to join in the Zionist pioneering effort and partly to the United States. This emigration did not include the more comfortably established of the city's Jews, despite the fact that many of them were active Zionists. Even the leaders of the Zionist parties made no effort to immigrate to Eretz Israel. They were supportive of their children who did so, but they themselves continued to believe that no evil would ever befall them in their home.

Chaim Mendel Friedman was among those who encouraged their offspring to make *aliya,* but first he made sure that his children finished gymnasium (secondary school), and that the boys received an academic education. My mother, Leah, graduated from the Hebrew Gymnasium in Grodno, the big city adjacent to Suwalk. Her diploma, dated June 1919, states that she studied "French Language and Literature, German Language and Literature, Russian Language and Literature, Latin, Jewish History, Algebra, Geometry, Physics, Chemistry, General History, and Psychology." Her niece Shoshana recalls that Mother's education and her continuing interest in philosophy and psychology led to difficulties in her relations with her fellow nursing students who had been born and raised in Palestine, and whose education was "grade-school only, and [whose] attitude to the profession was primitive." Her rebellious nature did not make relationships any easier for her either: "She had been a rebel since childhood and always acted in accordance with her own ideas, even when this meant swimming against the stream." Thus, recounts her niece, my mother decided to appear at her marriage to my father in October 1931 wearing not a white bridal gown but a flowered red dress! Unlike her brothers and sisters, she refused to return to visit Suwalk after she emigrated. Her father, who became a widower in 1930, carried on with his private business ventures and public activity and according to family members, "did not make *aliya* despite his desire to do so, because he could not bear to desert the Jewish community. He felt this was his responsibility, and the other community members felt likewise." Ch. M. Friedman died in 1938, one year before the outbreak of World War II.

In the months immediately following the German conquest of Poland, it became clear that Suwalk's Jewish community was doomed. In October 1939, the city was occupied by the German army, and after a short time in Soviet hands (between October and December 1939), all the Jews were expelled, some to Lithuania, some to Soviet-held territory, and some to the south. Most ultimately went to their deaths in the extermination camps.

ALIYA

The lives of the Friedman siblings who settled in Palestine were typical of those led by the not very large group of immigrants—no more than a few ten thousand—who had chosen *aliya* for Zionist ideological motives and had not immigrated after fleeing pogroms and other forms of persecution. The eldest sister, Frieda-Gila, arrived in 1919, but was deported along with some of her friends who were not allowed into the country.

They returned to Trieste, from whence they had sailed to Palestine, and remained there an entire year until, in 1920, they received permission to immigrate. Gila's friends went to Kibbutz Ein Harod, while she worked first as a nurse in Hadera, then planting trees on Mount Carmel; she subsequently joined the group that founded the village of Binyamina. She married Eliezer Beloch, a hydraulic engineer engaged in draining the Kabara marshes near Zichron. Eliezer later established a well-drilling company that specialized in deep wells, locating water in places where no one believed there was any to be found. When the company went bankrupt, he found work as a surveyor. The family moved to Pardess Hannah and later to Haifa. Gila worked in the field of immigrant absorption until the end of her days in 1961.

The eldest brother, David Aryeh, made *aliya* in 1925, served as ophthalmologist of the Herzliyya Gymnasium, and also ran a flourishing private clinic. He continued the literary activities he had begun while in Russia, and belonged to the circle of writers that included, among others, Sha'ul Tschernichovsky and Ya'akov Fichman. He edited the Jewish Medical Association's professional journal, *Harofeh,* from 1929 until his death in 1957 and wrote articles and essays in the field of medicine, as well as literary and art criticism. He was one of the earliest curators of the Tel Aviv Museum and a patron of the arts. Many of the artists he supported became, in the fullness of time, among the most prominent in the country.

My mother graduated in 1926 and was sent to work in a *tipat halav* (drop of milk) mother-and-baby clinic run by Hadassah in Tiberias and then to a tuberculosis sanatorium in Safed. When the disturbances referred to as "the 1929 incidents" began, my mother was already in Jerusalem working at a tipat halav clinic in the old city. Despite the fact that she was a midwife and hospital nurse, she decided to dedicate herself to the job of school and public health nurse. These were dubbed "green nurses" because of their green uniforms with a red Star of David on their triangular white collars. The green nurses cared for mothers and babies at clinics where they weighed and examined the infants, treated their illnesses, and prepared hot cereal and soup for them. The nurses also made house calls, taught mothers how to maintain a hygienic environment, and brought them modern ideas of what constituted a suitable menu for young children. In the primitive conditions that prevailed in the areas of the "old Yishuv" (pre-Zionist Jewish community), the nurses' work was quite demanding, and consisted primarily of battling health problems that were a product of inadequate sanitation, such as ringworm, trachoma (which, if untreated, can lead to blindness), and serious diseases affecting the digestive tract, including various forms of typhus and dysentery. In the harsh living conditions in the older sections of Jerusalem, especially in the damp cold of that city's winters, diphtheria and rheumatic fever were also endemic. My mother loved working among the *Haredi* (ultra-Orthodox) women of Mea Shearim, especially in the section called Batei Ungarn. These women, often the mothers of as many as six to eight children, had especially hard lives, and they reminded Mother of her own mother, with her black dress, her wig, her modest smile. Over the decades that she worked at this job, my mother cared for thousands of young families in Jerusalem's northern neighborhoods: Geula, Kerem Avraham, Mea Shearim, and others. In Jerusalem they used to say: "He who did not pass by way of Nurse Leah Friedman must have fallen into the hands of the teacher David Benvenisti."

After they married, my parents rented a two-room apartment in the Bucharan Quarter. The kitchen was a shack in the yard, at the far end of which stood the outhouse. After two years, they moved to roomier accommodations on the border of Geula, where I was born in 1934— but I am getting ahead of myself.

By the time of my birth, my father already held firm opinions regarding what he referred to as his "life's objective," a concept that encompassed his professional, national, and political aspirations. He had originally come to Eretz Israel with the intent of studying at a rabbinical college in Jerusalem. When he arrived, a sensitive young man of sixteen, he was greatly moved by the fact of actually being in the Holy City. Reflecting on his first Seder night spent outside the family circle and away from the city of his birth, he wrote: "Far am I, far from them, but where do my feet stand? In Jerusalem. And upon hearing this name, the obstacles recede, the homesickness vanishes." My father's *aliya* to the land was an expression of Zionist aspirations that had been nurtured by "emissaries" from Palestine—foremost among whom was the esteemed pedagogue Yitzhak Epstein—and also via direct contact with the Zionist institutions that were springing up throughout eastern and central Europe. But in my father's case, the religious component dominated. A journal entry dated April 1914 reads: "My initial education I received from my grandfather, N'Vinisti Shmuel [sic], at whose knee I was raised. With him I learned Torah, and his influence on me was immeasurable. He inspired me to appreciate all the religious points of view and to become a future bearer of the banner of religion, and to that end, I came to Eretz Israel." His original intent in coming to Jerusalem was "to carry the banner of religion in one of the places in the Balkans," and he did not flinch from writing the following sentence: "To Eretz Israel I am not bound; the Diaspora calls to me, and it is my duty to go there."

A short stay in Jerusalem caused him to rethink his "life's objective." The rabbinical college did not live up to his expectations: "The institute is not of a high level." He was unable to understand "how I had exchanged a religious social atmosphere full of wisdom and spiritual activity in my city (Salonika) for this institute in Jerusalem cut off from the life of the community." He decided to leave the rabbinical college and to enroll in the Hebrew Teachers' Seminary (where the language of instruction was Hebrew), joining his group of friends from Salonika who had arrived together in 1914. This was a hard choice, since he had long seen his vocation as studying for the rabbinate. Thus, at first he represents the decision as not binding: "At the present time I wish to complete my studies, and as time goes by, the objective of my life will become clear." But on the same day, he writes, "I am entering the Hebrew Seminary because I view it as the most important institution where the Hebrew spirit prevails, which is essential to a Hebrew youth who has set as his objective in life an involvement in intellectual pursuits." Elsewhere he elaborates: "The rabbinate and teaching have common characteristics. Their shared goals are to educate the younger generation in national and human values and to provide guidance for a decent life."

His decision to transfer to the secular-nationalist teachers' seminary came three months before the start of World War I, and the events of the war reinforced my father's inclination to devote his life "to furthering his studies in a pure Hebrew spirit in accordance with Zionist and nationalist values." Hence, he gave himself fully to the struggle for the exclusive use of Hebrew as the language of instruction and everyday use, and his journal abounds with references to the so-called language war. He also enthusiastically participated in the founding of a "group of Sephardi young people whose objective would be to dignify the image of the Sephardim," and he viewed the imparting of the history of those expelled from Spain as being of utmost importance.

His visits to the new Jewish villages filled him with pride and joy, but these emotions were tempered with criticism: "I imagined that the villages would be more nationalistic, but in all of them corruption is rampant; the essence, the inwardness is lacking. No longer are they animated by the ideal, but by materialism instead. Even the Hebrew language is not dominant in village life, the farmers' meetings being conducted in 'jargon.' Only the younger generation, the small children in particular, speak Hebrew. If striving for material things were accompanied by the aspiration to return to spiritual–nationalist deeds, then would we be able to boast about our villages. Now we have only a pretty exterior, but the soul is lacking." Nevertheless, in one place he writes appreciatively: "Boys are sitting on their land and breathing in its pure air. In the villages a new, free life is being fashioned, and the first foundations for the great edifice of the People of Israel have already been erected."

THE JEWISH LEGION

My father's commitment to the service of the Jewish people reached its peak following the liberation of Jerusalem in December 1917, when he participated in an event aimed at recruiting volunteers for the Jewish Legion of the British Army (Royal Fusiliers, 38th battalion; later 40th). For him, volunteering for the Jewish Legion had been a supreme act of pioneering, vital to the fulfillment of Zionism. In his journal, he quotes Berl Katzenelson (a leading figure in the socialist Zionist movement and one of the foremost advocates of Jewish enlistment in the British war effort): "The Jewish Legion adds a new meaning to our life in Eretz Israel; it is the need of the hour, just as the introduction of the principle of 'Hebrew labor' to our settlement policy was in the past." In a letter to a friend who had not enlisted, my father writes in October 1918: "The days were days of stormy heart and uplifted spirit, and the idea that captivated us before we undertook any concrete action, this idea has been actualized. With great diligence, we have continued our military studies in order to be prepared at the earliest possible opportunity to take part in a war for the liberation of our country."

He identified with the sentiments of one of the volunteers, who declared: "Our national soul has sunk in the mud and slime; we need to cleanse it, to bring to it atonement, and this atonement will come by the spilling of our blood; we need to spill our blood. We must show that we are not in the least an abject and contemptible people that accepts charity. We must show that we know how to spill our blood for the liberation of our land." Of the moment when he was handed the recruitment papers to sign, my father writes: "They gave me ten minutes to decide. These ten minutes were sacred to me, and I shall never forget them as long as I live. . . . In the end I came to the realization that I must volunteer *unconditionally* [underlined]. The nation calls and [we] must rally 'round the flag. . . My hand trembled when I wrote my name. . . . Here I am, now a Hebrew soldier, a son of my people. At that moment I dedicated my life to the liberation of my homeland."

His military service was a long process, which nurtured his nationalist and patriotic values and was rich in formative experiences that influenced the course of his life. In the last piece in the "Legion Journal" that he kept, he writes thus: "A period pregnant with adventure . . . unforgettable experiences . . . has come to an end. . . . We shall yet be aided by the military knowledge we acquired in the Legion in our role of defending the land. As for my friends and myself, we are today giving up the sword for the book."

But here lay his great disappointment: "Eretz Israel was liberated from the Turks, and we, though schooled in war, were not able to participate in her liberation. . . . Our primary function was fulfilled by others." The Jewish battalions played hardly any part at all in the fighting for Palestine, and my father's military activity was limited to guarding headquarters and camps for Turkish prisoners of war and escorting military trains. But despite everything, he continued to believe that the Jewish Legion had "another role that was as important as the first . . . to serve as the basis for a future Jewish militia. . . . Thus, many think that our battalion will act as a garrison force in the land." But this hope, too, rapidly faded; the soldiers of the battalion were not even permitted to go to the defense of Jerusalem's Jewish population, which was under Arab attack in April 1920, and ultimately it was disbanded.

KNOWING THE LAND

There was no stage in my father's life that was not infused with devotion to nationalist goals. His dedication to education and to imparting *Yediat Ha'aretz* ("Knowing the Land") to the general public frequently impelled him to reiterate his commitment to Zionist ideals when expressing himself on these matters, whether in writing or orally: "How severe the labor pains of our land," he writes to the schoolgirls he taught in 1928. "The way is full of obstacles, and sometimes the ground drops out from under our feet; many are the failures and many the affronts, and yet there is something here that you can rely upon so [that] your feet will not stumble and that, in spite of everything, accompanies you all along your way: . . . you know that there is a point to all this suffering—the sense of creation is palpable in everything."

My father's attitude toward our Arab neighbors was typical of his generation. It was characterized by almost complete disregard for their existence, with their being mentioned only in the context of acts of violence. The first such reference in his journal was in the winter of 1915: "Even in our land there is no rest. Among the Arabs there have arisen men who are inciting the simple masses to attack the Jews. Jewish youths have gathered in secret to set up self-defense for when it may be required and have sworn to sacrifice their lives for the peace of the land."

It was especially important to him that he be remembered as a member and officer in the Haganah, and in his archives he kept the papers announcing his appointment as "secretary of the Haganah committee" in Zichron, and as "commander [of] the detachment guarding the northern front (beside the hospital)." In a letter dated May 1921, he writes: "I was devoted body and soul to the defense of the village. At night I did guard duty, and I slept under the open sky outside the village, gun in hand and prepared for any eventuality. While on guard duty at night, and particularly on those nights when we anticipated an attack and prepared ourselves for battle, how happy I was. I did not think of death. My heart filled with joy, not because this might be my opportunity to fight and die for the homeland (I do not believe that a man is happy in anticipation of death, even for the sake of the homeland), but simply because I thought that this was a means by which I might resolve all of life's questions, and that all the struggles of my soul might come to an end, as well as all ephemeral strivings and hopes." He deleted his reflections on death from the letter as quoted in his autobiography.

He devoted considerable thought to the name by which Arab violence should be known: "incidents," "pogroms or massacres," or "war." A 1920 journal entry refers to "pogroms in Jerusalem"; however, in 1929, he writes to a friend: "On Friday the war began, and under no circumstances shall I agree to the word 'pogroms.' Use of this name is justified only in Hebron [where Jews were murdered with shocking brutality]." In his letter, he approvingly quotes the wondering question of little Ra'aya from the second grade, "What did we do to them [the Arabs] that they're attacking us?" In 1936, he pens the following description to a friend abroad: "The land is immersed in darkness, blood, fire, and clouds of smoke. 'Children are playing before us' [a biblical expression referring to the actions of irresponsible persons], destroying property, disrupting transportation; and the authorities, in their folly, stand idly by. When they locate the leaders, they do not harm, or even warn, them. And of course, we have to pay for all this. It should be noted that the Arab village is quiet, and the rioters are primarily rabble. The Jewish Yishuv calmly goes about its business, bites its tongue, and despite everything, continues its efforts and builds."

In the partition dispute of 1937, which saw the Jewish community split between those who supported the Peel Commission's report recommending the partition of Palestine and those who opposed it, my father stood with the latter: "There are rumors afoot regarding cantonization," he writes to a friend, "and we, where do we come down on this question? Will we permit them to divide our land? Will we hand the [Judean and Samarian] hills over to them? How right you were," he continues, "when you spoke out against the leaders who sent us to settle on the Shephela [coastal plain] and kept us away from the hills."

Teaching Knowing the Land had always been an activity requiring patriotic commitment, and the school subject *moledet* (homeland) was an important vehicle for indoctrination. In my father's words, it "was not like the mere study of geography but [was] like a course of studies embodying important nationalist-educational values." The hiking clubs that my father founded along with his childhood friend Nathan Shalem and others were much more than a simple leisure-time pursuit. The minutes of the Founding Assembly of the Ramblers' Society, held on 20 November 1927, quote Dr. Shalem:

> We may have a variety of objectives; however, the principal one is to know our homeland, and the principal means—hiking. And besides the primary objective of knowing the homeland, the athletic side of hiking is important as well. I visualize our society as taking the form of the alpine societies that exist in Europe and the rest of the world. This latter objective may have great importance. Take, for example, the fact that only with the help of Italian alpinists was Italy able to occupy the Tyrol, etc. [after World War I].

Nathan Shalem had studied at an Italian university and had been influenced in his thinking by the Italian nationalist movement and its hero, Gabriele D'Anunzzio. My father, on the other hand, had a less heroic vision. "We must hike and that's all. . . . Experience has taught me to shun publicity and large crowds. In order to even approach the realization of Shalem's program, we would have to hike for at least a year and know our strength." He did not, however, cease to emphasize the nationalistic objectives of the society, whose official name was the Eretz Israel Ramblers Society and whose motto was "Who shall give me leave to ramble in places that G-d has revealed to thy prophets and thy messengers?" (Yehuda Halevi).

THE RAMBLERS

In an article about the Ramblers Society published in 1933 in the Israeli daily *Ha'aretz,* the writer—identified only by the initials B. E.—describes the society's activities:

> Two young teachers, Dr. Nathan Shalem and David Benvenisti, founded the society, and for the past few years their enterprise has been growing quietly and without fanfare. This society, begun by a handful of Jerusalemites, has become a nationwide federation with numerous members and many branches; and from time to time, hundreds of young people leave behind our cities and villages, the conflict and arguments of political parties, uniforms and slogans, or the cafes, and journey to the wilderness of Judea, ascend the mountains of our land and descend into its valleys, come to the villages of our [Arab] neighbors and are guests in the tents of the Bedouin, and find their way to every forgotten corner and every place where no Jewish foot has trodden in our lifetimes. Thus do the Ramblers combine the beautiful with the effective: they enjoy the glories of nature and the fresh air, and at the same time, they are learning the lay of the land by "seeing it with their own eyes." . . . And to what the Ramblers are seeing with their own eyes is added an enormously powerful emotion: love—a deep love for the homeland, which contains within it the yearnings of countless generations of Jews.

At the seventh general meeting (or assembly, as it was called) of the Ramblers, in 1934, there was a lengthy discussion regarding the distinctive character of the society, its goals, and its bylaws. The question of acceptance of non-Jewish members arose. A member named Yanover proposed adding the word "Hebrew" to the society's name. My father pointed out that it was permissible according to the existing bylaws to bring in Arabs, as well as Jews. However, another member, Ben-Zion Lurie, stated that theirs was a Hebrew national society, and that therefore non-Jews should not be admitted. My father insisted that "non-Jews should not be denied the possibility of joining. . . . A person should not be denied this right because of his nationality." A vote was taken, and the decision was twelve to three in favor of having the society be open to everyone. However, the subject came up once more, this time in the context of the drafting of the membership application. In the first draft, it was written that members would be accepted who were known "for their proper relationship to the values of society and the nation." Nathan Shalem asked that this requirement be omitted, "because many and various are the doctrines of the parties and the different political currents, such that there is no objective criterion for the notion of society or nation." Y. Yisraeli requested that the words "values of Zionism" be added. In the end, the wording of the original draft was retained, with the proposal to omit the requirement regarding "national values" being defeated seven to five.

Some of the society's hikes were easy and short, but some were long treks that traversed remote and hazardous regions. The worsening security situation (e.g., the 1929 disturbances and the Arab Revolt of 1936–39) had a deleterious effect on the society's activities, but did not bring them to an end. One obvious result of the intensification of Jewish-Arab enmity was a sense that "[w]e must reexamine our relationship with the Arabs and particularly with the Arabs of the desert." This reexamination was of practical import for the society, since the Ramblers employed Bedouin as guides on their desert hikes and relied upon them. The most famous of these was Haj Abdallah al-A'ayan, a member of the Ta'amreh tribe, who lived in a cave near Herodion (east of Bethlehem) and had guided teams of English and German researchers even prior to World War I. He and my father were close friends, and Haj Abdallah often came to our home to visit with him.

With the outbreak of hostilities in 1929, my father was attacked for this policy: "What do you say about these Arabs of yours?" it was asked, meaning, my father writes, "about these guides from the Ta'amreh tribe with whom we were friendly on our desert trips and who had taken part in an attack on the Talpiot neighborhood [in Jerusalem] and looted homes there." His conclusion was the same as that arrived at by the Yishuv's leaders on every occasion that disturbances erupted—and especially when they were at their peak in 1937 and 1938: separation. "We need not always be dependent upon them for guidance along the trails of this country. We must reach all the hidden corners of the land, become familiar with every path, every mountain. The day will come when guides familiar with the country's trails will be common among our members." And indeed, within a relatively short period of time, the Ramblers' leaders had succeeded in freeing themselves from the necessity of employing Arab guides.

The importance they attached to doing their own guiding resulted in their investing a great deal of effort in collecting the details of their excursions in notebooks and subsequently editing them to produce a book that would be available to "Rambler, teacher, and tourist," as the title page proclaims.[2] The observations in the notebooks were informative, descriptive, and even occasionally written in a flowery style. For example, a hike to the Lower Galilee on the thirteenth and fourteenth of the Hebrew month of Nisan, 5691 (April 1931):

EVENING IN THE VILLAGE (SAFURIYYA — TSIPORI)

The sun sinks behind the Carmel Hills. The Beit Netofa Valley is slumbering and the Shazor Mountains stand guard over it. The muezzin calls to the faithful with flourishes of his beautiful voice. The village prepares the evening meal. The crescent moon spills its light onto the face of the village as it sleeps. The villagers' voices fade. Fog spreads over the Beit Netofa Valley.

We left the village at 7:15. The comrades were in good spirits. One commented, "Another day to stand in the open." He wished thereby to turn our attention to the pleasant scenery visible on every side. . . . At 8:10 we reached Khirbat Roma. It stands on a hill [whence the name Roma, *ram* being a height]. All around are beautiful valleys. To the north of Roma is Tel Wawiyyat, about which people would say: All the vicinity is valley and there is only one *tel;* the jackals climb up [it] and begin to howl; that is why they call it the Tel of the Jackals [*wawi, wawiyyat,* jackal, jackals]. At 9:40 we reached the foot of the mountain. Here there is a fork in the road. The path winding to the right on the mountain goes to Arraba, and the path that goes to the left turns toward Yodphat [Jotapata]. We arrived at Khirbat Cana, at the entrance to Wadi Daidaba, which descends to the West. We passed in front of the *khirba* and turned westward in a wadi separating the mountains of Daidaba and the mountains of Yodphat. We marched through the wadi and entered a beautiful world. The wadi is covered with an abundance of trees. To the left, the mountainsides are covered with plentiful trees, a bushy forest, carob trees, oaks, and blooming hawthorn: the farther we advance, the more tangled the forest. Wild almond trees, the kandoul, brilliant with shades of yellow, anemones, and even cyclamens. . . . At about 11:00, our feet brought us to Yodphat. . . . Encircling the summit of the mountain are large natural caverns that serve as enclosures for sheep and cattle, descending to the west are steps cut into the rock-face. . . . During our descent from the mountain, one of our members found two Hebrew coins: on one a date palm and on the other a star. At nightfall, we returned to Tsipori.

Occasionally the description is completely straightforward:

We leave the village and walk on a road bounded by *sabra* plants. Ten minutes later, the road divides, with one [fork] going to the right. We walk along the left fork among the olive trees (the right-hand fork follows the ridge), and after 35 minutes, we enter Sahel Safuriyya, a beautiful plain, and the road there is convenient for carts and small cars. The road passes between two stone walls, and most of the plain is to its left.

The material that had been gathered in the numerous notebooks was transferred to a two-volume book totaling more than 850 pages. This guidebook describes twenty excursions by car and by boat on the Dead Sea, eight tours of Jerusalem, and 162 hikes (including some in Trans-jordan, on Mount Hermon, in the Hauran, and in the Sinai). It includes introductory chapters designed to furnish the reader with general information about the country, its inhabitants, its natural features, climate, and history, as well as a Hebrew-Arabic conversation guide. The authors contributed material from their personal experience regarding preparations for a hike, guidelines for behavior while on the road, first aid, photography, map-reading, and also "etiquette and customs when visiting in Arab villages." For example:

> The hike's leader is to make sure that the hikers do not violate local customs nor make demands upon the village's inhabitants. . . . Should villagers come to welcome the visitors, the leader of the hikers converses with them about work, planting and plowing, harvesting and threshing. One may inquire as to the names of the mountains, places, and ancient ruins in the vicinity, and especially discuss historical matters. One does not speak about religion and belief, much less politics, except if the head of the household wishes it.

In their foreword to the guidebook, the authors define the objective of the hikes:

> Today, when we set out to educate the complete Jew, it is not sufficient to open to him the wellsprings of the spirit of Israel; rather, it is incumbent upon us to bring him into direct contact with nature, which has blessed our land with lovely vistas. . . . And you should be aware that love of the homeland is acquired also via the exertions of wandering and wayfaring, and the more hiking a person does, the more feeling for the homeland will take root in his soul. . . . And just as the earth serves as the foundation for the renaissance of the nation, so an acquaintance with the land provides the foundation for the renaissance of the nation's spirit. Because of this, the hikes must not be limited solely to the Hebrew settlements and readily accessible routes, but the entire land must be revealed to the eye of the Hebrew—with all its villages, settlements, and ruins.

This reference to "the entire land" took on special significance soon after the publication of the book, with the announcement of the Peel Commission's recommendations regarding the partition of Palestine. The authors' response was to write:

> The completion of the book took place at a time when the Hebrew public in this country was alarmed to hear the royal commission's recommendation to establish a Jewish state within very narrow boundaries. At that time, many were of the opinion that our work, as well, must be restricted to within the boundaries of the proposed state. Nevertheless, the authors have not deviated from the course that they laid out at the beginning of their work, out of a clear recognition that never in its life-

time have the Jewish People had but one land, which was set aside for them in its historic and natural boundaries, even though it has become a land of gentiles.

DISEMPOWERED

My father was fifty years old when the 1948 war began. He joined the National Guard, a unit of older soldiers who manned the major checkpoints that were set up along the borders of the Jewish neighborhoods of Jerusalem, and he was wounded in May 1948 by shrapnel. He and his middle-aged comrades, who had for decades hiked the trails of the land and knew every hamlet and valley, sat at home and mourned former students of theirs serving in the Haganah who had been killed on their way to carry out missions, often simply because they were unfamiliar with the terrain and had lost their way. My father was especially pained by the deaths of "the Lamed-Heh" ("the 35"), thirty-five young soldiers who had set out from the school building in Beit Hakerem one day in January 1948, headed for the besieged Ezion Block, not far from Hebron—many of whom he had taught. His frustration is evident in an exchange of letters with his good friend Pinchas Cohen: "Here you are, sitting at home, powerless to go and join these youngsters. . . . It would be better to take up one's walking stick and backpack and to walk ahead of these patrols, for why should they fall whose whole lives and all the future are before them?"

"I knew at the time that the young fellows had gone astray in the wilds," Cohen writes in his reply, "and you came forward, and you said that that was what had occurred. How right we were in our day and in the struggle we carried on—when we brought our school-age young men and women up to the hills to familiarize them with the trails of the homeland. I did this, and so did you, but we knew it was just a drop in the bucket. How many young people were around even at the best of times? The youth in general did not hike, and maps alone are not enough. Our cousins [the Arabs] follow their noses like a hunting dog sniffing the wind. . . . This matter is worsening apace, but that is what we anticipated from the beginning. We must not despair."

Then my father volunteered to lecture to soldiers—many of them new immigrants drafted straight off the boat—about the landscape and the communities where they bivouacked before and after battle. His descriptions of those days, though somewhat bombastic, are also almost euphoric.

> In those days (before the war), when we used to ramble in the Judean hills,
> we would plunge into a sea of recollections of the past—of the days when
> Judah surely dwelt in his land. . . . sensing the echo of the footfalls of our
> prophets. . . . and the presence of generation upon generation of Israel's
> heroes, who fought valiantly to restore the nation's freedom. However,
> upon arriving—after a lengthy trek—at villages built on mountaintops
> and hillsides and coming in contact with plowman and shepherd from the
> stock of Ishmael, we would be brought back to bitter reality. We would
> realize that only the smallest portion of the nation of Judea was now in
> these hills—how the times have changed. . . . And now it appears as if a
> sorcerer had touched the hills with his wand. The shadows of the past are
> brought back to life. . . . The descendents of the Hasmoneans—each man
> with weapon in hand, standing guard—grasping in their trusty hands the
> heritage of our forebears—the Judean hills. Judah dwells in his moun-
> tains, and the sons have returned to their borders.

The abandoned Arab villages and fields he describes thus:

> Vineyards and orchards with trees laden with earth's blessing of fruit; occa-
> sional farm plots are visible—plots of standing corn just ready for harvest,
> the whole crop bowing its head as if embarrassed by the weight of its load
> of kernels, which would not have the privilege of benefiting man or
> beast. . . . The ruins of the large houses that had been nests of murderers
> are testimony to the great battle that raged inside them. . . . After fighting
> bravely, the inhabitants scattered to the winds. . . . The enemy fled, leav-
> ing behind many casualties on the battlefield.

Pinchas Cohen, in a letter written in December 1948, gives a description
of my father guiding an excursion in the vicinity of Lod. A friend of
Cohen's had returned from the hike and told him: " 'A short little guy
was describing the places there, and he knew every stone and every wadi
[dry river bed] and every village and every valley.' I asked, 'And did he
go around without a hat?' 'Yes.' 'And he wore glasses?' 'Yes.' 'And does
his hair blow wildly in the wind?' 'Yes.' 'And does he speak as if knowledge of all the land is on the tip of his tongue?' He said, 'Yes.' I said, 'He
is my good friend David. You will see that is so—one of these days we
shall meet while helping numerous groups find the information they
seek, and all the land shall be overflowing with knowledge like water.' "

ALWAYS UNDER SIEGE

In a lecture that he gave on the eve of Rosh Hashanah (the Jewish New
Year) in October 1948, my father detailed the stages of Jerusalem's
growth and development and described how the hostile British authorities and their Arab cronies had devised a "satanic plan" to hem in the

city's Jewish population and to confine it to certain parts of town. The Arab neighborhoods, he contended, were being built as a "military operation" whose objective was to isolate the Jewish population living in the south of the city from their brothers in the city center. After the construction of the residential neighborhoods, "They [the Arabs] also commenced a systematic takeover of the Jewish commercial centers, which had acquired land in choice locations the length of Jaffa Road [Jerusalem's main street in British Mandate times] and the streets adjacent to it; Jewish merchants subsequently left Mamilla Street, the greater part of the [old] Commercial Center on Julian's Way [beside the King David Hotel], and the area from the Jaffa Gate [of the Old City] to the Russian Compound. Even in West Jerusalem, the people of the village of Lifta drove wedges of construction between Jewish homes, and on the Mount Scopus Road, rich Muslims built palatial mansions—in order to cut off our 'palaces of culture' [i.e., the Hebrew University] on Mount Scopus."

The Jews, a definite majority in West Jerusalem, were always "under siege" in my father's opinion, always cut off, always threatened. The Arabs, whose building activity was, in actuality, a matter of private, individual initiative, were supposedly acting according to a master plan in coordination with the British authorities. Conversely, in this scenario, the Jews were depicted as the passive victims of a fiendish plan of conquest, although nearly all Jewish building was initiated or supported by public or community bodies and motivated by the desire to dominate territory and secure transportation routes.

Everything, of course, fell into place with the liberation of Jerusalem during the 1948 war. "The detached islands, which had until then suffered at the hands of the cruel enemy, now served as a springboard for the conquest of the adjacent Arab-populated neighborhoods, and the work was completed. . . . Many tens of thousands of Arab residents fled at gunpoint, abandoning their homes, their possessions, and their magnificent and prosperous commercial establishments." "But," my father cautions, "the work will only truly be completed when we have restored the holy places that were lost to us and Israel's dwelling place in the Old City, as well as all our beloved shrines that were occupied, looted, destroyed, and burnt down by impure people." One can easily imagine my father's feelings when I came and told him that we had captured the Old City (the accomplishment of the occupation was still a secret at the time). In his view, the 1967 war was the final battle in a 2,000-year struggle: "Some 1,830 years had passed since the fall of Jerusalem—

with its cherished shrines—into the hands of enemy and foe in the days of Simeon Bar Kochba, 'president of Israel' [who led an unsuccessful revolt against the Romans 132–35 c.e.], until its restoration to Jewish rule," he writes. "With the pure blood of its courageous warriors, the IDF liberated the Western [Wailing] Wall and joined together the two halves of Jerusalem." In the guidebook that he hastened to publish, he meticulously inscribed the date: "Year 1 of the Redemption of United Jerusalem."

LIBERATION OF "THE ENTIRE LAND"

Throughout the 1948 war, and with the partition of the land in its wake, my father aired no extremist political views and was a loyal member of the ruling Israel Workers' Party (MAPAI), even becoming a candidate for the Knesset, although not high enough on the party's list to realistically expect to be elected. But his yearnings for those regions of the country that remained outside the borders of the new state reemerged immediately following the 1967 war and the occupation of the West Bank and territories under Syrian and Egyptian control. He wrote in July 1967:

> Before the Six-Day War, the most important parts of our land were outside the jurisdiction of the state of Israel. Our not being able to move about them freely meant that our appreciation of the significance of many chapters in our history was imperfect. Our victory in the war has broadened our horizons. Now we are able to journey the length and breadth of the land, to enjoy its abundance of sublime natural vistas, and to breath its air in all kinds of weather. . . . Colonization of the land, and especially in the areas that have been recovered from foreign rule, forges—through creative labor—our national bond to it [i.e., the land] and transfers to us the right of ownership. . . . Hiking is also an effective means for establishing proper relations with the Arab population that has possession of stretches of the liberated territory of Eretz Israel.

LATE RECOGNITION

For many years my father felt that the true value of his achievements had not been publicly acknowledged. All the honors he had received, including having been named Worthy of Jerusalem (*Yakir Yerushalayim*) in 1969, did not satisfy him. And then, at the age of eighty-five, out of the blue, he won the 1987 Israel Prize, the country's highest civilian award, for his life's work "in imparting Knowing the Land and love for the homeland." The judges' rationale for awarding him the prize included the following:

> From the very beginning of his active career, he strove to form devotees of Knowing the Land into an organized body and with friends founded the Ramblers' Society, which was the first group in Eretz Israel to deal on a permanent and ongoing basis with the organization of excursions and lectures and with conveying knowledge of the homeland. . . . Many are the outstanding scholars on the subject of Eretz Israel, and many the guides who are conversant with its trails; however, there walks among us today one man who has dedicated his life to the education of educators and has fostered generations of lovers of Eretz Israel. This is David Benvenisti—for his life's work in imparting Knowing the Land and love for the homeland, he is a worthy recipient of the Israel Prize.

My father's "life objective" of imparting Knowing the Land and love for the homeland found its most complete expression in the textbooks he wrote, in which an abundance of geographical, zoological, botanical, historical, geological, hydrological, ethnographic, and folkloric information is organized in strict accordance with the principle that he laid out when he described the methods for teaching Knowing the Land as "a course of studies embodying important nationalist-educational values."

My father published a series of textbooks about the various regions of Eretz Israel, designed for student and hiker alike, called *Our Land and Israel,* as well as maps and guides. In the opening pages of a booklet devoted to the hills of Samaria (1946), he writes:

> When our nation returned to the land [i.e., in the early days of Zionism], they remembered also the hills of Samaria—especially their northernmost region—scoring the earth with their plows and reviving the forests. However, the greater part of these hills—the good and fertile portion—still awaits redemption. Let us examine the natural conditions of the Samarian hills that are the source of their fertility. . . . Let us take note of the efforts made by our brothers to redeem the hills from their desolation, and let us celebrate the epoch of our courageous first pioneers.

At the beginning of the booklet on the Judean hills, he writes enthusiastically:

> In our day, when the People of Israel have gained control of our land and have set their plows to renew the face of the land, the Judean hills were privileged to be the first of the hills to be redeemed, even if not on a large scale. . . . Let us go up to the Judean hills; we shall walk their length and breadth and observe their structure and crops and their inhabitants, and we shall learn how we can restore their glory as in ancient times.

The information on the Arab population that my father saw fit to impart to the student of Knowing the Land was minimal. Moreover, he consciously and systematically ignored this large sector of Israel's citizenry. Of the city of Nazareth, he wrote: "It is the principal city of the Lower Galilee. . . . The towers of Christian churches are visible among the houses. Christian pilgrims visit there. According to their tradition, Nazareth was where Jesus had his home . . . Since the War of Independence, the Jewish community there has grown apace, and a new town called Upper Nazareth was built." The student does not even learn that the inhabitants of Nazareth are mainly Arab, not to mention anything about their way of life and their problems.

Regarding the 1948 war and its impact, my father wrote: "In the War of Independence, when the Arab armies were scheming to totally annihilate the Jewish population of Safed, and along with it the agricultural communities of the Western Galilee, the most courageous of Israel's warriors hastened to the aid of the city. After fierce battles, the entire city was reoccupied." The reader has no cause to suspect that Arabs lived in Safed and were, in fact, the majority of the population. After fleeing or being expelled outright in the wake of the war, they were uprooted from history as well—as if they had never been there: "In the old part of the city live painters and artisans . . . and they draw pictures of the vicinity's beautiful landscape and of interesting places inside the city." The homes of the Arabs and their mosques—now turned into art galleries—have been purged of any relationship to their original inhabitants. "On the western ridge of the Upper Galilee, the Jewish communities of S'as'a, Elkosh, Hosen, Parod, Kfar Shamai, Meron, [and] Peqi'in, were established, as well as others. On the Heights of Gush Halav . . . stand the villages of Safsufa, Kerem Ben Zimra, 'Alma, Bar'am, and others." The only reference to the Arab villages that were destroyed and in whose place Jewish communities were established is indirect: "The Arab villages retained the ancient Hebrew names from the era of the Second Temple and later." The Arab villages of Sa'sa', Deir el-Qasi, Suhmata, Faradiyya, Kufr Suma'i, Meroun, Safsufa, Alma, Ras al-Ahmar, and Bir'im—upon whose ruins and lands Jewish communities were built—sank into oblivion without a trace, and even their names, as my father tells it, were nothing more than bastardizations of the authentic Hebrew ones, an aberration of sorts, which was rectified with their "liberation," the expulsion of their inhabitants, and their repopulation with Jewish immigrants.

In early 2000, I published a book entitled *Sacred Landscape,* in which I describe the fate of the Arab-Palestinian landscape that was destroyed in 1948, its remnants having been covered over by the present-day Israeli landscape.[3] This book was a kind of challenge aimed at the cult of Knowing the Land—the cornerstones for which were laid, as described above, by my father and others. In a critique of the book, the Jewish American neoconservative orientalist Daniel Pipes, whose Israeli patriotism is evidently stronger than my own, wrote:

> This Israeli writer finds innovative new ways to injure his country—the introduction to *Sacred Landscape* may be the book's most interesting section. In it he recounts accompanying his father on mapping trips that played a major role in establishing "a Hebrew map of the land," then admits hating his father's success: "His map triumphed and I, his dutiful son, was left with the heavy burden of the fruits of victory." So that's it; Benvenisti's bizarre politics are symptoms of delayed filial rebellion. How pathetic.[4]

Delayed Filial Rebellion

When *Sacred Landscape* was published in early 2000, I indeed felt so distant and cut off from the heritage with which my father had striven to imbue me that perhaps there was a grain of truth in Pipes's diatribe. My moods and thinking, then and henceforth, were, without a doubt, a direct challenge to my father's lifework. Historical processes, a combination of fatigue and normalization, and violent intercommunal clashes have mercilessly gnawed away at the fundamental values of secular Israeli society, threatening its very cohesiveness. Revisionist historical research has given rise to critiques of the Zionist narrative and to a painful preoccupation with the darker chapters in the history of the Yishuv. I took part in the critique threatening the very essence of secular Zionism—love for the homeland—asserting that love can never be conscripted.

The educational enterprise of inculcating this "love for the homeland"—perhaps the most fundamental value in the education of Israeli youth both before and since the founding of the state—was based on the nationalization of the landscape, in both its physical and chronological dimensions. The land and one's ties to it—each relic of the past, each stone, each wadi, each wild bird, each thornbush, not to mention every tree Jews had planted and every house they had built—become the property of the Jewish nation, which cast its collective identity over the landscape, making it, too, "Jewish."

My father aspired to produce a generation of "natives" and saw the quintessence of their quest for "nativeness" in these lines by the celebrated poet Sha'ul Tschernichovsky: "Man is but a small piece of land. Man is but an image of his homeland's landscape." In fact, though, the founding fathers created the exact opposite. The landscape did not shape the soul of the Israeli-born sabra; rather, it was the committed inner landscape of the Israeli that shaped the external physical landscape. This model had no place for a direct personal connection with the land.

The cult of love for the homeland was an important element in shaping Israeli national consciousness, but its success was limited. Many of the children and grandchildren of those who where supposed to have been the first generation of Jewish "natives" in their homeland turned their backs on the cult, repelled by its chauvinistic fundamentalism. They created new forms of affinity with the land, no longer identifying with the "conscripted" culture of Israeli society. Those sabras who most closely approach the "native" ideal find in the landscape a source of personal satisfaction and pleasurable experience, but they reject its nationalization and insist on personalizing their love for it. Those who still strive to bind human beings in chains of indoctrination, obligating them to love their homeland, are not only fighting a losing battle, it appears that they are also trying to preserve principles that, although not explicit, are inherent in the cult of Knowing the Land—the alienation and dispossession of the Other.

TORCHING THE FORESTS

Efforts to alienate and dispossess the Other are evident in denying that the Palestinians feel an innate love for their homeland, as if love were an exclusive emotion, and the fact that another feels similarly would compromise one's own claim. I have written elsewhere not only that the Palestinians do, indeed, have an intimate, personal bond with their homeland, but also that they, unlike the Zionists, do not use their love for the land as a way to bolster a claim of proprietorship. The Arabs, I wrote, do not feel a need to conscript every eagle to their cause or to boast of "knowing every plant and every crevice," as if this "knowledge" carried the biblical connotation of sexual conquest.

The torching of forests by Arab Israelis following the killing of a number of Arab citizens by the police during demonstrations in the Galilee and central Israel around the beginning of the al-Aqsa Intifada

(October 2000) provides a convenient proof of Arab insensitivity to nature. It is only natural that attention has focused on this and other violent acts committed by Arab Israelis, such as attacks on Jewish passersby, destruction of infrastructure, and trashing of post offices and bank branches, which triggered murderous responses by the police. Alongside expressions of condemnation and shock at the hooliganism of marginal extremist elements, though, a grudging and hesitant understanding has begun to emerge for the deep-seated motives underlying the hatred and frustration: a recognition that these are the rotten fruits of continued discrimination against the Arab sector—of sewage flowing in the streets, chronic unemployment, inequities in the allocation of public resources, of land expropriation, and political and social alienation.

Only one form of violence has received universal condemnation—the burning of forests—being touted as an example of the "primitive impulses of the Arab 'sons of the desert.'" Even staunch champions of Jewish-Arab fellowship were appalled by these acts of arson and confronted their erstwhile comrades with their feelings: "Those who love their homeland do not destroy its natural beauty. This primitive vandalism is inexcusable!"

Israelis could barely fathom that the verdant forests—with their pleasant secluded areas and picnic spots—are more than just "green lungs" or examples of silent natural beauty, that, in fact, they are one more aspect of an all-out struggle over disputed territory. Indeed, many of the forests that were set ablaze had been purposely planted to conceal any evidence of Arab habitation—villages, cultivated fields, orchards, and cemeteries—their planting intended to bury that stratum of the country's history, without trace and without memorial.

Those who enjoy spending time in the woods and who were shocked by attempts to set them ablaze—have not been aware that human beings whose homes were once in these vanished villages live among them, for whom these green forests are a constant reminder of their catastrophe. But of course the Israeli picnickers are incapable of understanding this, because it seems to them that were they to permit themselves to be exposed to all this pain, their faith in the righteousness of the Zionist enterprise might be shaken. Their desperate need to protect themselves from the cognitive dissonance aroused by such an understanding results in their interpreting Arab rage in the context of material deprivation only, for if its significance were to be understood on a deeper level, they fear it would amount to heresy.

MAKING THE DESERT BLOOM?

Planting forests was at the heart of the cult of "making the desert bloom" promoted by the Jewish National Fund (JNF), which culminated each year in planting ceremonies on Tu Bishvat, the Jewish "New Year of the Trees." "This became," my father wrote, "an important vehicle for imparting a love of nature, of the homeland, and of productive work, not only among Jewish children in this country or in the Diaspora, but also in the hearts of everyone in the Yishuv." The JNF, through its educational branch, the Teachers' Council of the JNF, was the principal agent of Zionist propaganda in Jewish schools in Palestine. And, as he describes it: "The Teachers' Council made a point of introducing—into both the formal curricula of the schools and their informal student activities—concepts and basic elements of Zionism, with the objective of giving the children a place in the [new Jewish] mosaic being constructed on the nation's soil, gaining their cooperation in the redemption of the nation by means of the redemption of the land, and finding ways to make the idea of the rebirth of the nation real and tangible to them."

My father was active in the Teachers' Council from the time of its founding in 1926 until the day he died. In the last years of his life, bitter arguments sometimes broke out between us over the issue of "making the desert bloom" in the occupied territories. On one occasion in the mid 1980s, returning from an excursion to the Jordan Valley full of wonder at the flourishing agriculture in that region, he commented admiringly, "Look how they are making the desert bloom!" I called his attention to what had been done on the other side of the Jordan, where cultivated fields stretched to the water's edge, and pointed out that, "years ago the Palestinians in the occupied territories were prohibited from working their fields and were even refused access to them 'for security reasons.' The fields lay fallow, and their water was taken by the Jewish settlements that were established there during those years, whose inhabitants were, of course, permitted to enter the area. And you call this 'making the desert bloom?'" "Of course it is making the desert bloom," he retorted, "Why are you being a PLO propagandist, for G-d's sake?!"

DEVASTATION IN THE NAME OF LOVE

During my frequent trips to the occupied territories, I have encountered the devastation wrought in the name of love by those with pretensions to a monopoly on love for Eretz Israel—the settlers. Settlement expansion and road-building activity carried out on the West Bank have totally and irretrievably obliterated the biblical landscape of Judea and Samaria. Lovers of Eretz Israel "who know every stone and every tree because they dwell in the landscape" (i.e., the settlers) have embarked upon a comprehensive campaign to ensure that the territory will remain "in the hands of the Jewish people for eternity." With the permission and financial backing of the government, they expanded the built-up areas of the settlements, planting house trailers on every hilltop and issuing permits for cemeteries for the burial of Jews whose bodies are flown in from abroad.

But the actual "pioneer" that "goes before the camp" has been the yellow bulldozer and the lengthening ribbon of asphalt behind it. Hundreds of kilometers of "bypass roads" have been built "to irrevocably secure the place of the Zionist settlement project in the biblical landscape, where our ancestors walked." The insane project with the aim of ensuring the security of those traveling to isolated settlements and of bypassing areas under Palestinian control has earned many responses, all of them in the context of politics and security. In such an atmosphere, there was no chance at all for anyone to seriously consider what the price of this feverish road-building has really been—the terrible price in terms of irreversible damage to the extremely fragile landscape, the very same biblical landscape that was the pretext for the whole operation. Before long—once all the unimportant deliberations about the future of these regions and others, marked off on yellowing maps, have sunk into oblivion—people will stand on the hills amazed that the bulldozer driver's hands did not tremble as he laid waste the valleys and bisected them with wide swaths of asphalt, mounds of spilt earth, and massive concrete bridges. And all of this has been done in the name of love for Eretz Israel. A prodigious amount of audacity is needed to call this brutal rape "love." The ravaged landscape cannot scream "Rape!" and its true lovers are silenced by the fear that their outcry might be interpreted as a political statement.

My father's reaction would have been different from mine. Like all members of his generation, he was an enthusiastic supporter of every development project. "Building the country": the absorption of millions of immigrants and the creation of an economic infrastructure to support them, the establishment of settlement faits accomplis for political and security-related objectives—these were the essence of his brand of Zionism. He believed that the boundaries of the Jewish collectivity were determined by the extent of Jewish settlement, and he therefore followed with interest and pride the construction of—and in—the pioneering communities of pre-state times and the early days of the state. His first words upon returning from an excursion were invariably, "It's developing well." What is interesting is that my father's devotion to the cult of "development" coexisted with its diametric opposite: his care for relics of the past, for planting trees, for research into historical geography, archeology, and geology. But this is a false dichotomy. Both his ambitions regarding the caring preservation of the past and his enthusiasm for development and change were mobilized in the service of nationalist objectives. Homes and communities populated with Jews were a way of gaining possession of the open spaces; development and change, the preservation of nature, and the study of relics of the past were all assertions of proprietorship. To him, the natural environment—no less than a house that had been built or a tree that had been planted—was a Jewish national asset. And we have already seen how my father regarded the occupation of the territories captured in the 1967 war and the establishment of the first settlements as being a direct extension of the Zionist settlement project in which he had participated since 1913.

Nonetheless, certain remarks that he made in the course of the 1980s hinted that he might have begun to entertain doubts as to the Zionist legitimacy of the urban settlements being built in close proximity to the Green Line separating pre-1967 Israel from the occupied territories. He was also alarmed by inflammatory right-wing slogans designed to coerce the "love for homeland" that he had so strongly championed. But he was already old and tired and did not have the strength to rethink his deeply rooted beliefs and perceptions. Perhaps he also lacked the strength to contend with the ruinous consequences of unbridled development coupled with massive immigration, which imperiled the landscape of the homeland and its quality of life; he continued to be impressed by "the developments."

ENVIRONMENTAL NIGHTMARE

I—whose involvement with the landscape dates back to halfway through the second decade of my life—found myself halfway through my seventh decade gripped by despair in the face of the ecological disaster unfolding before my eyes. There was no place that I recalled from childhood that had not become an environmental nightmare. In this there was, unquestionably, an element of nostalgia; but there is no doubt that the land had been transformed into a wasteland of asphalt and concrete and masses of hideous architecture, the result of aggressive planning practices, nationalistic arrogance, and the avarice of contractors. My sorrow at witnessing the obliteration of the landscapes of my childhood was mingled with a great deal of anger at the fact that this destruction was in large part the product of political impulses masquerading as patriotism—love for the homeland—but in fact, destroying the homeland.

Usually, criticism of Zionism's accepted conventions and of hallowed national myths was confined to a relatively small collection of post-Zionist groups and to revisionist "new historians." Intellectual conservatism, establishment interests, and a nostalgic snuggling up to a heroic past worked together to cause any person who dared cause a crack in the façade of Zionist mythology to be accused of sacrilege. Such criticism started to be heard coming, albeit with considerable hesitation, from the mouths of influential individuals who make use of statistical and demographic data and usually steer clear of intentionally provocative arguments.

Disquieting data regarding population density and growth, and the resultant soaring pace of housing construction and urban development, are impelling academics and "Green" activists alike to wonder aloud about the likely consequences of continued devotion "to the Zionist ethos based on encouragement of Jewish immigration and the conquest of the desert" and about the chances of maintaining a reasonable standard of living for Israel's population. If development goes on unabated, they caution, the result will be an ecological disaster that will "seal the fate of Israeli society."

If, indeed, the Zionist dream has been revealed to be dangerously flawed, the slaughter of some sacred cows—such as the Law of Return and the Zionist dedication to "clothing the land in a mantle of concrete and mortar"—may be in order. Nonetheless, there are Greens who balk at radical pronouncements questioning "basic tenets of Zionism that must not be relinquished." They point out that it is not population growth alone that is creating the ecological crisis, but also the standard of living. In fact, well-to-do families with few children consume far more natural resources than do the multi-child, low-income families of "religious people, Arabs, and Mizrahim ["oriental" Jews, i.e., mainly those from Arabic-speaking countries]." The problem is that both those who challenge the Zionist ethos and those who fear that "expressing opinions so far from the mainstream will make it even more difficult" to avert disaster are ignoring, consciously or unconsciously, one crucial element that contributes to the exacerbation of the problem: it is not only the citizens of Israel whose existence is dependent on the region's environmental resources (i.e., air, water, and land), but millions of Palestinians as well.

All of these statistics concerning population density, expansion of the area earmarked for housing, development of infrastructure, and air and water pollution are based on data gathered in Israel within the Green Line. But this line, which just may have geopolitical significance, is a fiction when it comes to environmental considerations. Anyone involved with land use or environmental planning knows that the territories on either side of the Green Line comprise a single bioregion. Both populations are sustained by the same water resources and breathe the same air. What's more, the growth of Israel's population and of the area required for housing are creating increased pressure for the establishment of additional "nonideological" settlements in the areas of the occupied territories that are an integral part of metropolitan Tel Aviv and Jerusalem. It is estimated that almost ten million people are already (2007) living in the territory that really should be of concern to the Greens (the whole of Eretz Israel / Palestine), and by the beginning of the second decade of this millennium, some twelve million will be living there.

Introducing the Palestinian factor is not to the taste of the Green activists, of course, and for obvious reasons they've heard enough "opinions far from the mainstream" of the Jewish population, and they are not interested in adding political controversies to the ecological debate—especially ones liable to divert the discussion to issues perceived as irrelevant and to thereby make it even more difficult for those contending with the collapse of the Zionist dream.

Over and above these considerations, all of those concerned with this issue—be they adherents of the "Zionist ethos" or its challengers—base their positions and forecasts on a common assumption: that the rate of usage of the natural resources shared by the Israelis and Palestinians will remain at its present level. That means that the Palestinians in the territories, who make up 40 percent of the population, would continue to control just 8 percent of the water resources and 11 percent of the land, while their per capita income (which has such a great influence on resource consumption) would remain approximately one-tenth of that of the Israelis. Even those who reject the ethos of settlements hold fast to the conviction that Israel has the right to retain a near-monopoly on the region's resources, with the Palestinians having to make do with the leftovers. And if they should demand a more equitable share, the same old arguments regarding the looming ecological debacle will be trotted out to prove that the Palestinian claim is unreasonable and courts disaster.

This assumption, however, cannot withstand the test of reality. Halting the growth of the Palestinian population and the rise in its standard of living is impossible, as is stemming the pressure on the shared resources of the region caused by these factors. What this means is that the dimensions of the coming ecological disaster are far greater than predicted, and the challenges to the Zionist ethos must go beyond critiques of "immigration and making the desert bloom," to include questions regarding Israeli-Palestinian coexistence and the right of the two peoples to live in dignity in their common homeland.

Is it any wonder that these opinions are regarded by some as evidence of my "delayed filial rebellion"? Even that could be considered an understatement.

EMOTIONAL TIES

Is there truly nothing left of the values that my father strove to instill into me, just as he tried to implant them in everyone of my generation?

The answer is that he succeeded far more than is possible to determine from a superficial examination. The final test lies not in the presence or absence of sentimental or nostalgic declarations of love for the homeland, but rather in those moments when one's affinity for a piece of land called "homeland" clashes with one's other values or ties, resulting in cognitive dissonance and emotional distress. There was never any doubt regarding my political positions on questions of principle regarding the necessity of partitioning the land and the establishment of "two states for two peoples"—the Israeli and the Palestinian; that is, of course, so long as this was still a realistic option. But I was not party to the efforts of the Israeli Left to divest itself of all emotional ties to the occupied territories out of the conviction that the settlers' nurturing of such ties was nothing but a cult of blood and land. I could not bring myself to join those who renounced a sense of belonging to the occupied territories and regarded it simply as a pretext for taking over the land of another people. As early as 1967, when I arrived on the West Bank as a conquering soldier, I wrote:

> For us, native-born Israeli soldiers in our mid-thirties, . . . the story of the West Bank did not begin in 1967. The various districts of the West Bank were a part of my childhood landscape. I often hiked in the areas around Bethlehem, Hebron, and the Dead Sea with my father. I grew up on sto-

ries of the excursions he had taken in the Judean desert. I read the guidebooks that he had written, and I helped him to publish writings by his friend Nathan Shalem dealing with the Judean desert. With this emotional baggage, I crossed the minefield on the Bethlehem Road and traveled southward with my unit to the Etzion Block and from there to Hebron. The maps in my father's desk drawers became three-dimensional waking dreams. To members of my generation and to my older comrades in arms, the West Bank was not a strange land. When we again reached the River Jordan, we climbed Mount Gerizim and Qarn Sartaba, and nineteen years (1948–67) were erased as if they never had been. The physical and human landscapes, the food, the smells, speaking Arabic—rusty from disuse— had suddenly revived the Palestine of our childhood: the authentic, beautiful land of our imaginings.[1]

The distance between these feelings and what my father felt as he hastened to revise his guidebook, in which he wrote about "the liberation of regions of the homeland," was indeed very small. But even then, I asked myself: "What is the connection between this emotional vertigo and political attitudes? Must a deep sense of belonging translate into acceptance of concepts such as domination, annexation, imposition of Israeli law? Must a humanitarian sensibility, belief in equality among nations, empathy for political and communal suffering necessarily override this sense of belonging, transforming these familiar regions into alien occupied territory from which we must withdraw as quickly as possible?"

REMBRANDTS IN JERICHO

In the course of deliberations regarding the handover of Jericho and its environs to the Palestinian Authority (PA) in the context of the Oslo Accords, this sense of belonging, of affinity for our historic heritage on the West Bank, collided with the desire to achieve peace via partition of the land. In the fall of 1993, prior to Israel's withdrawal from the Jericho region, the Israeli Antiquities Authority embarked upon wide-ranging archeological excavations with the purpose of ensuring that no relics of the Jewish past would fall into the hands of the PA, especially not ancient scrolls like those that had been found hidden in caves near the Dead Sea decades before.

The initiators of "Operation Scroll" did not disguise their intention to conduct salvage excavations prior to the handover of the area to PA control, and their action was interpreted as an act of illegal seizure in contravention to the 1954 Hague Convention for the Protection of Cultural Property in the Event of Armed Conflict. The critics of the operation sought to portray it as the theft of cultural artifacts belonging to a subject population and likened the Israeli archeologists to the colonialist grave robbers of the nineteenth century who made off with the treasures of ancient Greece, Asia Minor, Babylonia, Egypt, and Palestine and transported them to museums in Europe. This attitude was articulated very clearly in the sarcastic comment: "Suppose they had pictures by Rembrandt in the Jericho Municipal Museum. What a horrible temptation that would be!" In other words, the caves in the Judean desert were the cultural property of the Palestinians and were now about to be restored to their ownership; so Israelis' attachment to the scrolls was akin to their coveting one of Rembrandt's paintings.

From this alienated perspective, one's national cultural heritage is treated as if it were a matter of bourgeois antique collecting, the whole point of which is to display treasures of the past in one's living room, or in a museum for tourists—or to deal in them. Anyone who shared the profound feelings aroused by the discovery of the Dead Sea Scrolls—an event that left few Israelis unmoved—and knew how important they were to the formation of the "Israeli experience," could not but hang his head in sorrow. He also could not avoid seeing how this way of looking at things reflected the destructive influence of the Israeli-Palestinian conflict and was, in fact, a reaction to the distortion and corruption of the Jewish national and cultural heritage at the hands of fundamentalist nationalists who have made use of it in their efforts to justify every act of dispossession; of theft of land from Palestinians, transforming them into strangers in their own homeland. The sense of loathing with which the supporters of reconciliation and coexistence with the Palestinians regard the pagan cult of stones and saints' graves has resulted in their attempting to distance themselves from it by renouncing any metaphysical connection to objects in the occupied territories and by deliberately dissociating themselves from historical sites located on the other side of an arbitrary geopolitical boundary.

This reaction is just as simplistic as the blood-and-land cult that produced it is primitive. Sites and objects that embody the cultural heritage of the people of Israel are not found only within the boundaries of the state, and anyone who seeks to expunge his or her sense of subjective belonging to them—labeling them "Palestinian" and treating them as material objects and nothing more—is doing violence to the values of the cultural heritage with his or her own hands. Damage to this heritage does not occur only through the destruction of physical objects, but also—and perhaps primarily—via an alienated attitude toward them. One who does not differentiate between national heritage and a sense of historical continuity, on the one hand, and their exploitation for political and nationalistic ends, on the other—one who does not cultivate the former and reject the latter—is fostering alienation and educating a generation that will be contemptuous of every show of patriotism or, on the contrary, will purposely search out destructive mythologies to follow.

It is impossible to ignore the fact that cultural heritage, archeology, and historiography have been fully mobilized in the service of the Israeli-Palestinian struggle. Just as archeology is utilized to discredit the Palestinians' legitimate affinity for their homeland, the other side invests significant effort in attempts to refute the existence of any connection between the Jewish people and their homeland and to represent such claims as Zionist propaganda. Those who claim in official publications that "the Jebusites are the ancestors of the Palestinians" and that "the Jewish presence in Palestine disappeared, unlike the Arab presence, which persisted under Babylonian, Persian, Greek, Roman, and Byzantine rule" are unlikely to be very interested in unearthing relics specifically from the era of Bar Kochba, say. Conversely, those who destroy Arab cemeteries and turn mosques into galleries or restaurants are in part displaying their unease at the sight of the physical manifestations of the Palestinian heritage within Israel proper. Considerable time will have to pass before it becomes possible to relate to the cultural heritage of the Other with equanimity and not regard it as a threat to one's own cultural identity.

My father would have been proud of me if he could read these lines.

THE VIEW FROM MOUNT NEBO

As I stood on the summit of Mount Nebo in Jordan, soon after the signing of the peace treaty with Jordan in 1995, it became clear to me that historical-emotional attachment is not identical to political affinity. On my return, I wrote:

> On the road sign bearing the name "Jordan," which stands near the border crossing in the Beit Shean Valley, someone had spray-painted the words "Eastern Eretz Israel." One may assume that the graffiti artist was thereby expressing his belief that the eastern bank of the Jordan was our patrimony—"The Jordan has two banks, this one's ours and so is that," in the words of the anthem of the right-wing Beitar youth movement. Let's hope that he and his ilk visit the Hashemite Kingdom of Jordan, because

if they do, they will eventually learn to differentiate between emotional attachment and historical connection, on the one hand, and claims of mastery and the impulse to dominate, on the other. In other words, how does one request a visa to visit the "cradle of our nation"?

The landscapes—physical, historical, emotional, and political—that are revealed from the summit of Mount Nebo outline true perspectives of what is happening on this [i.e., the west] side of the Jordan, and thus lend new meaning to the biblical description: "And they beheld . . . all the land of Judah to the farthest sea." Beholding one's home in Jerusalem or Ein Gedi, the patches of greenery and outline of road—Israeli passport in hand—one can give oneself over to the powerful emotions aroused by the sight of the mountains of Gilead and the wilderness of Moab, and by Dibon, Heshbon, and the river Arnon, without these feelings being translated into a lust for domination. The Bible that acts as his guidebook does not serve as a title deed. Close scrutiny by the Jordanian police does not prevent one from feeling the profound sense of belonging inspired by the ancient verses recounting the tragic death of Absalom, son of King David, in the woods of Gilead or the courageous struggle of the Zealots at Makhor (Machaerus) during the great revolt against the Romans, or from reading the inscription on the Stele of Mesha [a monument of the biblical king of Moab] in Hebrew, which was also the language of the ancient Moabites. All of these raw materials—from which the Jewish-Israeli national mythology was fashioned and which impart a sense of rootedness that animates Israeli political claims—here remain confined to the realm of feeling. From here, the true lineaments of the Israeli cult of the homeland are apparent, and we may even learn the lesson that a historical connection is not necessarily identical to political association.[2]

In the summer of 1995, the government of Israel, headed by Yitzhak Rabin, was asked to determine the boundaries of the territories that would be transferred to the Palestinian Authority in accordance with the Oslo II guidelines. According to the first draft of the map, the government agreed that Rachel's Tomb, located on the Jerusalem-Bethlehem border, be turned over to the PA. This decision aroused a great furor and fierce opposition from right-wing circles, which viewed "the handover of Rachel's Tomb" as striking at the very root of Israeli and Zionist survival and as constituting an ideological and metapolitical confrontation. The Left, for its part, regarded the Right's protest as "undermining the political [i.e., peace] process and giving encouragement to the extreme Right to continue rioting." In their opinion, Rachel's Tomb was simply a convenient pretext—a sentimental weak spot that was being exploited by the opponents of the Oslo process to assail the government's position in the negotiations.

My own emotional relationship with this site led me to express understanding for the feelings of those who regarded the handover of Rachel's
Tomb as an assault on national values. I believed that the debate over
Rachel's Tomb provided a blatant example of lack of sensitivity and
absence of real listening to the feelings of one's political rivals, which only
contributes to the gratuitous intensification of the confrontation between
Left and Right. Rachel's tomb is one of the cornerstones of Jewish-Israeli
identity and not just another "holy place" dear only to the hearts of religious people who prostrate themselves on saints' graves in hopes of having their prayers answered. Our matriarch Rachel, beautiful wife of our
forefather Jacob, symbolizes—by her sorrow-ridden life and tragic
death—motherhood, compassion, hope, and the redemption of the Jewish people. No Israeli-Jewish child, religious or secular, can fail to recognize the words of Jeremiah 31:15–17: "A voice was heard in Ramah,
lamentation, and bitter weeping; Rachel, weeping for her children,
refused to be comforted for her children, because they were not. Thus
saith the Lord, Restrain thy voice from weeping, and thine eyes from
tears; for thy work shall be rewarded. . . . And there is hope in thine
end . . . that thy children shall come again to their own border." This
place, "on the way to Ephrat, it is Bethlehem," has been sacred to the
Jews for some two thousand years. It is one of the few sites in Eretz Israel
that have always remained exclusively in Jewish hands.

When Moshe Dayan decided in 1967 not to include Rachel's Tomb
in the territory annexed to Jerusalem following the Six-Day War, he did
not do so out of disregard for the importance of the place; on the contrary, he believed that the profound affinity for this site would be
stronger than geopolitical borders, and that the Jewish ties to "the cradle of the nation" would be able to span arbitrary jurisdictional boundaries. Now that it has suddenly become apparent that Rachel's Tomb
is "four hundred and sixty meters from the Jerusalem border," this
religious-national site has become a bone of contention between the
supporters of peace and the settlers. The insensitivity regarding Rachel's
Tomb no doubt arose from the fact that the settlers have turned the holy
places into weapons in the struggle against the peace process. However,
feelings shared by hundreds of thousands of Israelis should not have
been ignored and, indeed, sensitivity to them might have broadened the
circle of the supporters of reconciliation. Peace is not simply a process
of negotiation; it is also a means for the realization of national aims and
for the forging of a national identity.

NATIVENESS

The conflicts and contradictions that threaten to open cracks in the edifice of Zionist mythology, to whose construction my father dedicated his life, in no way contradict my sense that he succeeded in the principal mission that he took on: to make of me a "native" in my homeland. They perhaps even strengthen it. I have had no need for the Zionist ideological superstructure, the indoctrination, or the self-justifications. As I wrote in 1988: "For me the claim was a foregone conclusion. It depended only on my basic sense of belonging to the land. My starting point was 'native.'"[3]

I was not unique, and I do not give credit for this success to my father alone; but I can serve as a typical example of my generation—Jews born in Palestine in the 1930s. We and our older siblings are succumbing to natural attrition, and today no more than 1 percent of the Jewish population of Israel were born in the country and were of kindergarten age or older at the founding of the state in 1948. But we were exposed to the cult of Knowing the Land from the day of our birth, and it turns out that the priests of this cult—my father among them—had no mean success: they did succeed in turning us into natives.

It is difficult to determine whether or not this was an inevitable, natural process, an outcome of the very fact that we were born and raised here, and to what degree our education and its content influenced our propensity for nativeness. But the end result is not in dispute, as Israel Bartal writes: "The experience of the Land, its past, its landscapes, and its population are a part of the natural and taken-for-granted experience of the locally born person. He can ask the tough questions, openly deal with delicate subjects . . . and expose the complexity of the objects of his research, the relative nature of things, and the multiplicity of meanings associated with the sources being studied."[4]

In fact, this experience has come to be so "natural and taken-for-granted" that many of those born and bred here after us do not concern themselves at all with "the experience of the country" as a collective mythology that demands close-knit comradery. Many of them have chosen an urban lifestyle, turning their backs on the out-of-doors, and others have personalized their affinity for nature and local history, rebuffing attempts to force on them a cultlike "love for the land." And a fair number regard the ideological settlers in the occupied territories and their supporters, who purport to be the true heirs of the Zionist pioneers, as a gang of proto-fascists who idolize blood and soil.

That does not mean, however, that "nativeness" necessarily finds its expression in the adoption of moderate political positions. On the contrary, this "natural" connection to the homeland—free of ambivalence and requiring no self-justification—is actually liable to reinforce a tendency toward extremist attitudes, because of the deeply rooted perception that there can be but one "native" collectivity in the homeland, and that the Palestinians must, therefore, be divested of their status as natives and must become mere resident aliens. For these Jewish "natives," there is no longer any need to search out rights dating back to the biblical period or to postulate mythological roots in the homeland as a defense against attempts to portray the Zionist enterprise as a white settler society and therefore as a form of illegitimate colonialism. Today's thriving Israeli society—firmly planted in its homeland and having evolved a rich and varied culture in its own Hebrew language—requires no vindication for them, and anyone who dares to challenge its legitimacy risks being denounced as an anti-Semite.

When I was a youth, the Jewish community in Eretz Israel had to fight for its legitimacy. Jews constituted a minority compelled to defend itself against the claim that it was nothing but a collection of immigrants scheming to take over a land that did not belong to it. Now, in my old age, the tables are turned, and the Palestinian people finds itself in the position of having to struggle for recognition that it, too, is a legitimate collectivity whose homeland this is, and not just a "gang of terrorists."

The "nativeness" we acquired was largely derivative, and thus was variously perceived as confused or as multidimensional, as suffering from vagueness and ambivalence or as being blessed with a wealth of nuance and the ability to accommodate a multiplicity of viewpoints. It was all in the eye of the beholder.

For many years, I regarded references to the Israeli-Palestinian struggle as a conflict between a settler society and an indigenous population as anti-Israel slurs. In 1988, I wrote:

> The fallacy in the depiction of Israel as colonialist becomes clear upon examination of the following facts: the Zionist movement's origins are in the Jewish religion—an ethnic religion with a solid national foundation. The Zionists did not come to Eretz Israel because they were searching for "elbow room," but rather because they wished to return to their homeland. They labored with a strength born of ideological motivations, and their objective was to found a new egalitarian society based on "self-labor" [i.e., a do-it-yourself ethic], not on exploitation. Unlike the white settlers of Europe's overseas colonies, they came to Palestine without the

sponsorship of a mother country. They established a distinct sociopolitical system, and did not become an upper class ruling over the "natives"
and exploiting them.[5]

This was how I viewed the Zionist movement, whose character had
become "colonialist," I believed, only after the occupation of the West
Bank and Gaza Strip. I regarded the settlement of the occupied territories as a corruption of Zionism, not as an expression of its inherent
nature: "Concepts that are not in themselves colonialist became—due to
the change in circumstances—a mask for classical colonialist activity. . . . Flourishing suburban communities (in the occupied territories)—
erected on confiscated land and guarded by the Israeli armed forces—
were invested with an aura of 'pioneerism' *[halutziut]*." I came to the
conclusion that "Zionism's fate has been like that of other revolutionary
movements, which became corrupt because their principles ossified, and
that went from being in the vanguard of progress to being the standard-
bearers of reaction." I continued, with sadness and regret, "When I see
the symbols of the settlement of the land and the conquest of the wilderness in their new incarnation, I cannot but discern my own symbols—
distorted by the heat of 'strange fire' in the shattered vessels of my
generation."[6]

At that time, I still utilized the tools of logic when analyzing the conflict, and I still saw reality through the lens of nationalism: "When one
describes the conflict in Eretz Israel, its binational character is evident;
i.e., in Eretz Israel there is deep-seated antagonism between two national
groups, both of which aspire to sovereignty over the same territory."[7]
The inevitable conclusion of this analysis was clear and could be summarized by the Israeli Left's old slogan "Two states for two peoples." But
even then, in the 1980s, I had doubts as to the suitability of this model,
because it did not account for the many aspects of this conflict that were
absent from other binational conflicts but were frequently found in disputes originating in clashes between native and immigrant populations—
primary among these being the intense focus on the issue of control of
the physical space, a common feature of settler-native confrontations.

It was convenient for me to think that the national model had applied
to Israel during the period prior to the 1967 occupation, and that the
Jewish settlement of the territories had distorted it. However, the imposition of "de facto binationalism" (see chapters 6–7) in the form of the
quasi-permanent domination of one nation by the other (expediently
referred to as "a military occupation") only acted to exacerbate inter-

communal friction in such a way that the perspectives of the conflict reverted to their most basic, atavistic, and emotional level. The 1993 Oslo Accords and their faltering implementation were a desperate attempt to deal with the conflict rationally. Mutual recognition between Israel and the PLO was perhaps the crowning achievement of the effort to employ a rational approach. But the "settler-native syndrome" quickly regained ascendancy in a worsening cycle of bloodshed: land grabs, settlements in the heart of the local population, and violent responses that in turn provoked retaliation.

"NATIONAL" VERSUS "SETTLER" MODELS

Little by little, I arrived at the conclusion that to attempt to understand the conflict using a rational model was to employ an instrument that was not accurate enough to expose the underlying reality. At that point, I reread an account of the deterioration of the relationship between British colonists in Tasmania and the aboriginal population. The renowned British historian James (later Jan) Morris, after describing years of mistreatment of the latter by the former, comments:

> Despised, debased, and brutalized themselves, their numbers precipitously declining, now [the aborigines] were often the aggressors. . . . It did not take long for the white community to convince itself that the Europeans were the aggrieved party, and soon the classic settler-native syndrome was far advanced. . . . [Settlers and administrators alike]—all were reaching the conclusion that life in Tasmania would be much happier if there were no Tasmanians.[8]

Israelis were not convicts transported to a distant colony, as were the first white Tasmanian settlers, and the Palestinians are not hunter-gatherers without previous contact with the West, but the syndrome is familiar. Jewish settlers who moved into the territory of the indigenous Arabs encountered violent opposition from the latter and reacted as if they (the settlers) were the aggrieved party and the "natives" were the aggressors; and thus there evolved a cycle of mutual violence that has yet to end.

The "settler-native" model has been analyzed in countless academic studies, and I have chosen to present here a summary that was prepared by Dr. Erez Tzfadia as part of a research project that I directed in 2001–2:

> "Settler societies" are those founded by colonists, mainly European, in territories where there is already a native population. With the passage of time, the settlers become the dominant group, both politically and eco-

nomically, and they refer to themselves as the "founders" or the "first settlers." Later waves of immigrants are integrated into the state or nation
with a status inferior to that of the founding group, but superior to that
of the natives. This results in the development of a society that is hetero-
geneous in terms of ethnicity, class, and race, and that tends to retain and
reinforce this ethnic and class stratification throughout the process of
nation building. During this process, the boundaries of the nation are
defined and expanded to encompass the founding and immigrant groups
[and to exclude the natives], as is the pattern of allocation of wealth
within the society and the region.

This model is at work in Israel as well: the founding group of Euro-
peans can be equated with the mainly Ashkenazi Jewish immigrants who
came to Israel from Europe during the period of Ottoman and British
Mandatory rule—impelled by nationalistic aspirations—some of whom
embraced the values of the Zionist movement. They are the prototype of
"Israeliness." The "natives" are the Palestinians. With them, and with the
Arab world of which they are a part, the state of Israel has for many years
been embroiled in a territorial struggle. The "immigrants," in the case of
Israel, are identified as two distinct major groups: the Mizrahim, Jews
from Muslim countries in Africa and Asia who immigrated to Israel during the first two decades after the establishment of the state, bringing with
them an Arab "oriental" culture; and the "Russians," immigrants from
the former Soviet Union—some half of whom are non-Jews—who arrived
in Israel during the 1990s. The project of building the Israeli nation and
state, which was carried out in the shadow of the conflict, gathered the
Ashkenazim, Mizrahim, and Russians to its bosom while leaving the
Palestinians out.[9]

I erred in my thinking when, as observers from the Left are wont to do,
I divided the history of Zionism, or the history of the Israeli-Palestinian
confrontation, into pre– and post–1967 war periods, which supposedly
differ in essential ways. To this way of thinking, the situation that
obtained prior to the Six-Day War changed fundamentally on the seventh day. But the passage of nearly two generations has proven that
1967 was not actually a point of disconnection, but its opposite—the
period between 1948 and the 1967 war representing a hiatus in the
fighting—and that the Six-Day War was in fact the final battle of the
1948 war; the partition of the land carried out at the signing of the 1949
armistice agreements (which held for eighteen years) was obliterated in
one fell swoop with the Israeli conquest and occupation of the territories. And the nineteen years between 1948 and 1967—during which
Eretz Israel / Palestine was divided into two distinct geopolitical units—
had not been a long enough period of time to psychologically separate
the respective communities from their territories "across the border."

The designation of the land within specific political and administrative boundaries—artificial and absurd as these might be—as "the homeland" is a dynamic well known in the experience of the developing world. There, the borders of colonies, drawn to suit imperialist interests, defined the national identities of the indigenous communities that dwelt within them, and not vice versa. Here in Eretz Israel / Palestine, this dynamic was not fully played out. The Palestinians on the West Bank, despite the fact that a Jordanian identity had begun to take hold among them, persisted in maintaining their emotional connection with the areas from which they had been expelled in 1948. The Jews, the overwhelming majority of whom had become reconciled to being cut off from the West Bank, reverted—almost immediately following the beginning of the occupation—to cultivating a religiously and nationalistically based affinity for what had once been "the cradle of the nation." The violent political confrontation between the Israelis and the Palestinians also had not changed in any fundamental way, only altering its character to suit the new circumstances; nor had the settler-native syndrome really changed, if anything becoming increasingly severe in the absence of the moderating influence of the British, who had acted as a mediating third party during the Mandate.

QUESTIONS OF IDENTITY

It is difficult to say which was the cause and which the effect. Was my understanding of reality from a "native" point of view the outcome of the Zionist education I had received, combined with the emotional affinity passed down to me, or had my disgust at witnessing the descent of both Israeli and Palestinian nationalisms into the depths of extremism, xenophobia, violence, and killing awakened in me my "native" identity—one purporting to cast off nationalism and to pursue fellowship among Arab and Jewish "natives"—or was it all just a question of the chicken or the egg? One way or another, I found myself inclined toward defining my my worldview as "native," or "neo-Canaanite." It is an attempt to transcend nationalism and construct an identity based on a "native" affinity to the land. Admittedly, it is a romantic and artificial concept, but it is posed against the current national extremism. At least there is no harm in it. I feel everything created by human beings—by any human being—in this land combines to form a rich and glorious cultural heritage that influences the lives and experience of all who live there. No one has the right to rewrite or erase parts of it. The destruction of the

Other's cultural landscape, whether material or conceptual, would turn against the destroyer, leaving him impoverished and rootless. My political positions, as well as my attitudes toward other questions of identity became increasingly esoteric, since public discourse was, and is, conducted within the "nationalist" model. Both Palestinians and Israelis emphasize and cultivate—and confront each other with—their respective national identities, and they affix this identity to the disputed territory. Both sides cling to aspirations of "self-determination" and to consequent claims of sovereignty over a defined piece of territory, and these aspirations also focus the debate on questions such as geographical partition and "unilateral separation," as I elaborate below (chapter 6). I find my thinking totally irrelevant to Israeli public discourse, and this is also the attitude toward me.

The concept of a "native" attachment to Eretz Israel / Palestine is not widely accepted in Israeli society for various, often contradictory reasons. It is regarded by the Zionist establishment and in right-wing circles as a betrayal of Zionist values and as undermining the privileged position granted by the Zionist establishment to those who act as if nothing had changed since the days of Theodore Herzl, Chaim Weitzman, and the pioneers of the second and third *aliyot* (sing., *aliya,* waves of Jewish immigration to Palestine in the early twentieth century). This intimate, native connection to the land is perceived as negating one's connection to the Jewish people and, especially, to its sufferings, which are viewed as having endowed it with an absolute entitlement to a sense of self-righteousness as the "quintessential victim."

Attachments suggestive of "post-Zionism" are perceived as anti-Zionist, which comes perilously close—in the view of the Right—to anti-Semitism. Moreover, even the Zionist Left is united in viewing those who identify themselves as post-Zionists with a degree of mistrust bordering on hostility. A blend of Israeli-Jewish ethnocentrism and anti-Palestinian sentiments with strong elements of religious fanaticism is promoted as "neo-Zionism," a national ideology that tries to serve as a unifying myth within Israeli society. The Zionist revolution is purported to be a "permanent revolution," although it can hardly plaster over the deep cracks in a society that has lost its cohesion.

ASHKENAZI SABRAS' GUILT

Voices predicting the immanent breakup of Israeli society into its component parts are increasing in strength and number. Accompanying this trend, there has also been an upsurge in the expression of hatred toward my sociocultural subgroup, "sabra sons of the founders." Those who were here first are being labeled as the ones to blame for all the hardships experienced by Israeli society. Hostile pronouncements have come from all quarters: the Right and the Left, social activists, intellectuals, sociologists, Mizrahim, and "post-Zionists," all competing to confirm the guilt of the founders' offspring.

Lev Greenberg, a political sociologist from Ben-Gurion University of the Negev, states: "In Israel there are classes of citizenship, and the first-class citizens are the sabra warriors, the native-born offspring of the "founding generation." These "children of the founding elites" have permitted themselves to appropriate the symbols of the nation and "to reinstate the dominance of the Ashkenazi military-officer class at all costs," as well as the "secularism and Ashkenazi culture at its core." The repeated attempts by the founders' heirs to create national symbols in their own image "now seems pathetic," Greenberg concludes.

Baruch Kimmerling writes that the "OKhUSaLim" (an acronym created from the initial letters of "Ashkenazim" and the Hebrew words for secular, old-timers, socialist, and nationalists)

> built this society and this state, were victorious in the 1948 war, uprooted a considerable portion of the Arab population from within the territory of the state, and absorbed a colossal number of immigrants, grinding them in the cultural and political grist-mill [of the state] to make of them a new nation via the mechanism of the pressure cooker [the more intense cousin of the American "melting pot"]. . . . The OkhUSaLi personages [now] coming to the end of their political road are the link joining a yesterday clothed in splendour—though hateful in the eyes of many—and a future bearing a number of alternatives, some of them contradictory.[10]

Hatred for the elite made up of native Israeli offspring of the founders unites immigrants from the Arab world—who resent being discriminated against and relegated to the margins of society and Israeli cultural life, their traditional family structure destroyed—and those from the former Soviet Union, who detest the socialist Left and the remnants of the communist ethos. Even though there are those who proclaim that the era of rule by this elite is over, we are cautioned that they still comprise the dominant social stratum in the economic, cultural, and other aspects of society and have been able to find new sidekicks among Moroccan and Russian Jews. "As a result of this," writes the social commentator Yossi Yonah, "their hegemony endures—a march of folly on the backs of these new acolytes."[11]

PROUD "MAYFLOWER" HERITAGE

Many of the "founders' sons" are unaware of the hostility directed at them, in part because they exist within the protective bubble surrounding members of their set and are therefore not exposed to the accusations being leveled against them; nor do they read the scholarly sociological analyses describing their arrogant, holier-than-thou attitude and denouncing their appropriation of privilege. There are, however, others who acknowledge the allegations of arrogance, feel guilty about their mistreatment of "the new immigrants," and make dramatic public apologies for their "terrible deeds" during the large-scale immigration of the 1950s. They are apologetic about their elitism and join ranks with their harshest critics, some even leading the chorus of recriminations, since they are such smooth talkers.

I, too, was once a part of this reproachful choir, but I have apparently mellowed with age; and now, entering the eighth decade of my life, my perspective has changed. I am engulfed by a sweet nostalgia for my childhood and youth; and in addition to that, I am filled with pride and joy at belonging to the "tribe" of the founders' sons. What's more, I feel the need to defend myself against attack and even to launch a defiant counterattack of my own: "I am a proud 'Mayflower' descendent," "the salt of the earth." I feel no guilt or inferiority, nor do I regard myself as a robber. On the contrary, it is only thanks to us—the founders and their children—that our defamers and critics are here to complain. What would their fate have been had we not been here to welcome them?

The list of charges against the "sons of the founding elites" is long and the accusations are grave, giving a vivid (and in my opinion a distorted and ungrateful) picture of how a small group of Ashkenazi Jews (an ethnic subcategory designed to highlight the contrast between European and "oriental") allegedly manipulated their way to control of the Zionist enterprise. By means of a sophisticated combination of political daring, modern ideas, single-minded devotion to their objectives, and charismatic leadership, this group succeeded in creating the canonical myth of the *halutz,* the trail-blazing pioneer who set the political and ethical standards for the Zionist movement and the Jewish Yishuv in pre-state Eretz Israel. By assuming that role, it is charged, the "founders" successfully claimed special privileges for themselves and their children. Using money belonging to the Jewish people, they established and laid the foundations for the political, economic, settlement-related, and cultural institutions of the Yishuv, placing them under their own leadership and grabbing the key positions.

In the course of the 1948 war, they expelled the Palestinian Arabs from their homes and took over their land and property. Upon the arrival of the large wave of Mizrahi immigrants between 1948 and 1952, they did, it is true, go to the trouble of granting them political rights; however, they consigned them to the margins of society and settled them in hazardous border regions or in abandoned Arab villages and neighborhoods. Concentration of the means of agricultural and publicly held industrial production in the hands of the Ashkenazi old-timers forced the majority of Mizrahim into the role of unskilled labor. As a result, the latter find themselves at the bottom of the economic heap. Moreover, the Ashkenazi elites maintained a monopoly over the definition of "Israeli" identity (secular, Western, predominantly urban) and, through coercion targeted at the Mizrahi community, brought about the widespread loss of Mizrahi identity, the breakup of the traditional Mizrahi extended family unit, and, ultimately, the abandonment of a culture stigmatized as "inferior."

The humiliation of the Mizrahim and their resentment at being forced to abandon their ethnic identity resulted in intercommunal tensions that not only have not subsided but have increased with time, their political and cultural repercussions threatening to pull apart the flimsy seams that are barely holding Israeli society together. The hegemony of the "sons of the founding elites" allows them to dictate Israel's economic objectives and its security and peace policies—and news of the end of this hegemony is premature.

The Israeli novelist Amos Oz, in a strongly worded article, enumerates "the sins of MAPAI" (forerunner of the Labour party), the party that represented the founders and their progeny in the early years of the state. Allegedly:

> The greedy, oppressive, scheming MAPAI, whose venomous and manipulative, octopus-like tentacles reached out in all directions, strangling the Palestinians and persecuting religious Jews . . . had the goal of gathering everyone [i.e., Jewish communities from around the world] here in order to destroy their identities and suppress their heritages with the help of its satanic "pressure cooker" . . . so as to turn them all into cannon fodder for imperialistic wars and into [the] "hewers of wood and drawers of water [of Israeli society]."[12]

Oz, of course, rejects all of these allegations and has reduced them to absurdities in order to demonstrate how unjust he regards them to be. His intent is to show MAPAI in a favorable light and to influence his audience "to join me in nostalgia, not nostalgia for what once was here, but nostalgia for what might have been here; nostalgia for what nearly was here." And Amos Oz has earned the support of Ben-Dror Yemini, a journalist described as "the descendent of families that came to Israel [sic] from Yemen in the early 1920s," a group of immigrants the discrimination against and deprivation of whom figure prominently among "the sins of the Ashkenazi founding fathers." Yemini also has a score to settle with "the Mizrahi intellectuals who carry the banner of Mizrahi pride" and mourn the shameful loss of "Mizrahi values: family, humaneness, and tolerance" and the destruction of their cultural identity. "It is true that the Mizrahim have been oppressed in Israel," writes Yemini, "socially, culturally, economically, politically—all under the steamroller of this supposedly Western and democratic state. But where would we be . . . had we not been subjected to the steamroller of oppression? Where would we be were the state of Israel not an extension of the West. . . . [b]ut an oriental state in the style of its neighbors? What exactly is the alternative that might have been?"[13]

CHAPTER 3

Jerusalemites

It is amazing that Amos Oz, that "shining icon of Israeliness," felt the need to respond to the accusations of discrimination and arrogance on the part of people of his background with the counterclaim that the Ashkenazim, too, had been miserable and poor and had suffered scorn and deprivation. Oz's book *A Tale of Love and Darkness* is laced with vignettes of the hard lives of "the poor Ashkenazim." Oz describes the book as "not exactly an autobiography . . . a novel, as well, but not exactly a novel; a historical panorama, but not exactly a historical panorama,"[1] so he can permit himself a degree of poetic license. However, his responses to an interviewer's questions about the meaning of the book are clear and pointed. The interviewer, Ari Shavit, comments: "In any case there is an element of the sociological here. When one digs a little beneath the surface, it turns out that even the story of the old-time Ashkenazi elites is one of difficult transitions. Amos Oz's story is no less a tale of hardship than are those of Shlomo Ben-Ami and Eli Amir [sons of 1950s Mizrahi immigrants, who secured prominent places for themselves in Israeli political and cultural life]." Oz replies:

> I don't know which was easier. . . . Perhaps when it comes down to it, it was easier for me, since in some sense people who came from Europe did, after all, feel more like "subjects" and less like "objects." But it is true that there was some DDT even in our story [Oz is referring to the spraying of Mizrahi immigrants with insecticide as they disembarked, which they regarded as symbolic of their humiliation]. . . . They sprayed my grandfa-

ther with Flit (bug killer) when he arrived at Haifa Port. . . . The milieu of
the story is, indeed, that of poor Ashkenazim: how poor Ashkenazim
lived, what poor Ashkenazim talked about, what they furnished their
two-room apartments with. . . . In this book, I'm writing—among other
things—about the desperate effort by poor Ashkenazim to make a good
impression, and I write about the feelings out of which this effort arose,
the perception that they were despised on principle, and had been for generations upon generations.[2]

CHILDHOOD IN JERUSALEM

I rub my eyes and shake my head. I don't understand. I myself was born
on Yosef Ben-Mattityahu Street, opposite the corner of Zefaniya Street,
in the same neighborhood where Oz was born, albeit five years prior to
Oz. My mother the nurse used to weigh the infant Amos at the local
tipat halav mother-and-baby clinic. And many of the characters that
populate Oz's book are modeled on actual people living in Jerusalem in
the 1940s and 1950s who were well known to my parents; some were
even close woman friends of my mother's. How is it, then, that I fail to
discern in my parents' lives the misery of "the poor Ashkenazim" that
Oz describes, "the desperate effort to make a good impression" and
"the perception that they were despised"? That was simply not the
atmosphere in my parents' home, and I suspect that, were Amos Oz's
parents still living, they would be insulted by his interpretation of their
lives. In any case, living in two rooms was not an indication of poverty
in those days. My parents' home boasted three rooms, and my mother
rented one of them out "to help cover expenses," but she never felt herself to be "poor and despised." My parents' lives were not easy; things
did not always go smoothly, neither their relations with their surroundings nor within the family. But despite their arguments and my "difficult" personality, I think I had a normal childhood. How many children
born during the Arab Revolt of 1936–39, World War II, or the 1948 war
can—as can I—say that their childhood was so normal that they recall
its traumatic events only as an indistinct blur?

A NEW EPIC?

It took me some time to understand that in *A Tale of Love and Darkness,* Oz has launched his own counterattack against those who assault
"the sons of the founding elites." Avirama Golan, an Israeli literary
critic, writes:

> [T]he Zionist narrative lost its legitimacy with dizzying speed, becoming
> the butt of the "new historians," cultural researchers, sociologists, liter-
> ary critics, and extraparliamentary entities, left and right. The linkage of
> postmodernism and post-Zionism, along with the seduction of multicul-
> turalism, inflicted considerable damage. It undermined and battered the
> national narrative. National narratives do not stand on their own. They
> are a binding force that creates social solidarity. . . .
>
> Oz, sitting in the middle of all this, watching his countrymen shunted
> to the sidelines, felt a desperate need to restore the legitimacy of the
> national narrative. His age, his standing, his reading of the map and his
> real anxiety at seeing this exploitation of fading memories, spurred him
> on. With replenished strength, he launched into a mission that he felt
> duty-bound to perform, considering where he was on the social spectrum,
> weaving a tapestry of memory, personal and public, rich in detail and
> broad in scope.
>
> What *A Tale of Love and Darkness* did was free Zionism from its
> musty corner, allow it to cough up all the dust, and encourage it to sing
> out again, loud and clear.[3]

What I have been witnessing is the creation of a "national narrative," maybe a new epic, not mere nostalgic reminiscence, or even a literary masterpiece; and who am I to comment on its historical accuracy?

In 1937, when my family moved to a new home at the far end of the Jewish neighborhood of Rehavia, we found ourselves on the border of the Arab neighborhoods of Shaheen and Katamon. I heard the news of the outbreak of World War II while on the bus carrying me to my first day of school in the first-grade class of the Beit Hakerem Elementary School. My parents, it turned out, had made two serious mistakes that influenced the course of my school life. First of all, they had made (successful) efforts to enroll me in school a year ahead of others my age, thereby guaranteeing that for many years I would be the youngest in my social group, with all the problems that accompany this status. Secondly, they sent me to the school where my father served as principal; hence my situation was always precarious: on the one hand, I was expected to be well behaved and a high achiever, and on the other hand, I permitted myself to be a nonconformist.

All the events of World War II are, for me, associated with trivial incidents. The great battle of Stalingrad is linked in my mind to the episode of my being thrown out the window (on the ground floor, of course) because I had disturbed the big boys when they were sticking thumbtacks in their war maps to mark the shifting position of the fronts. The battle of El Alamein is inscribed in my memory because we had gone to the (Arab-owned) Rex Cinema to see a film about the war in the Western Desert and had gotten into a fistfight with some Arab children. On VE Day (8 May 1945), the day following Germany's surrender to the Allies, our class was on the train passing near Zichron Ya'akov on our annual school outing, when the train suddenly stopped and Australian soldiers wearing those broad-brimmed hats of theirs jumped off and began shooting in the air and handing out Mandatory shilling coins.

I learned of the Holocaust only in 1946, and the descriptions of the atrocities that I read then gave me nightmares that persist to this day, rendering me incapable of even watching a film like *Schindler's List.*

SIEGE

In the summer of 1946, following the intensification of terrorist acts by the Jewish underground, the British established "security zones" in Jerusalem, one of which stretched from the upper end of Gaza Road— where I lived—in Rehavia and along the border of the Talbiyeh neighborhood, which was inhabited primarily by Arabs. The security zone was set off by barbed-wire fences, and at its entrance the British had erected a fortified position constructed from sandbags, where they installed a permanent guard post manned by combat soldiers. This post retains an important place in my childhood memories, because it was there that I witnessed the end of the British Mandate with my own eyes.

On the morning of Friday, 14 May 1948, I was playing with my brother Rafi near the checkpoint, and we could still see British soldiers sitting behind the wall of sandbags. All of a sudden, they got up and left, leaving behind them piles of rifle bullets—which we collected and handed over to the Haganah soldiers who arrived on the scene immediately after us. The Haganah swiftly gained control of Talbiyeh—which, being in the security zone, was nearly empty—and my brother and I followed in their wake and entered empty homes whose doors had been battered down, gathering food left behind in the pantries and kitchens. At that time, Jewish Jerusalem was under siege and subjected to constant shelling; and the shortage of food, and especially of water, was acutely felt in our household. The food that Rafi and I collected that day helped us to weather the siege without having to go hungry.

The period of war and siege lasted some eight months (December 1947–August 1948). Nonetheless, in our home, evidently unlike that of the Oz family on Zefaniya Street, the prevailing mood was not that of "frightened animals [in] underground [burrows]"; hence that period was not engraved upon my memory as traumatic. Amos Oz's childhood

in the same city was apparently characterized by continuous fear and
dread:

> There was certainly dread . . . there was anxiety . . . and disaster was in
> the air . . . since anywhere you walked in Jerusalem you saw the [Arab]
> villages all around; all they had to do was make a fist, and the city would
> be crushed from all sides. . . . But what I remember most of all—and it
> sends shivers up and down my spine to this day—is the two green lines we
> found one morning in 1947 on the gate of our house and on the adjacent
> houses, because the Arabs had passed through the neighborhood during
> the night marking the houses: who would live in which house, who would
> "inherit" which house.[4]

I suspect that Oz needed to portray his childhood thus in order to provide a basis for his present political and ideological stance vis-à-vis the
Palestinians:

> When I see the "hawkish" hysteria on the one side and the "anti-
> colonialist" hysteria on the other . . . I am conveyed back to my begin-
> nings: When I was a boy during the siege of Jerusalem, for eight months
> we sat in underground burrows like frightened animals; and they starved
> us and deprived us of water, and they shelled us every two min-
> utes. . . . When I wrote this book, I realized, to my horror, the degree to
> which we have our backs to the wall. . . . On the other side of this line
> ([on the side] controlled by the Arabs) there hadn't been partial ethnic
> cleansing [as on the Israeli side of the line], but complete ethnic cleansing,
> the absolute ethnic cleansing of Jews.[5]

Like the Mizrahim, the Palestinians cannot claim to have a monopoly
on persecution, nor can they pretend that their victimization is unique.
Amos Oz, too, was an unfortunate victim, it seems, and the Arabs were
cruel, even crueler than we were. "If this is a matter of 'if you live, I die,'
then I will live and you shall die; it is better that you die," Oz declares.[6]
This from a man who unabashedly represents himself as a peace activist,
who, as he tells it, has suffered—along with his family—for his activism
on behalf of reconciliation between the two peoples.

Unlike for Oz, however, for me the siege of 1948 was a time of adventure: I cycled daily to school along the borders of the Arab neighborhoods; during the shelling, I lay on our veranda identifying the types of
incoming artillery shells by the sound of the blast as they left the barrel
and the whistle they made in flight; I assisted the truck drivers from the
convoys that brought food into Jerusalem and then got stuck in the city
for weeks at a time; I helped the Haganah soldiers at their post on the
border of Rehavia confiscate booty from looters who had ransacked the

homes of Arabs who had fled from the adjacent neighborhood of Katamon, and stood in line to receive our ration of water as it was doled out
from a small tanker on our street. On Gaza Road, the mood was not one
of anxiety but of resolve.

MUTUAL ALIENATION

Our house on Gaza Road was on the border of the Arab Shaheen section, in the western part of the Katamon neighborhood, and of the Talbiyeh neighborhood referred to above. Decades after the fact, it is hard
to explain—or to understand—the sense of mutual alienation that set
the Jewish neighborhood and the nearby Arab neighborhoods apart, in
two distinct worlds. On my "mental map" (and I am sure also on those
of our Arab neighbors), the Arab (or, in their case, Jewish) neighborhoods were indicated by white patches, symbolizing terra incognita.
There, in that Other landscape, were houses and human beings that had
meaning for us only as the objects of our political hostilities and fears
for our security, but in no way, shape, or manner, as subjects in their
own right. As an adult, I made an intellectual and emotional effort to fill
in the white patches and to understand the vanished Palestinian world,
the world of my neighbors who had been uprooted from their homes.
And then, at about the time I completed my book on the vanished Arab
civilization, *Sacred Landscape: The Buried History of the Holy Land
since 1948*, an autobiographical memoir by Edward Said, my neighbor
from the other side of the British roadblock, appeared. Said was
Jerusalem-born, like me, and roughly my contemporary in age, and his
home and mine had been just a few hundred meters apart, but his childhood and mine could not have been more different.

Said's point of view reinforces my sense of the blindness governing
one's view of the Other. In his autobiography, where he describes a
childhood divided mainly between Cairo, rural Lebanon, and Jerusalem, he writes that "Jerusalem . . . seemed to have a more homoge-
nous population [than Cairo], made up mainly of Palestinians."[7] He
writes this even though two out of three people that he would have met
on the street outside his immediate, mainly Arab, neighborhood were
Jews (100,000 of the city's 160,000 inhabitants). The only Jews he
refers to by name in his description of Jerusalem are the midwife who
delivered him, his pediatrician ("a Dr. Grunfelder . . . known to be the
finest in Palestine"), and one Jewish classmate. I, similarly, can only
name a single non-Jewish friend, the son of our Bosnian (i.e., European

Muslim) neighbors, the Mushabaks, with whom I quarreled more than I played.

SAID UPSET

Edward Said clearly remembered the checkpoint on Gaza Street, recalling how "nervous Tommies at the barbed-wire barricade . . . examined [his] zone pass suspiciously" when he passed by on his way to school, looking older than his twelve years.[8] He lived the comfortable life of an urban, well-to-do Palestinian, steeped in Western culture, in an elegant home in Talbiyeh—enjoying leisurely drives around the neighborhood with his older cousins in his aunt's family's light green Studebaker—until bullets began to fly in Jerusalem. In a critique of an interview with Said that had appeared in the *Ha'aretz* weekend supplement on 18 August 2000, I wrote:

> At the historic moment when the British evacuated the checkpoint and departed the city, we were there collecting the discarded ammunition, but Edward Said was already living in his Cairo home, whence the family had fled immediately after the first shots were heard in late 1947. Said's need to present the Palestinians as hapless peace-lovers who fell victim to the Jewish forces of evil is so profound that he is incapable of coming to terms with the cowardice and treachery of the Palestinian elites—including his own family—at the time of the 1948 war. A Palestinian intellectual less well known than Said, Prof. Hisham Sharabi, painfully accepts responsibility for his part in the betrayal perpetrated by "the educated people and 'effendis'" who fled, abandoning "the ignorant masses" to their fate. Said's tormented conscience compels him to employ harsh language, even causing him to justify the Palestinian rejection of the 1947 partition plan, thereby also justifying their taking the initiative in the opening of hostilities, which ultimately led to their ruin. In Said's opinion, however, he himself is not obliged to acknowledge any responsibility for his family's and community's contribution to the catastrophe. Moreover, he denounces those who stayed behind and are now attempting to preserve what is left. Compared to the Palestinians who stayed, this New York intellectual will always be the greater patriot, and there will always be enough guilt-ridden Israelis willing to accept full responsibility for what took place and to absorb Said's every insult in a kind of self-flagellation.
>
> As I read Said's memoir, I reflected on his pampered childhood and on my own childhood. Said and those like him had never understood the power of the desperation in my parents' hearts, and by the time they did understand, it was already too late. Now Said permits himself to cry over his lot, and I'm supposed to feel guilty for our victory—for the sacrifices my parents made, for the fact that we stayed and fought, while he and his ilk fled. Isn't it about time Said's spell were broken, allowing us to speak

the mangled language of the market square, in which the real dialogue takes place?[9]

Said was tremendously upset when he read the English translation of my article, and wrote a letter to the editor of *Ha'aretz* that demonstrated that my criticism had hit a raw nerve:

> Crude, blustering demagogue that he is, Benvenisti enjoins us to use "the mangled language of the market square," which to judge by the sheer awfulness of his writing is hardly the best medium either for clear thought or for logical exchange. As a result he resorts to personal abuse and every exploded myth of Zionist *hasbara* [propaganda] that his resentful brain is capable of. . . . He neglects, however, to mention his own shabby role in the ethnic cleansing of Jerusalem right after Israel's conquest of the city in 1967. Along with Moshe Dayan and Teddy Kollek, he participated in the forced removal of hundreds of Palestinians in order to clear the space before the Western Wall. That he feels no guilt or even embarrassment nevertheless strikes me in the end as being as uninteresting as the details of his family's history that he regales us with shamelessly in the process of slandering mine. He neither has a consciousness of who he is nor a capacity for orderly and consequential thought. How he expects anyone to believe his ranting about the Palestinians' responsibility for their own dispossession is quite staggering. It is especially unseemly, even indecent, for a member of his people to speak so gloatingly about the misfortunes of others. Never mind that he can't face the truth about what Zionist forces were responsible for in 1948 in the deliberate routing and dispossession of hundreds of thousands of civilians (as acknowledged by every historian who has consulted the Israeli archives), but to suggest that the four million Palestinian refugees deserve their fifty-year-old suffering is to reveal a depth of hatred that one would have thought Benvenisti, clamoring for attention as he does, would have best left hidden.
>
> Besides, suppose for a moment it is true that the Palestinians left because of the treachery of their leaders or their middle class. What is supposed to follow from that? Most civilians abandon their houses to protect themselves and their children during war. Israeli residents of Kiryat Shmona regularly used to run into shelters when there were rocket attacks. Millions of people leave their homes during wartime, most recently in Kosovo and Bosnia. Is Benvenisti seriously suggesting that because all these people left like cowards, they therefore should be punished by not being allowed to return? Unwittingly perhaps, Benvenisti reveals the utter bankruptcy of what has for years been the Israeli argument about the Palestinian refugees. First, it was that neither they nor the Palestinian people existed. Second, it was that they left because their leaders told them to. Third is Benvenisti's variant, that their cowardly leaders and intellectuals traduced them into leaving. So? How is not allowing them back to their homes commensurate with any of these fake arguments? The fact is that it isn't and never was

commensurate: and hence the imperative of the Palestinian right of return.[10]

Said's impassioned attack only reinforced my pride in my parents and their generation, who raised my older friends and me. We did not flee the country, but stayed and fought and won. And as to my myopia regarding my Palestinian neighbors, it admittedly persisted for many more years, until 1967; and as I commented earlier, their tragedy penetrated my consciousness even later. In this I was not unlike many others. For indeed, numerous Israelis look upon the years between 1948 and the outbreak of the 1967 war as a calm, almost idyllic period, because during that time Israeli society felt freed, by and large, from the relentless nightmare of Israeli-Palestinian confrontation. A slogan frequently on the lips of Israel's left wing, "Back to the 1967 Borders," expresses not only a yearning for the reimposition of the Green Line dividing Israel proper from the occupied territories, but also the desire to travel backward in time to a period when we were able to externalize the Palestinian problem and treat the conflict as if it were a war between sovereign states. The intercommunal warfare between Rehavia and Talbiyeh, Tel Aviv and Jaffa, had been effectively wiped from the Israeli consciousness, and the Palestinians who populated the neighborhoods and villages that bordered ours became in our eyes refugees without a national identity—whose very presence was taken to be an Arab plot designed to embarrass the Jewish state. The 1948 war became fixed in our minds as a defensive war waged by the fledgling Jewish state against the invading armies of the Arab world. After the war came "infiltrators" who murdered innocent Jews in frontier communities, Syrian threats, collaboration between the Jordanian Arab Legion and the fedayeen (Palestinian irregulars), and arms deals between Egypt and the Soviet bloc in preparation for "round two." Every attack against Israeli civilians was seen as further proof of Arab refusal to come to terms with the fact of Israel's existence, and every piece of evidence pointing to Israel's responsibility—in the form of military provocations—met with charges of anti-Semitic defamation, since, of course, "Israel's hand is always extended in peace."

THE YOUTH MOVEMENT

Like everyone else, I believed that Israel was a Jewish "nation-state" immersed in the noble work of "ingathering of exiles" while at the same time persisting in its efforts to establish a new, just society based on the visions of the prophets of ancient Israel and the fathers of modern socialism. In the winter of 1948, in the midst of the war, I joined the Tnuah Meuchedet (United Movement), the socialist Zionist youth movement set up by the MAPAI party. Like the other youth affiliates of the Israeli labor movement, my movement, too, educated us for the "realization" of Zionist and socialist ideals, that is, either joining one of the existing kibbutzim or founding a new one. My entire social, emotional, and intellectual life was given over to "movement" activity—with an intensity characteristic of life within the "bubble" inhabited by members of my generation and social class, that of the "sons of the founders." Inside this bubble we led a sheltered existence—with well-appointed homes and prestigious schools, a wealth of social and cultural activities—shared exclusively by those of our social stratum. All around us, the world was in upheaval, hundreds of thousands of impoverished immigrants (primarily Mizrahim) lived crowded together in *ma'abarot* (temporary immigrant settlements) and tent camps, while we carried on with our normal lives: wearing our blue youth-movement shirts, laced at the throat with red or white (by the more Marxist-oriented Hashomer Hatza'ir), we debated from dusk till dawn the relative merits of Marxism-Leninism and "constructive socialism," the Eretz Israeli version of which is described by Zeev Sternhell in *The Founding Myths of Israel, Nationalism, Socialism, and the Making of the Jewish State* as "a socialism of conquest of the land and building the Jewish economy . . . [whose] primary aim was to create a strong economic infrastructure . . . [and that was] never an aim in itself but a tool for the advancement of national objectives, an incomparably effective mobilizing force."[11] We went on grueling hikes in the desert in order to toughen ourselves and to demonstrate our love of homeland and our scouting skills, and we dreamt of the day when we, too, would set out for kibbutz life and Zionist "realization" or would take our places as officers in the army that was even then being forged from the pre-state underground military organizations.

SYNTHETIC ISRAELINESS

Our parents were busy with their mission of "immigrant absorption," with building a state and society from scratch, as Amos Oz describes as being the case with MAPAI: "Its head was above the clouds, and its eyes were, for the space of two generations, fastened on the stars and bound to a vision more gripping than any, and at base, also just and humane."[12] Us they trained to follow in their footsteps, to implement the blueprints they had drawn up. They unapologetically groomed us to serve as an elite that would inherit the privileges they had amassed; they aspired that we, "the first generation for redemption," should be the very personification of "Israeliness," an object of emulation for the new immigrant masses. The Hebrew we spoke—with its own peculiar slang—the community singing, the exceptionally informal style of dress, the sarcastic humor, the modern first names, the folk dances, the military and geographical knowledge, the rough exterior and sentimental interior of the sabra, the secularism—all were meant to aid in constructing a new image for the immigrants, who would look upon us as role models—as products of the Israeli "pressure cooker"—by whose example Israel's diverse ethnic communities would become truly One Nation.

This synthetic Israeliness became, as well, a rallying point for world Jewry, a symbol of the New Israel that had risen from the ashes of the diaspora communities destroyed in the Holocaust. Our parents could not have succeeded in creating the "new Israeli" had they not poured all their strength into our education. My father's devotion to this cause exemplified the energies invested by his generation and mine of educators—school and kindergarten teachers, as well as youth leaders—in this project. But their dedication and talent would not have sufficed were it not for the stirring message on their lips, a romantic tale of the rebirth of a nation, suffused with the loftiest social ideals. The real key to the success of this educational venture, however, lay in the amazing success of the whole Zionist enterprise. One found it easy to identify with the rousing saga of our struggle for national independence and to be full of pride in the part played by one's tribe—and oneself—in the marvelous success and in the knowledge that you had been here from the very beginning. And we, the young objects of this educational effort, took it all *very* seriously: we played at living the utopia, and we established a splendidly narcissistic society.

No wonder those who did not "belong" hated, envied—and emulated—us. We had only ourselves to blame for their negative attitude. However, few of us felt that we were the beneficiaries of injustice or wrongful privilege. We hadn't stolen anything from anyone. On the contrary, we had given our all to "absorb" the others, those who had come because of persecution and because they had no choice, unlike our parents, who had immigrated of their own free will and out of a sense of ideological commitment to the realization of Zionism. Nonetheless, claims that we were arrogant, that we had an unjustifiable degree of control over the centers of political and economic power, and that we were contemptuous of the newcomers' culture grew in intensity as various groups of immigrants became more firmly established and began to demand their rightful place in the Israeli power structure.

For our part, we paid little attention to the immigrants' outrage and sense of deprivation or to their envy of our position since, on the whole, these assumed a political form: support for Menachem Begin's right-wing, expansionist Herut party, which had declared war on the MAPAI establishment. We had been brought up to hate and despise the revisionist movement from which both Herut and ITzL (the National Military Organization, or Irgun) had sprung, and we regarded Begin and other followers of Ze'ev Jabotinsky as "enemies of the working class" and political adventurists tainted with fascism. This hatred and attendant mistrust dated back at least to the murder of the Zionist labor activist Chaim Arlozoroff in 1933, for which the revisionists were blamed; and found expression, for example, in the 1948 sinking of an Irgun munitions ship, the *Altalena,* by command of Prime Minister David Ben-Gurion, who viewed its presence as the prelude to an attempt to overthrow the elected government of Israel. Begin was seen as a demagogue whipping up the masses to bring down the governing regime and wipe out the achievements of the Israeli labor movement. The fact that many of Herut's (and later the Likud's) supporters were new immigrants from Arab countries enabled us to discount their hostility as being the result of a "primitive" response to incitement and, therefore, beneath contempt, not to be taken seriously.

In 1953, I was recruited along with my fellow youth leaders and the older teens from the movement to converge on Jerusalem to fend off an anticipated attempt by Menachem Begin and his "gang" to mount an assault on the Knesset in an endeavor to thwart Ben-Gurion's efforts to gain approval for his decision to accept reparations from Germany. Each of us carried a wooden pickax handle and sported a red armband; we hid in the basements of houses near the Knesset building, awaiting the Herut attack. A bloody clash was averted only because the army and police themselves succeeded in repulsing the inflamed demonstrators. The dismissive and disdainful attitude harbored by the bulk of the Ashkenazi elite and other MAPAI supporters toward Menachem Begin and his party was ultimately to have serious repercussions after the Likud victory and consequent takeover of the reigns of power in 1977.

THE KIBBUTZ

In the summer of 1951, after completing my secondary school studies, I—along with fellow youth-movement graduates from Jerusalem, Petah Tikva, and Kiryat Haim, both male and female—had joined the army as a group within the framework of the Nachal ("Fighting Pioneer Youth") corps. The Nachal program was based upon a brief period of army service (three months) followed by a longer period of living and working together on a kibbutz as preparation for life as an "independent commune," during which time we were still in uniform and under military command. About a year after joining the army, in the fall of 1952, we were sent to Kibbutz Rosh Haniqra on the Lebanese border, where a thinning in the ranks of its founding members had obliged the movement to send "reinforcements"—that is, we were to join this kibbutz rather than found a new one of our own.

Nachal was modeled on the Palmach, the legendary pre-state military organization that had combined agricultural labor with military maneuvers. This combination, which acquired symbolic meaning ("Sheaves and Sword" or "Rifle and Plow"), had originally arisen out of the prosaic need of Palmach units to earn their keep by working on kibbutzim. Nachal had no need to finance its activities; however, the amalgamation of military activity with work on a kibbutz—which was, of course, romantically represented as the continuation of the "Sheaves and Sword" ethos—also had a totally prosaic objective, maintenance of a structure for recruiting a young workforce that could be directed to kibbutzim in need of reinforcement. The kibbutz was perceived as the optimal environment for the flourishing of the halutzic ethos, whence it might radiate Zionist and socialist values upon Israeli society as a whole. And we, the "pioneering" elite, were destined—through strenuous agricultural labor—to "realize" all the exalted social ideals embodied in the visions of the biblical prophets, in the *Communist Manifesto*, and in David Ben-Gurion's speeches—dancing a tempestuous hora dance all the while. This was the adventure of a lifetime, which all of us recall with pangs of nostalgia, and which nurtured a sense of intimate and lasting fellowship that has endured for fifty years and more.

The truth of the matter, however, is that even back in 1952, this was all a sham, since the circumstances that had given rise to the necessity for halutzic "realization" had already changed utterly: fulfilment of the needs of the state now required that young people like myself dedicate ourselves to service in the many fields that were in desperate need of an educated workforce with leadership potential—in the army, the economy, and government bureaucracy. Instead, we were spending our days at exhausting and tedious agricultural labor—in communities that, in the end, would prove to have no lasting impact on the underlying values of the Israeli economy—engaged in what was merely a ritual that purported to embody values whose time had, in any case, passed. Indeed, there were already nagging doubts as to whether the kibbutz (as a socioeconomic institution) would last, or whether the heroic effort to establish these nuclei of an egalitarian, "pioneering" society was not just another utopian experiment like any number of others that had been undertaken, only to be abandoned, in Europe and America.

We could discern the yawning gap between the pretensions of the kibbutzim and their actual role in the shaping of Israeli society. There is no doubt that the kibbutzim enjoyed a degree of political, economic, and ideological influence far out of proportion to their numbers (generally a mere 3 percent of the Israeli population); however, their contribution—both direct and indirect—to immigrant absorption and to the solution of the other tremendous problems facing the young state was marginal (although perhaps we should exclude from this assessment the significant part played by second-generation *kibbutznikim* [sing., *kibbutznik*, kibbutz members] in the army and the security apparatus, and of course recall the kibbutz movement's dominance in the agricultural sector and control of land and water resources, which were vitally important).

Life on a kibbutz—with all the romance of the "conquest of the desert," the intense comradery of late adolescence, and the sense of mission—was difficult and, more to the point, boring. The hardships of physical labor, the Spartan living conditions, and the distance from the city and cultural centers spawned serious misgivings. It became harder and harder for me to see haymaking and fruit-picking as activities leading to "the ennoblement of humankind through socialism," in the words of one of the slogans we used to declaim. Is it any wonder that I jumped at the opportunity to leave for a post as an adult youth-movement leader, first in Rehovot and then in Tel Aviv?

ATTACK ON THE OLD ETHOS

For me, 1953 and 1954 were years fraught with ideological crises and personal doubts. David Ben-Gurion, our indomitable leader, had launched a frontal attack on the old ethos and was calling upon the nation's youth to redefine their pioneer ethic and to join "statist" (*mam-*

lachti in Hebrew) ventures such as the army, government bureaucracy, and looking out for the welfare of new immigrants. Although he dared not lay a hand on socialist symbols like the red flag and the "Internationale," in practice he dismantled the labor-movement-sponsored stream in the educational system (*zerem ha-ovdim*) and denied the Histadrut trade union federation the crucial role it had previously played in affairs of state. For those of us who had been brought up on the official slogan "The best [go] to the kibbutz," this was terribly hurtful. All of a sudden one could be a halutz sitting behind a desk in a government office in Tel Aviv or pursuing a career in banking or other "bourgeois" occupations. My colleagues and I continued to lead youth groups in accordance with the same traditional socialist Zionist principles, but I could not avoid being influenced by the qualitative change I saw taking place among the members of the old-time elites, who were giving in to the allure of consumer capitalism with barely a qualm.

Indeed, the "new" historians paint an even less heroic picture of the pre-state halutzic period than this, claiming that all the revolutionary-socialist-halutzic rhetoric was nothing more than a cover for the strong-arm policy vis-à-vis the Arabs and a way of maintaining control of the governing institutions of the Jewish settler community and the World Zionist Organization. Be that as it may, the old slogans are long gone now, and the symbols of class solidarity—the red flag, the "Internationale," the blue shirt—have been folded up and stashed away. There is no longer any necessity to pretend: making money, a bureaucratic career, and a hedonistic, bourgeois lifestyle have become accepted practice, with no need for a veil of hypocrisy.

HIKES

The chances of my returning to kibbutz life appeared slim, and in the meanwhile, I immersed myself in the challenging activity of leading young people on tough desert treks. This was not merely the idle pastime of an adolescent adventurer, however, but also a statement of cultural/class identity: I was carrying on the glorious tradition of the Ramblers' Society that my father founded and of the famed Palmach desert patrols. Over the next few years, I led thousands of youngsters on demanding hikes "from [Mediterranean] sea to sea [of Galilee]," to the Judean desert and Masada, to the farthest reaches of the Negev, and the hills of Eilat on the shores of the Red Sea. These hikes made a lasting impression on the participants, who still talk of them half a century later. One of them, when asked to describe my role as youth leader, replied: "He excelled in everything to do with knowledge of the land and was the unhesitating scout, a man who was confident of his way. By contrast, for many other scouts, the story was, 'How did they lose their way?' He, even if he lost his way, had an almost metaphysical reason that one could not argue with, because he was a person in whom scouting ability was combined with charisma."[13]

Drinking water was strictly limited on youth-movement hikes, as a way of strengthening one's character. This "water discipline" was an inherent aspect of the "cult of the homeland" and reflected the Spartan Zionist ideology. The difficulty of these hikes was a major part of the experience, and intentionally so. *Hanichim* ("trainee" hikers) who could not stand the hardships and "broke" were dragged to trucks that were waiting a few days' walk away; and the *hanichim* carried the trauma of this desert torture with them for many years. "I was a *hanich*," recounts one, "who plodded along in the long line of hikers and tried with all my might to love the desert, but tried even harder—with every ounce of strength that I had—to make it to the end of the hike."

These hikes, crisscrossing the wilderness, served as a way of proving that we "owned" the desert and wastelands, as well as a way of demonstrating a Jewish presence for the benefit of the Bedouin inhabitants of the desert, who had been banished from the open spaces and concentrated on the Beersheba plateau. The supreme expression of the Jewish-Israeli claim to proprietorship over these areas was the wholesale renaming of all of the geographical locations and topographical features throughout the Negev and Arava. A National Naming Committee was appointed by Ben-Gurion, who set out its objectives: "We are obliged to remove the Arabic names for reasons of state. Just as we do not recognize the Arabs' political proprietorship over the country, so also do we not recognize their spiritual proprietorship and their place-names." The committee eradicated the ancient, "organic," and picturesque Arabic names, which had been determined and accepted via a lengthy evolutionary process whose origins are shrouded in mystery and replaced them with Hebrew ones. On our hikes we still used the Arabic names, however, since the committee completed its work in 1951, and detailed maps bearing the Hebrew names came out only later in the 1950s. But there was an additional reason for our stubbornness in continuing to use the Arabic names: it was an ostentatious allusion to our sabra roots, to the fact that we were members of the "old-time" generation of desert scouts. In 1959, my father and I together produced a booklet entitled

Guide for the Teacher and Youth Leader, which gave detailed descriptions of routes for desert hikes. It was my first published book.

The transition from the life of youth-movement leader to that of university student was smoother and less traumatic than I had anticipated—although for many years I avoided visiting Kibbutz Rosh Haniqra, where I had been a member, because of the shame I felt at having left.

CRUSADERS AND ZIONISTS

My choice of university courses reflected both my areas of interest and my membership in the privileged halutzic elite. I enrolled in the economics program in order to ready myself for a government career, at the same time joining the MAPAI-affiliated student association. Not long afterward, I was elected chairman of the universitywide student federation (1957–58) and also general secretary of the National Student Union. Years later, someone pointed out that of all those who had held the latter position, I was the only one who had not become a government minister or, at the very least, a member of Knesset. This was not surprising, as my understanding of the job had been anything but conservative. In 1958, for example, I led a student strike protesting an increase in tuition, and as a result the government appointed a committee of experts to determine the criteria for setting tuition levels. When the committee made its conclusions public, the student federation decided to launch a strike protesting them as well. Opposing this strike because I regarded our agreement to the formation of the committee as constituting a commitment to accept its conclusions, I resigned my position and—at my own expense—took out an ad explaining my actions. The strike collapsed, and my recompense was a deluge of anger and scorn. So ended my career in student politics.

This freed me to turn my attention to a subject with which I was already quite familiar: the historical geography of Palestine, and I had the privilege of being involved in a project of lasting value, the creation of a map of the Holy Land under the Crusaders. "The Project," as it was called (using the English word), was a monumental undertaking conceived by our teacher, Professor Yehoshua Prawer, in the course of which we read through all available primary sources from the Crusader period, summarizing the information on the places described therein and recording it on file cards. Since the quantity of source material was so huge—comprising historical and geographical descriptions, itineraries, chronicles, and feudal charters in a variety of languages—the card files, too, were immense, filling numerous metal boxes, which rested on a large trolley. The task allotted to me was to pinpoint the geographical locations of the Crusader and indigenous settlements and to designate their exact positions, thereby making it possible to chart the pattern of habitation in the Crusader period for a map that would appear in the historical section of the *Atlas of Israel.*

For me, there could not have been more thrilling work than that which Professor Prawer had assigned me. For example, I read a document recording a grant of land by Hugo, Seigneur of Caesarea, to the canons of the Church of the Holy Sepulcher in the year 1166, in which the following details appear: "[The boundaries of the granted area begin] on the hill adjacent to the garden of Fiesse [or Dfiesse] at the place where a spring issues forth from the aqueduct beginning [on the opposite side] of the road that comes from Braicet to the village of the Church of the Holy Sepulcher [Fiesse] and turns eastward beside a cave between two hills and reaches a small hill . . . and beside a lime kiln continues in a straight line that divides Fiesse from the lands of the village of Sabarim of the Hospitaller Order." The area described in the document is well known to me, and all the features it describes (with the exception of the Arab villages, which have been destroyed) are there to this very day.

In the case of the above example, Claude Conder had already confirmed the identity of the places in the late nineteenth century. However, in similar instances, where the settlements or topographic features had not yet been identified, I would look for hints in the settlements that were already identified or the location of the geographical area in question, followed by a painstaking search through the register of place-names of the British Palestine Exploration Fund for places with similar-sounding Arabic names whose location approximated the putative site.

Thus, in the course of more than two years of work, I succeeded in ascertaining the location of 830 places referred to in the literature, several hundred more than had been identified in the preceding hundred years by scholars such as Baron de Ray, C. Conder, C. N. Johns, and F. M. Abel. I shall never forget the day in mid 1960 when Professor Prawer showed me the introduction he had written for the map, which he had signed with both our names—he the famous professor and I the undergraduate whose first piece of research this was. Our map remains the standard record of Crusader-era settlement patterns to this day.

In other areas of my work on the historical geography of the Crusaders, however, I was to see hypotheses that I had posed and conclusions that I had reached contradicted by young scholars. At one scientific conference, where I was serving as chair, two researchers presented papers proving conclusions of mine to be erroneous. "I am fortunate to have had the privilege of chairing a meeting at which my cherished theories were cut to shreds," I remarked. "That is the way of science." But what I did not understand at the time was that I was able to allow myself the luxury of such generosity of spirit toward these junior scholars only because I had already left this field and turned my attention to other matters. My colleagues who had put their trust in my now disproved conclusions could not lightly permit themselves such revisions, since their ongoing research was being challenged—and so they carried on the debate without me. Later in my life, I lost that spirit of generosity and became annoyed when researchers and historians plagiarized my work or ignored my contributions. I realized, however, that one is lucky to have had one's hour of glory and should not bemoan falling into anonymity. Obsessively opening a book at the index to search for reference to one's name is seldom rewarding.

Like a true patriot, I became involved in Israel's *hasbara* ("explanation") aimed at thwarting Arab propaganda equating Zionists with "Crusaders." "This comparison," I wrote in 1973, "is completely baseless." Unlike the Zionists, the Crusaders were colonialists tainted with a propensity for "apartheid"; they were a minority in the land and produced no culturally independent society of their own.

> The stability of any society is dependent to a large extent upon its rural population. In the case of the Crusaders, even the third- and fourth-generation settlers had developed neither a spiritual relationship with the homeland nor a sense of belonging to the land. The Crusaders, who refused to become tillers of the soil, who feared to sally forth from behind the protective walls of their fortified cities, could not be "natives" in the full sense of the word. The small minority that succeeded in striking deeper roots was unable to persuade the others, since the continuous waves of immigration from Europe brought with them elements who constantly reinforced the cultural influence of their countries of origin across the Mediterranean Sea. . . . And when the end came, those who survived sailed their boats back across the sea . . . and the colony that they had established ceased to exist. Few mourned its demise. Even those born in the Latin kingdom of Jerusalem were not dispirited; they had places to return to.

> Israel is a totally different sort of phenomenon than the Crusader kingdom. It was established without the military support of any other state and is therefore not a colonialist initiative. Zionism is not a religious movement (as were the Crusaders), but a national movement with defined

political objectives. Zionism (unlike the Crusaders) established an autonomous economy that was not dependent upon the exploitation of non-Jewish natives. Zionist settlement activity has extended throughout the entire land (in contrast to that of the Crusaders). Israeli society has become firmly established, with its own culture and language and a magnificent array of educational institutions. Those born into this society have sunk their roots deep into the landscape and have become imbued with a sense of belonging to their people, their culture, and their land. And finally, Israel is a state whose citizens (unlike the Crusaders) have no other homeland to return to.[14]

Even as late as 1986, when it was already clear that Israeli rule in the occupied territories had created an apartheid-like situation and contained many of the elements of a colonial regime, including the exploitation of the population under occupation, I persisted—despite all of this—in stating that the comparison with the Crusaders was "stupid" and "absolutely absurd."

INSTANT "ORIENTALIST"

During my student years, and even afterward, when I worked for the Government Tourism Corporation, I had neither contact with nor even an intellectual interest in the Arab population. In fact, I had no interest in interethnic conflicts at all. Like the great majority of Israelis, I externalized "the Palestinian problem," in my mind, turning the Palestinians themselves into "infiltrators" or simply "refugees," whom I conflated with the rest of the "Arab World." As far as I was concerned at the time, the Arab minority living on the margins of Israeli society was, at best, irrelevant or, at worst, a "fifth column." The 1967 war and the conquest of East Jerusalem turned me into an instant "orientalist," but only because Jerusalem's mayor during that war, Teddy Kollek, chanced to meet me on the street and offered me a job as his aide for "Old City Affairs." This was not my first encounter with Kollek. I had worked under him at the Government Tourism Corporation and afterward had been recruited to his election campaign when he first ran for the post of mayor of Jerusalem in 1965.

The story of our work together and of the policies regarding the city's Arab population that we set and carried out has already been told in extensive detail in my books *Jerusalem, the Torn City*[15] and *Conflicts and Contradictions*,[16] and also by other writers. A summary of my role in this work, written in 1983, ends on an apologetic note.

I began my involvement in Jerusalem's municipal affairs as a pragmatic, process-oriented practitioner. I believed that my duty was to alleviate hardship, to minimize tension, and to foster coexistence. I had no set political goals except coping with the immediate symptoms of the conflict, which were serious enough. My Israeli-Zionist ideology, my professional training, and my liberal world-view clashed all too often, but I was not confused by the contradictions. I was merely a troubleshooter. I did not hesitate to be party to a decision to demolish the house of a terrorist before his trial—and to issue a building license for the same house a few months later. I tried to limit the extent of land expropriation but set up an office to compensate Arabs for confiscated land. I participated in overseeing the works at the Western Wall area, but cooperated with the Muslim authorities to safeguard their property there. I fought a decision to retaliate to a grenade attack by evicting innocent civilian Arab families from their houses, but once the decision was made, I volunteered to carry out the eviction peacefully and humanely. I approved a request to build an Arab war memorial but ordered the removal of other memorials built illegally. I tried to reinstate the Arab municipal government, dispersed after the annexation, but organized massive Arab participation in the first Israeli municipal election after the annexation. All these actions were inconsistent as far as a desired goal is concerned, whether partisan, professional, or ideological. There was only a consistent effort to deal with the symptom of a malaise that already seemed endemic. But in a city where electricity is "Jewish" and "Arab" and two ethnic blood banks exist, there is no place for an administrator whose job is to deal impartially with community relations. My actions were scrutinized on two levels: Israeli partisan actions seemed appropriate, normal, and obvious—and were therefore ignored; actions aimed at helping Arabs seemed harmful and unpatriotic—and were therefore deplored. As most Israeli officials stayed away from the Arab population, I found myself dealing almost exclusively with Arab problems. No wonder all my actions were perceived as ideologically "pro-Arab."

The ideological role was forced upon me and, given my temperament, I took up the challenge and made my position clear. It was only a matter of time before I had to leave. Other people stayed within the system and tried to pursue the symptomatic approach. I admire them, but what worries me is that with the institutionalization of the dual, unequal system in Jerusalem, their role had willy-nilly become ideological. The mere fact that they stay in office legitimizes the system. People say that if these people are still there, it cannot be that bad. As the years turn into decades I wonder how much I myself contributed to the legitimization of the system. It may well be that my genuine, humane attempts to lessen communal tension and alleviate hardship made it easier for the "partisans" to impose their ethnocentric goals with minimum opposition and optimal public relations. But what else could I have done?[17]

In 1978, a journalist who had closely followed Kollek's and my shared endeavors over the years wrote:

Kollek gave Benvenisti carte blanche in East Jerusalem. Teddy set high policy but Meron's contribution in East Jerusalem was decisive. If there was an argument, Teddy always gave way in the end. Says Benvenisti: "I fertilized his thinking but without his dynamic personality and his *bitsui*-ism [focus on getting things done] things would have remained sterile." . . .

Says someone who has worked with Benvenisti: "Temperamentally as well as by training he's an historian. He has a need to play a role in the historical development of Jerusalem, particularly at this time and I had the feeling he was preparing himself as the person who would take these critical decisions."[18]

HEROIC FAILURES

I left municipal government some nine years prior to the outbreak of the violent events referred to as the first Intifada, which, in Jerusalem, began in December 1987 and went on for five years. The Intifada made a mockery of any illusion that our tolerant policies toward the residents of East Jerusalem had created the conditions required for stable coexistence. Mayor Kollek continued his policy of "tolerance" throughout the Intifada years, only very occasionally reacting harshly to violent acts of protest by the Palestinians. This policy remained, as it had been from the beginning, an attempt to mollify the Arab populace through the improvement of municipal services. In Kollek's opinion, improving their standard of living was supposed to convince them that they were being treated fairly and equally. This paternalistic, apolitical, and incurably optimistic attitude suffered from two defects. Firstly, Kollek did not have in hand the financial resources to adequately invest in the Arab population; and even when he had enough money, he did not make an effort to ensure its equitable distribution between Jews and Arabs: the Arab population of East Jerusalem received less than 5 percent of the municipal budget. However, even had he invested more financial resources in the Arab sector, this would not have sufficed to pacify the city, and only a member of the old colonialist generation could have believed that money could "buy off" a people with nationalist aspirations. In reply to a journalist's question at the time, I stated:

Teddy is an optimist, whereas I was born here and have a different picture of the situation. The conflicts here have made me very pessimistic—while Teddy has been trying for twenty years to force his optimism on this violent and obdurate city. It's clear to me, however, that had he not believed in the effectualness of his policies he would not have done anything. I am only sorry to see him suffering so much and taking the current situation as a personal affront. In this tragedy called Jerusalem, there needs to be one figure that everyone loves to love, for if not, we all will be devoured by despair—and Teddy is that point of light that makes the surrounding evil all the more visible. He truly believed that Jerusalem was a mosaic of ethnic communities, whereas I maintained that the city was a collection of mutually alienated islands. And what should I say to him now? "I told you so"? He would answer, "You were right, but you didn't do anything. You just sat there in your 'bubble,' whereas my failure was a heroic one."

A reporter once asked me, *"You're a historian. Do you sometimes examine your own deeds from that point of view?"* My answer was:

All the time. And that is what makes my heart ache with a sense of futility. I have been conducting a feeble rearguard action without any chance of altering the key processes. I am not the king of England or Caesar Borgia. The bulldozer driver makes more of a difference than do I. I only tried to make "the morning after" more livable. . . .

And were you able to improve the prospects for "the morning after"?

In 1968 someone tossed hand grenades onto the road leading to the Wailing Wall. Moshe Dayan came and said we must evict all the Arabs living on the Wailing Wall Road, despite it's being clear that it was not they who were to blame. Three tank units were brought in. I requested four hours of grace in which to evict them peacefully. I went from house to house with my aides. I explained the situation and cried along with them. We helped them drag their belongings outside. Thus the need to employ force did not arise.

You ask if this was worth something? It wasn't worth anything concrete, but not one child cried. I did not diminish their hatred. I occasionally see one of the people who were evicted; he looks at me, and I know what he's thinking. At such times I reflect on the job I did. Perhaps I made the occupation tolerable instead of intolerable. Perhaps I did wrong.

Three years ago I was awakened in the middle of the night and was told that some Arabs had, without permission, erected a monument to their soldiers killed during the 1967 war. I gave instructions to have it dismantled immediately, to take the memorial plaque to the police station, and to summon the person who had put up the monument to come and claim his plaque. Another would have hesitated and waited until morning, but I knew that once the monument had been touched by the first rays of sunlight, it would become a political shrine and its removal a political issue. So long as the plaster was still wet, it would be possible to remove it. You ask why this is important? It's not really important, except that Jerusalem had one more peaceful morning. [Some months later, Jerusalem's Arab residents erected a prominent war memorial with a permit from City Council].

How can you survive as a politician where you must accommodate a situation that can change from one day to the next?

The answer is, don't be a politician. . . .

With your political skepticism and the Cassandra-like prophesies you express, you will not have a long political career. The voters prefer unambiguous candidates.

Then the voters can go fuck themselves.

Is this for the record?

I'd rather have a conversation like this with you than be mayor.

So . . .

> I don't know. Maybe I'll work on my Crusader books. Maybe I'll go to Harvard. I made a thesis proposal to them on the subject of decision making in ethnically divided cities. But I would go crazy sitting at Harvard for two years. That's not the real world. I need to create a world of my own, since it appears that I'll not manage in this one. Next April I'll be 45 years old and I still don't know what to do with my life. Maybe nothing.[19]

At the time, it did not occur to me that at the age of 45, I would indeed part company with public life as a politician or official and embark on the hand-to-mouth—or more accurately, research grant-to-research grant—existence of an academic. After a brief and unsuccessful attempt to get elected to the Knesset in 1981, I applied for my first grant. My mother was concerned about my future. She bemoaned the fact that her firstborn son "did not have financial security and didn't have a steady job." "What will happen when you have to retire?" she worriedly asked.

BELFAST AND JERUSALEM

The first stage of my new journey was to return to the classrooms of Harvard, which I shared with students the age of my eldest son. The title of my doctoral dissertation (degree awarded 1982) was "Administering Conflicts: A Comparative Study of Public Administration in Belfast and Jerusalem." In the introduction, I wrote:

> In Jerusalem and Belfast, both groups [Jews and Arabs in the one, Protestants and Catholics in the other] perceive themselves to be a besieged minority; minority and majority are equally prejudiced insofar as they interpret events in dichotomous terms. Total dichotomization is a charac-

teristic condition of societies at war. Indeed, the conflicting groups both in Jerusalem and in Belfast perceive their conflict as a war or as an "intense conflict." They would agree that their respective conflicts conform to the definition: "A conflict is intense when the issues at stake are thought to be of the greatest importance, involving the segment's social identity, its most sought-after material rewards, its most cherished cultural values or its perceived inalienable rights."[20]

Yet the emphasis on the conflictual elements of the situation tends to underplay the basic difference between societies at war and polarized societies. In war, both real and perceived environments are dichotomized; whereas in Jerusalem and in Belfast, the real environment is still a fairly integrated urban system. Perceived dichotomous communities strive to concretize dichotomy by creating a dual physical and social environment. However, that impulse clashes with the necessity to keep the urban system intact. Both conflicting groups rely upon the efficient supply of municipal services and life-support systems. Without it, they would not be able to pursue their endless conflict. In wars, the only interaction of the conflicting parties is through gun-sights. Polarized societies interact in the streets, in factories and through the common sewerage system. Wars are waged until one side is victorious or until both sides are exhausted. Then, everybody can go home. Communal conflicts are endemic, and have no ultimate solution. Even under the most severe confrontations, life goes on.

The encapsulation of the binational conflict into the urban setting makes Jerusalem and Belfast comparable cases. Both are extreme cases, because societal, cultural and political conditions created a very complex and multi-dimensional conflict. They are not unique. Other cities in the same class are Beirut and Nicosia. Brussels and Montreal would represent a somewhat lesser degree of dichotomization. Ethnically segmented American cities would be even milder cases.

The very fact of my drawing a comparison between Jerusalem and Belfast infuriated Teddy Kollek. "Jerusalem is not and will never be Belfast," he stormed, attributing my attitude to my recent ouster from City Hall. To him it was evidence of my frustration at having been removed from a position with influence on municipal policy. Before many years had passed, projects dealing with comparing "divided cities" and "polarized societies" had spawned a real industry. Scholars and politicians alike collected research funds to set up teams to study various aspects of the divided Holy City and its possible analogues: Brussels and Jerusalem; Berlin and Jerusalem; Montreal and Jerusalem; Israel, South Africa, and Northern Ireland. Even Teddy Kollek was placated and admitted that, given the events of the Intifada, his hoped-for "multicultural city" would not be realized in the space of a few decades but "might take a hundred years."

Ironically, the aversion to comparing Jerusalem and Belfast evaporated when the violence in Northern Ireland abated and it was Jerusalem that had become the city riven by violent confrontation. The comparison, which supposedly hinted at an irreparable rift—conveying the opposite message than the "unified city" propaganda—suddenly came to signify a coveted ideal: "If only we could learn from how they are coping with the tensions in Belfast!!"

I wrote these impressions of Belfast after a trip there in 2002:

> It's hard to believe, but a man returning from Belfast comes back charged with optimism and hope that even in Jerusalem all is not lost. Anyone who remembers the warnings sounded in the late seventies and early eighties regarding the danger that Jerusalem would become another Belfast—that the intercommunal violence would degenerate into Northern-Ireland-style clashes—now says to him/herself, "Would that today's Jerusalem were like Belfast is now."[21]

Circumstances had changed to such a degree that the comparison itself appeared baseless: how was it at all possible to equate a pair of communities that, after generations of violent conflict, had resolved to give up violence and to confine their strife to political channels with a pair of communities whose relations seemed increasingly defined by confrontation, delegitimization, and mutual terrorization? Perhaps it is a matter of different placement on the historical continuum from confrontation to reconciliation, with Belfast a generation ahead of Jerusalem—on a positive trajectory somewhere between a political settlement and reconciliation—whereas Jerusalem is stuck far behind, perhaps even sinking deeper into the depths of alienation and reliance on violence.

A Jerusalemite visiting Belfast will immediately notice the similarity between his or her own ancient city and the British-Irish city, whose appearance is so different. In both cities, the world is divided in two: "us" and "them," "ours" and "theirs." Both are divided cities where tribalism expresses itself in the realm of interpersonal relations, in political configurations, and especially in a territorial homogeneity that paints the cities' neighborhoods in the national colors of their warring factions: orange and green in Belfast, blue-white and green in Jerusalem. No less than twenty-five demarcation lines—walls constructed of brick and corrugated iron—separate the Protestant and Catholic neighborhoods, their function underscored by massive murals illustrative of the residents' respective national identities. These terror-inducing boundaries, euphemistically termed "peace lines," are foci of intense violence; and the number of barriers not only has not declined since the 1994 cease-fire agreement between the Catholic and Protestant militant organizations, it has increased. In Belfast, one learns the difference between political arrangements and real intercommunal reconciliation. Since the "Good Friday Agreement," or Belfast Agreement, of 10 April 1998 (see chapter 7), which set in motion a process designed, among other things, to foster participation in the governing of Northern Ireland by all sections of the local community, segregation between Catholics and Protestants in the city has increased to such a degree that today it is referred to as "voluntary apartheid."

The decrease in the level of confrontation between the communal militias did not do away with violence in Belfast, but only altered its character. Now it is directed inward, manifesting in the punishment of "those who deviate from the party line" and criminal elements, as well as in juvenile violence and wars between drug-trafficking gangs—which goes to show that the elimination of an external threat intensifies internal disputes, and that "peace" is not utopia. In fact, many members of the Protestant majority are enraged at what they perceive as "sweeping concessions" by their government and leaders, whom they regard as having sold their birthright to the Catholics and as having sacrificed their political interests and sacred symbols. This, too, is part of the price of "painful compromise," and it bears within it the potential for the destabilization of the process.

If that is the state of affairs in Belfast, what was the source of my optimism? I drew it from the way in which the political, academic, and societal elites have been managing public affairs and influencing public discourse. Their activity has been characterized by avoidance of anything not designed to build bridges and the eschewing of the use of emotionally charged language. For example, one does not hear the term "terrorism" or the epithet "terrorist"; after all, "a terrorist with blood-stained hands" served as education minister in the Northern Irish Executive formed after the devolution of power provided for in the Good Friday Agreement. If such a thing is possible in Belfast, perhaps in Jerusalem, too, all is not lost.

THE LAST ROUND

In 1993, when Teddy Kollek was running for another term as mayor of Jerusalem, he proposed that I return to civic politics and run again, after almost twenty years, for the post of deputy mayor on his ticket. I agreed and joined the campaign. I looked upon this as having come full circle:

I had been with him in his first campaign in 1965 and was now again in his latest—he being already eighty-two years of age and I nearly sixty. The failure was huge and galling. I served an additional year as a member of the City Council but finally resigned because I could no longer stand the style and behaviour of the new mayor, Ehud Olmert, a Likud man.

Olmert did everything within his power to inflame the ethnic tensions in the city. He both initiated and rushed the excavation of a tunnel running the length of the western face of the walls that border the Temple Mount—threatening the structural integrity of some of the homes it undercut—and in September 1996, he organized an opening ceremony that triggered bloody riots in Arab sections of the city and on the West Bank. Olmert instigated other provocative actions as well, such as attempting to interfere with the curriculum being taught in the Arab schools of East Jerusalem, waging a campaign of demolishing "illegal" homes (i.e., those built or added onto without the requisite permits, though building permits were next to impossible for Arab Jerusalemites to obtain), and the continual disruption of the activities of Orient House, the center of Palestinian political activity in East Jerusalem. Olmert also supported the settlers who were attempting to penetrate to the heart of the Palestinian areas of the Old City and the "City of David" (the village of Silwan, just outside the Old City walls) and taking over dwellings there. He even went so far as to participate in fund-raising events on behalf of Ateret Kohanim, a "charitable" society that employed especially aggressive tactics of questionable legality for the acquisition of Arab properties in and around the Old City.

On top of these provocations, Olmert also chose to impugn the reputation of his predecessor, Teddy Kollek, charging Kollek with having intentionally neglected East Jerusalem and having acquired his reputation as "the guardian of the Arabs" merely by dint of successful public relations that were a cover-up for his lies and ineffectual policies. This attack from a right-wing, Arab-bashing quarter was unexpected and disingenuous. Kollek had really been "Mr. Annexation" and bore responsibility for implementing Israel's policy of aggressive control over East Jerusalem, although his approach was more complex than those of others. Unlike the central government, Kollek did not believe that it was possible to annex land without the people living on it. For that reason he fought for—and barely succeeded in obtaining—the granting to Jerusalem Arabs of the benefits of the Israeli welfare state, freedom of movement throughout the country, despite their not being citizens, an independent educational system, relative freedom of the press, and exemption from the Absentee Property Law, which transferred the homes and land of the many thousands of Palestinians who had happened to be residing elsewhere for any period of time during the hostilities of the 1948 war to state ownership via the Custodian of Absentee Property. Evidence of the success of Kollek's approach can be seen in the East Jerusalemites' reluctance to give up these rights should the Palestinian Authority be granted jurisdiction over their neighborhoods.

The issue of Jerusalem remained on the agenda only because, notwithstanding Israeli efforts to the contrary, the Palestinians have succeeded in establishing a vigorous national community in the city, in large part thanks to Kollek's policies, even if these were tainted with paternalism. Teddy Kollek paid for his heroic attempt to impose his harmonious, universalistic, and humane worldview—the product of his liberal Viennese education, his life experience, and his personal proclivities—on a city enveloped in ruinous hatreds. He endeavored to divert his constituents' attention from their everyday hardships and to persuade them that there is more to life than their nationalistic quarrels. He believed that the establishment of a zoo that both Jewish and Arab children could visit, a joint youth orchestra and shared cultural institutions, and conducting a relaxed dialogue while smoking a narghile (oriental water pipe) in a Damascus Gate café could eventually create an atmosphere in which a solution might more readily be achieved. There was a time when many Jerusalemites cherished this sweet illusion. When it evaporated with the first Intifada, even Kollek was shattered: "Coexistence is dead," he lamented. He was the first to admit publicly: "We really have done nothing for the Arabs." "Now I think that [getting peace] may take a hundred years," he said.

MYTHS AND STATISTICS

The annual *Shenaton statisyi li-Yerushalayim* / *Statistical Yearbook of Jerusalem* details the changes that have taken place in the unified city during the preceding twelve months in the areas of demography, employment, the economy, welfare, transportation, construction, and public services, using scores of tables and thousands of pieces of data. The yearbook's editors are professionals in their fields, and the publisher, too, is not a person one would suspect of an intent to fudge data to suit her political views. It is, however, difficult to shake off the sense that the mode of presentation of the data contributes to a picture consistent with

Israel's official political positions and obscures facts liable to discomfit the city fathers.

Particular emphasis is always given to the findings that "every third child in Jerusalem lives below the poverty line" and that Jerusalem "is the number-two city in the country (after B'nei Brak) in terms of poverty." These general statistics refer to the whole population of the city and do not differentiate between Jews and Arabs. Were the data broken down to show the percentage of Arab children living below the poverty line, it would be evident that the incidence of poverty among Arab children is nearly three times that among Jewish children. The huge gap between the two communities in terms of income level, welfare, delivery of public services, funding of education, rate of unemployment, and all the other socioeconomic indicators is not deemed worthy of comment. It crops up in only a few pieces of data, such as those showing that housing is twice as crowded in the Arab sector as in the Jewish.

The disparities between Jews and Arabs are so great that any average figure purporting to present the status of Jerusalem in relation to other Israeli cities is meaningless, and in the worst case, deliberately misleading. Any data that treat the city as one political, economic, and social unit are by definition meaningless because the depiction of Jerusalem as a unified city is itself a fiction. The necessity of maintaining this fiction requires that the data be manipulated to support it. The use of numbers, which are—by their very nature—"objective," lends an air of "scientific" reliability to what is actually a way of shoring up positions dictated from above in accordance with government policy requirements.

Evidence for the strong connection between statistics and politics can be found in the never-ending preoccupation with the issue of the "demographic balance" between Jews and Arabs, a subject that rates particular attention in the Statistical Yearbook. It is well known that in Jerusalem the "desirable" demographic ratio of Jews to Arabs in the city's population was determined many years ago to be 72 percent to 28 percent. Professional demographers are quite aware that this "demographic balance" is a fictional construct, since it was created in the very beginning by the intentional manipulation of municipal boundaries so as to incorporate into the "unified" city a minimal number of its Arab residents. Had the boundaries been drawn in conformity with urban-planning considerations rather than political ones, the demographic distribution would have been different. Today, in fact, there is demographic parity between Jews and Arabs in the Jerusalem metropolitan area, which extends well beyond the city's municipal boundaries.

Professionals, however, can be expected to represent the prevailing situation in the divided city unambiguously. One way of defining this situation is: Jerusalem is inhabited by two distinct societies, both of them "normal" in the sense that each comprises a full array of socioeconomic strata and displays a high degree of cultural cohesiveness. These two societies live in close proximity (sometimes even overlapping), and hence their mutual relations are "abnormal." This is an uncomfortable state of affairs for those who seek to perpetuate the fiction of the "unified city" and who therefore attempt to mask the divide with the aid of "averages," lest the obvious conclusion—that the "abnormal" relations require a political solution—be drawn.

THE ALCHEMY OF JERUSALEM

In May 1999, Ehud Barak was elected prime minister and set up a government that made it a priority to step up the pace of negotiations for a permanent status agreement with the Palestinians. Both the official deliberations and those held behind closed doors included discussion of the fate of Jerusalem (hitherto a taboo subject), in the wake of which hoards of academics and politicians came forward with "programs for the solution of the problem of Jerusalem," for publication or for submission to the government for consideration. All this frenetic activity, which went on for years, made me skeptical, even cynical. I, of course, refused to take part in any of it and instead expressed my feelings on the matter openly. I felt that despite their divergent positions, the interests of politicians and academics are not so very different, both being influenced more by personal and professional motives than by anxiety over the future of Jerusalem.

This is a serious accusation, though often considered justified when leveled against politicians—but academics? Yet it can't be avoided: The "peace plans" industry is one of the crops that thrive on the rotting soil of the continuing conflict—right beside another burgeoning industry, that of "security and protection." Much money, prestige, and ego is wrapped up in this industry. It is financed by wealthy funding agencies whose directors have been convinced by the academics' assurances that they have in hand the magic formula for "the solution." This kind of activity provides the participants with a good living, while turning out recycled versions of their predecessors' "solutions."

Surely there is no harm in promoting positive ideas; except that on occasion the rational models articulated in these peace plans unwittingly lead to an outcome the opposite of that intended by their proponents. When a conflict is not ripe for resolution, and the only way of managing it is by taking advantage of the haziness surrounding the issue, the formulating of models and proposals may actually exacerbate matters to no lesser degree than would outright incitement. "Peace plans"—by forcibly imposing their theoretical models upon the conflict—bring existing differences of opinion into sharper focus, thereby clarifying for those involved the degree to which their positions are in opposition.

The unresolved problem of Jerusalem has engendered a longing for "creative solutions" that will break through the deadlock. The outlook based upon this longing is that there is no problem that the human brain is not capable of overcoming and that the solution depends upon the concocting of a magic formula that will melt down the stones of dissention and transform them into silver and gold.

And indeed, the greatest experts in a variety of fields—they too infected with a Pollyannaish optimism—have banded together to provide magic formulas, their activities having already developed into a whole new branch of research. Those who share in the belief that speculative thought has the power to bring about a "happy ending" are sure that even in the event that this does not come to pass, public discourse will at least have been nourished by fresh ideas that may alter hidebound conceptions. Others, more skeptical, may notice parallels between these "creative solutions" and the "science" of alchemy. The alchemists of old also believed in their ability to achieve "the good of mankind" by transforming common materials into gold, and opinions were divided regarding them as well. Some saw them as the heralds of progress, and others as charlatans.

The gaping chasm between speculation and reality is revealed in the words of a distinguished law professor who was one of the scholars to propose innovative solutions to the problem of sovereignty in the Old City: "The problem," she said, "is that Yasir Arafat did not take my course in international law." That is to say, the obstacle to progress was Arafat's ignorance. Had he but been "exposed" to recent innovations in the field of international law, a solution would be within reach. His stubborn attachment to Muslim symbols of sovereignty that have existed for more than 1,400 years had put him on a collision course with Israeli claims that are buttressed by a mix of nationalist-religious concepts and occidental notions of sovereignty. Apparently, only scientific innovation is capable of bridging this abyss. But the proposed experiments are remarkably similar to those of the alchemists, which, by contrast, were always pursued in reliance upon the Creator.

There is supposedly no harm in theoretical experiments, since they contribute to a discussion that may be able to demolish positions that have hitherto been sacrosanct. But playing with explosive materials was always an occupational hazard of alchemists. So long as all parties held opposing views, the negotiations were, of course, deadlocked; and the situation "on the ground"—transitory and internally contradictory as it was—produced a status quo that was pragmatic and relatively stable. Innovative experiments, however, are stirring up a hornets' nest of malevolent and combative forces that have acquiesced—albeit only just—in the situation, since it was perceived as temporary and not requiring the adoption of a decisive position.

Experience teaches that the road to the hell of religious and interethnic violence is paved with the good intentions of those searching for "creative solutions" to insoluble problems—who believe in their ability to come up with magic formulas, but who, by the very act of proposing their creations, are pushing a solution further away. The perception that the path to a happy ending is blazed by purveyors of magic potions is no less simple-minded than the archaic notions they are designed to overthrow. Alchemy was a stage in the development of a science that ultimately led to revolutionary achievements. When the conflict over the Old City is ripe for resolution, that resolution will rely on tried-and-true principles and not on magic formulas and "creative solutions."

HEAVENLY AND EARTHLY JERUSALEM

In December 2000, following the failure of the Camp David summit and the publication of the Clinton Parameters,[22] I wrote the following column expressing my feelings in regard to the ongoing efforts to solve the enigma of Jerusalem.

> In his will, my late father stated that he did not wish to be "gathered to his ancestors" buried in the Sephardic "al-Buraq" section of the Jewish cemetery on the Mount of Olives [in East Jerusalem], preferring instead to be interred at the Har Hamenuhot cemetery [in West Jerusalem]. "I do not believe that you will have the strength to hold on to the Mount of Olives and to ensure free access to it," he said.
>
> Yesterday I discovered that according to one of the maps of the proposed division of Jerusalem between Israel and a future Palestinian state presented at Camp David and endorsed by President Clinton, my home in

the Abu-Tor neighborhood would be within the sovereign territory of the Palestinian state. And according to the well-known declaration, "Not for [the Arab village and refugee camp of] Shu'afat did we pray for two thousand years," the road I travel every day will be located "in another country."

I met an Arab friend of mine, Shue'ib Shaheen, at the Butchers' Market; and he asked me when he would have to return his Israeli medical insurance card, and where exactly the border between his state and mine would run—since his shop is located at the intersection of the boundaries of the Christian, Muslim, and Jewish quarters of the Old City.

According to documents published so far, sovereignty over the Temple Mount will be "sliced" in such a way that the bottom layer, "at the thickest part of the mount," will be Israeli, and then we shall be able "to uncover the ruins of our holy temple." For fifty years I have pursued my interest in Jerusalem's past, but never have I heard (except in fanciful fables) that remnants of the Holy of Holies might be concealed in the ancient cisterns that cover much of the lower slope of the Temple Mount. Perhaps they intend to invest the Jewish affinity for this place with substance by sanctifying reservoirs and cesspools, just as was done with "the Wailing Wall tunnel."

Ever since the recent publication the Clinton Parameters [following the failure of the Camp David summit in June], bemused Jerusalemites have been coming to me and expressing their feeling that the whole discussion is divorced from reality and is nothing but a pathetic attempt at employing empty words to bridge an abyss of contradictions. The bridge imagery is not coincidental, since when I attempted to find out from my "sources" how it might be possible to implement the "division of Jerusalem along ethnic lines," it became clear that civil engineers specializing in bridge construction would be much in demand: a bridge from Arab Silwan to the mosques on the Temple Mount, a bridge from the Jewish Quarter to the Mount of Olives, bridges to create "territorial contiguity" among the Jewish neighborhoods of East Jerusalem. The vertical division of Jerusalem, with variations on the theme of the Earthly Jerusalem (below) and Heavenly Jerusalem (above)—sometimes we are below, as in the case of the Temple Mount, sometimes above, as in the case of the network of bridges—does not cease to preoccupy our statesmen.

My confusion persists, and no wonder. On the one hand, I should be awestruck by the historic breakthrough that promises to bring an end to the conflict at long last—after all, my whole life I've worked for peace. On the other hand, what will become of my ancestors' graves, of my basic sense of security, of my relations with my Arab friends, and of my perception that a city is a living organism that must not be dissected with the blunt scalpel of alienated healers? What is to be done with my sense of a universal connection to this city that encompasses the ties of others and exists in harmony with their traditions and cultures? Why should I be required to huddle in an ethnic ghetto and hand over the Church of the Holy Sepulcher to Arafat? Why do they insist on imposing "separation" on Jerusalem, a strategy that—in the name of "an end to the conflict"—will only augment the alienation and hatred?

If "ending the conflict" is more than an empty slogan mouthed by our statesmen, why are they setting a historic precedent by declaring that peace requires the erection of walls that sunder the heart of the city, when wall-building has, up to now, been an outcome of war? Why do they not understand that Jerusalem is more than the sum of its ethnic parts, and that the "separation" model must be replaced by one of "sharing"? And if conditions are not yet ripe for "sharing," perhaps this rush to reach a permanent solution is a serious mistake, and we need to foster a gradual process based on the rudimentary beginnings of sharing that already exist.

Don't worry, my sources reassure me. We are working on "the details," and these will surely mollify you. In any case, they tell me, I must trust my leaders—the very ones who are exploiting the mystique of power. But then, why are they hastening to proclaim the Clinton Parameters as such a historic event, and not telling the truth—that everything depends on "the details" that will take many years to work out, and that only then will come "an end to the conflict"? God is hiding in the details, and his prophets should display more humility.[23]

OBSERVATIONS FROM AFAR

From the mid 1990s on, my involvement in Jerusalem affairs became that of an observer from afar. Only occasionally did I reveal the intensity of my feelings: my anger and frustration at what was being done to the city of my birth by all the arrogant, power-hungry, hate-mongering boors—promoters of a destructive mythology—who found in Jerusalem a convenient platform from which to preach to the converted.

Every year, Jerusalem celebrates a holiday called Jerusalem Day. When the idea was conceived of adding this day to the calendar, already overloaded with patriotic memorial days, it was known as "Jerusalem Liberation Day." But it soon became clear that this name was false and cynical; the liberation meant subordination of the Arab population, and the day became a day of mourning for one-third of the city's residents.

Then they began calling it "Jerusalem Unification Day," until the Intifada arrived and tore asunder the illusion of "unity." By default, the present banal name, "Jerusalem Day," remained, but the event itself is not as neutral as its name: it is an expression of Jewish antagonism and xenophobia, a chance to hold arcane ceremonies of allegiance and to nurture nationalistic and religious myths. As it grows more routine, the day is drowning in a deep yawn of boredom; perhaps it is no coincidence that the only secular groups that celebrate in the streets of Jerusalem—other than religious zealots on parade—are members of the "pioneer" communities, the kibbutzim and moshavim. Thus, a population living off its past glory and present-day real estate speculation salutes a city locked in the dream of its past grandeur and present misery. How symbolic it is that a few weeks before the Jerusalem Day celebrations of 2005, it was revealed that the famous song "Jerusalem of Gold" by Naomi Shemer, which had become the city's unofficial anthem, is derived from a Basque folk tune.

The statistical data clearly reflect a widespread disappointment and weariness with the "Jerusalem syndrome": the number of people leaving the city—notably the young, the secular, and the professionals—is continually growing. In 2004, no fewer than 18,000 left the city. The civic leaders pursue those disenchanted Jerusalemites and attempt to keep them in the city by extending the municipal boundaries to include all the satellite suburbs that the escapees have set up. Fast train lines to Tel Aviv and Modi'in, "ring roads" with tunnels and bridges, giant construction projects, and a haphazard patchwork of houses hastily erected by Palestinians hoping to hold on to land earmarked for Israeli expropriation are turning a vast area, stretching from Modi'in and Beit Shemesh in the west to the outskirts of Jericho in the east, and from Ramallah in the north to the outskirts of Hebron the south, into one gargantuan metropolis. Throughout this huge urban expanse, chaotic planning, an unrelenting intercommunal struggle for hegemony over the physical space, and chronic violence prevail.

This grotesque expansion of Jerusalem signals the implosion of the "eternal city." The inherent absurdity of attempting to extend the sanctity of Jerusalem to encompass hundreds of square miles and more than one million people is becoming apparent. Committees of experts have been busy formulating plans that place the city's Palestinian neighborhoods outside the boundaries of the municipality, and the governing apparatus of the state has been acting as if the inhabitants of Palestinian East Jerusalem were not legal residents of Israel. In this way, claim the planners, most of the city's problems will be wafted away, as if by a magic wand. Some three-quarters of the inhabitants of the eastern part of the city will lose their status as residents of Israel, thereby solving "the demographic problem" that so perturbs the city fathers: the Arabs, who currently make up one-third of the city's population will be reduced to about 10 percent of its inhabitants.

The monetary savings, the experts maintain, will be huge: there will be no need to fund welfare services like health insurance, National Insurance, guaranteed income supplements, and the rest of the transfer payments for the Palestinians, and the municipality will be saved the necessity of developing municipal services for and delivering them to that sector. Abrogation of the rights of the Palestinians in East Jerusalem—who alone among the millions of noncitizen Palestinians under Israeli control have been accorded more or less reasonable living conditions—does not trouble the collective Israeli conscience. The insolent presumptuousness of first annexing territory without so much as a "by your leave" to the population and then—upon realizing the error of this policy—abruptly depriving them of any benefits they may have experienced under this imposed regime is not looked upon as the height of colonialist arrogance, but rather as radical and leftist.

Continued Israeli control of the Old City and its environs is intended to mitigate criticism from the nationalist camp over the loss of the outlying neighborhoods. The so-called "Peace Camp" cheered the Likud, when, with the disengagement from Gaza (see chapter 6), it supposedly demonstrated that it had "finally adopted the ideology of the Left" and was ready to abandon the taboo on challenging the idea that Jerusalem would always remain "united" under Israeli rule. One might even foresee the old myths about the eternal city beginning to undergo a slow process of contraction: before long, the phrase "Jerusalem, the holy city," in Hebrew and Arabic, may once again be applied to the original site alone—the Old City and what is known as "the Holy Basin" surrounding it. This area will be turned into a museum-like "heritage site," a center for pilgrims and tourists, administered jointly by representatives of the communities involved.

Attempts to use the name of Jerusalem to promote seditious sentiments based on religion and nationalism will be unsuccessful, because the heroic illusions associated with this name will have lost their power. The remainder of the metropolitan area will remain conflict-ridden and difficult to govern, but those responsible for it will, at least, be freed from the need to cope with the heavy burden of the tragic past conjured up by the name of Jerusalem, which coats every temporal problem with a veneer of eternity.

The thought of changing the municipal boundaries would not have arisen had the absurdity of constructing the "Jerusalem envelope" separation wall not become evident. This monstrous wall has created insoluble complications and made normal life impossible for the Palestinians: sixty thousand Palestinians with Israeli identity cards suddenly found themselves on the "other side" of the wall and have been cut off from their businesses, schools, and medical centers in East Jerusalem; many of these then moved back across the wall, causing rents in Arab Jerusalem to skyrocket.

Construction of the wall has also had grave political and legal consequences for Israel. The route they chose more or less follows an arbitrary line that was hastily sketched in June 1967, lacking any logic, be it urban, security-related, or political. This 1967 line earned the sobriquet "the arak and cigarette border," since it had been drawn in such a way that a distillery and a cigarette factory would remain beyond the municipal boundaries of the "reunited city." At the time, its whole objective was to annex territory devoid of Arab inhabitants and to keep the populated areas outside the city limits. Almost forty years later, when the developed urban area of Jerusalem that extends beyond the city's artificial borders had acquired a population numbering in the tens of thousands, the powers that be were attempting to preserve the 1967 line "with only essential adjustments," the objective of which was to illegally annex more land for Jewish expansion.

The wall's designers made no effort to provide evidence that their choice of route for the wall was based on security considerations; after all, it is impossible to explain why a concrete wall that bisects a town and truncates roads is of value to security, and why the Palestinians who live on the other side of the wall are more dangerous than those who live on "our side." Instead, so as to be able to use "security arguments" to justify the drawing of a political boundary cutting off the northern West Bank from the Bethlehem and Hebron "canton" (see chapter 6), the Israeli authorities concocted a groundless ethno-urban theory the purpose of which was to foist upon a diverse population of some quarter-of-a-million Israeli identity card holders the spurious collective identity of "East Jerusalem Arabs." This group of people, upon whom the Israelis have, out of the kindness of their hearts, bestowed blue (i.e., Israeli) identity cards, "must" behave as if they are different from their brothers and sisters who have found themselves living on the other side of the arbitrary line of "the Jerusalem envelope."

This theory also states that the East Jerusalem Arabs are not inclined to be involved in terrorism, because "they have something to lose" and they are interested in safeguarding the benefits that Israeli residency entitles them to, in contrast to the residents of the West Bank. This attitude is characteristic of colonialist regimes, which are convinced that it is within their power to define ethnic identities and attitudes—creating them out of thin air—to mold them within borders and enclosures, and to dispense with them when there is no longer any need for them.

The designers of the "Jerusalem envelope" regarded East Jerusalem Arabs—a fictional entity invented when the city's arbitrary borders, including twenty-eight villages, were drawn—as "good Arabs"; and should they dare "to make trouble," they know how to deal harshly with them. The danger that the very fact of the wall's construction, the difficulties of access that it causes, the land confiscations it required, and the division of families all increase the hatred and nourish the impulse for revenge does not perturb the wall builders; according to their racist thinking, Arab terrorism is genetic. In any case, the planners knew that the objective of the wall had less to do with security than with psychology. The Israeli public wanted a wall against fear so much that no one dares ask questions.

Steps were quickly taken to amend some of the worst mistakes that had been made without forethought, but the authorities failed to comprehend that the problem lay not in the wall's route, but in the very attempt to impose a physical barrier, thereby shredding the urban fabric of Jerusalem and cutting entire populations off from access to large parts of their world.

As long as the separation between east and west—or between Jews and Arab—was "soft" and quasi-voluntary, it was possible to preserve the complexity of the city, to have intercommunal contact of some sort, and to maintain the status of Jerusalem as a metropolitan hub. Now that separation is enforced by physical barriers, and inhibitions that formerly prevented the transformation of fellow Jerusalemites into a class of people with inferior rights (by stripping them of social benefits in the name of their "national liberation") are vanishing. The entire city has become a dead end, no matter what the route taken by the separation line.

The dream of a pluralist and open city that maintains tolerable coexistence among ethnic elements is fading. This dream was common to Jews and Arabs, and its remnants can be seen in the Arabs' efforts to maintain their personal legal status as Jerusalem residents, even though this had originally been forced on them. Many will say the dream of a united city was futile from the outset, since it was brutally imposed by the Israelis. Nonetheless, it contained an element of hope that perhaps tolerable relations across the ethnic fault line were a possibility.

Jerusalem has indeed become dead end: a border city in which dwells a Jewish community surrounded by a hostile population, a city whose urban space is dissected by a system of roadblocks, and that is cut off from its surroundings by a wall; a neglected and dirty city whose treasury is depleted and whose populace is impoverished and self-absorbed; a city where no one believes anymore in the impassioned slogans and heroic illusions once inspired by its name.

In many senses, Jerusalem has regressed to its pre-1967 status as a divided and fossilized city on the frontier. It is certainly true that its population has trebled and its area has increased fivefold since then, and that the walls that once cut through its heart have long since been dismantled. In their place, however, have arisen new and even mightier barriers.

Perhaps there is an important lesson in this. Jerusalem has always been a city with a cyclical history, and—in the words of Dan Pagis's poem: "Within her are all the magicians / masters of necromancy / yearning for the sign / that will descend upon her from the heavens / and will transform her face, and bury her soul in a pile of dust, and will consecrate her / forever, at their feet, as a cemetery."[24]

CHAPTER 4

"The Ceremony of Innocence Is Drowned . . ."

The early 1990s saw great expectations and messianic hopes in Eretz Israel / Palestine. Before long, however, it became clear that the peace process had encountered serious, perhaps even fatal, difficulties. It is not my intent here to chronicle the deterioration of this process—from the day the 1993 Declaration of Principles was signed by Israel and the Palestine Liberation Organization (PLO), to Prime Minister Yitzhak Rabin's assassination in 1995, to the outbreak of the al-Aqsa Intifada in 2000, and beyond—but it may nonetheless be useful to summarize the landmark events of the Israeli-Palestinian conflict over the past fifteen years:

LANDMARK EVENTS

13 September 1993—Declaration of Principles agreed upon by Israel and the PLO

28 April 1994—agreement regarding the transfer of authority and the establishment of the Palestinian Authority (PA)

4 May 1994—agreement to hand over Gaza and Jericho to the PA

26 October 1994—signing of the Israeli-Jordanian peace treaty

28 September 1995—the Oslo II agreement—the transfer of areas A and B to the PA

4 November 1995—the assassination of Yitzhak Rabin

22 November 1995—Shimon Peres becomes prime minister

February—March 1996—multi-victim suicide-bombing attacks

21 April 1996—Operation Grapes of Wrath in Lebanon; Peres does not implement the promised withdrawal from Hebron

31 May 1996—Benjamin Netanyahu becomes prime minister

17 January 1997—Netanyahu signs over a portion of Hebron to the PA

17 May 1999—Ehud Barak becomes prime minister

11–25 July 2000—the Camp David Summit

28 October 2000—outbreak of the al-Aqsa Intifada; disturbances in the Arab-Israeli sector

23 December 2000—publication of the Clinton Parameters for a solution to the conflict

27 January 2001—the end of Taba meeting between Israel and the PA

6 February 2001—Ariel Sharon becomes prime minister

January 2003—Sharon's second cabinet

20 March 2003—the invasion of Iraq

30 April 2003—the Road Map for peace presented

13 June 2004—the Israeli cabinet endorses revised plan for disengagement from Gaza

August 2005—Israeli withdrawal from Gaza and dismantlement of settlements completed

January 2006—Ariel Sharon hospitalized

January 2006—Hamas wins Palestinian elections

March 2006—general elections in Israel; Hamas forms a Palestinian cabinet

May 2006—intensification of Palestinian missile attacks on Israeli towns around the Gaza strip and Israeli retaliation

July 2006—Hezbollah kidnapping of Israeli soldiers; massive Israeli attack on Lebanon; eruption of a new Lebanon war

This crucial period has been extensively described and analyzed. I have chosen in part here to use material drawn from columns that I wrote for the Israeli daily *Ha'aretz* during those years, under the subject headings "Violence," "Negotiations: Oslo and Beyond," and "The Crisis on the

Left." Although I have sought to preserve the immediacy of my reactions, the articles have been edited to fit the context of this book.

VIOLENCE

The Israeli Right has pursued a violent and provocative campaign against the peace process since well before the Oslo Accords, especially the settlers in the occupied territories. After Yitzhak Rabin's 1992 election victory, "anti-peace" efforts intensified and turned ugly. Right-wing extremists did not hesitate to issue veiled—and sometimes open—calls for the prime minister's death. Rabin was assassinated as he left a huge peace rally in Tel Aviv on 4 November 1995.

Rabin Assassinated

Violent death at the hands of an anonymous murderer is, sadly, a frequent fate of leaders. In its wake, the people, stunned and grieving, struggle to find meaning in the event. Why? And what now? They grasp at historical parallels that help them relate rationally and with a measure of emotional distance to what has just taken place: the assassinations of Lincoln, the Kennedys, Martin Luther King Jr., Mahatma Gandhi, and Anwar el-Sadat. All of these parallels, however, are embedded in historical and psychological contexts that are specific to them, save only the fact of the meeting between assassin and victim. The two principals—the murderer pulling the trigger and the victim in the last moments of his life—knew very well the reason for the deed and its political significance.

Nevertheless, the fatal encounter on 4 November 1995 was more than just a political assassination, and more, even, than a deed of fratricide. The finger on the trigger belonged to a young man from an economically deprived immigrant community who was born to the messianic madness that arose following the "miraculous" Israeli victories of the Six-Day War (1967), and had grown up in the shadow of the Yom Kippur War (1973). The killer was convinced that he was acting in accordance with a divine decree to prevent the handover of the patrimony of the Jewish people to those whom he identified with the Amalekites, biblical arch-foes of the Israelites. His bullets brought down a man born five years after the Balfour Declaration (1917) pledging British support for the establishment of a Jewish homeland in Palestine to parents who had come to this land out of a desire to create a new country and a just society; a man whose fabled heroism had provided his murderer with home and heritage; a man who had reaped the putrid fruits of the occupation with his own hands, and who looked upon himself, therefore, as entitled to cast away the poisonous harvest.

Murderer and victim were both native sons of this country, but contrary to the myth that "a man is an image of his homeland's landscape," the Israeli is a reflection of his or her generation, its life experience, and its worldview. The clash between sabras who are a part of the rationalistic and pragmatic-secular political culture and those who espouse nationalistic, fundamentalist religious views is both profound and bitter.

This confrontation, however, is not in and of itself sufficient explanation for the murder; for this was no simple political or ideological deed: it was an act of patricide. The heir murdered his father, because, to his mind, his father was scheming to rob him of his inheritance. Multitudes of Israelis sensed the powerful and terrible meaning of this deed, and they grieved over the dead man as over a revered father who had passed away—with an intimate grief that transcended political differences.

Euologies of Yitzhak Rabin depict him as one of Israel's founding fathers, or even as the last of them, but this was not so; in fact, he was the most outstanding representative of the "second generation." The founding fathers, members of Rabin's parents' generation, were the ones who spawned the Zionist revolution, who formulated its political and social objectives, and who shaped the myths on which their children were brought up. Before the second generation, "the first generation of the Zionist redemption," they set the task of accomplishing the mission whose substance and objectives they—the founding fathers—had determined for them; and the sons, "ever ready to obey" (in the words of the pre-state Palmach anthem), faithfully carried out the commands of their revolutionary fathers and did not challenge the soothing myths that had been invented to reconcile a humanistic-socialist value system with circumstances that dictated the use of force in achieving the goals of Zionism. They rallied to the fulfillment of the halutzic ideal, becoming experts at farming and at raising chickens, out of a belief—planted in them by their parents—that they were battling, not the Arabs, but the desert. In time, they themselves became living legends, their exploits inspiring phrases such as "few against many," "purity of arms," "sheaves and the sword," and indeed (by virtue of their sacrifices in the 1948 war), "the silver platter" (on which the state was "presented" to the people).

Yitzhak Rabin was the archetypal member of the second generation, for decades dutifully playing his part in the establishment of military, economic, social, and cultural institutions, all of which could be lumped together under the rubric of "security." Thanks to the loyalty he thus displayed, he earned the confidence of the founding fathers who, their own energies flagging, appointed him as the first Israeli-born prime minister.

Rabin's sense of loyalty to the legacy of the founding fathers persisted even after the departure of the last of them. It was eighteen years after his installation as the head of the nation before he managed to summon up sufficient moral fortitude to challenge the two basic assumptions that had guided the Zionist project ever since its first encounter with the "unanticipated" hostility of the country's Arab population: first, that there is only one legitimate national collectivity in Eretz Israel, and that the Jewish people's claim to the entire homeland is therefore absolute; second, that the Arabs understand only the language of force.

The moment he shook the hand of Yasir Arafat, Yitzhak Rabin began redefining Zionism's fundamental precepts. He proclaimed the victory of Zionism, thereby bringing to an end his role as a son continuing in his fathers' footsteps. Now, he supposed, he would himself be able to be a "founding father"—of a new Israel—and to guide the sons following after him in shaping a new era.

But this was not to be. A patricidal young man—acting out, in his madness, historical and psychological forces of reactionary fanaticism—killed the founding father of the new era. Perhaps it was Rabin's fate, like that of Moses, to stand at the summit of his own Mount Nebo and see the Promised Land "but . . . not go over thither."

The violent death of such a man arouses powerful emotions of grief and bereavement. The assassination of a revered leader is often perceived, in historical perspective "as the fitting pinnacle of the man's glorious life and work," as Pandit Nehru wrote of his friend Mahatma Gandhi. Now this member of the second generation who went on to become a founding father in his own right was gone; everything depended on his heirs. So far, however, they have failed.

· · ·

The immediate causes for the eruption of the new cycle of violence in Israel/Palestine will forever remain shrouded in controversy. It is, however, universally accepted that the al-Aqsa Intifada that started in October 2000 has been the cruelest and bloodiest of all the outbreaks of

Israeli-Palestinian hostilities with the exception of the 1947–48 war. The fifth round of intercommunal warfare between Israelis and Palestinians—after the Arab Revolt of 1936–39, the war of 1947–48, the 1981–82 invasion of Lebanon, and the first Intifada (1987–92)—has attained terrible new heights of brutality and contempt for human life. Its violence has provoked extreme reactions from many quarters.

Defining the "Enemy"

The characterization of the al-Aqsa Intifada as an out-and-out war between the Jewish and Palestinian peoples has earned almost universal support in Israel, which also traced a direct line from Arab hostility toward the Jewish Yishuv at the very outset of the Zionist enterprise straight to the al-Aqsa Intifada, and regarded the situation as the final battle of the War of Independence.

The old image of the struggle over the West Bank and Gaza as "the seventh day of the Six-Day War" has fallen from favor and quietly been replaced by its portrayal as "unfinished business" from the 1948 war. There is apparently nothing new in that—after all, this has always been the position of the Israeli Right—except that their [i.e., the right-wingers'] position was strengthened by the fact that the Palestinians, too, conveyed the same message, in both word and deed. The latter justified their acts of violence as "a legitimate struggle against the occupation," but the attitude that the 1948 war is unfinished business is reflected in their [i.e., the Palestinians'] demand for "the right of return" and in attacks on targets within the Green Line, not to mention the rhetoric of an ever more powerful Hamas, whose supporters continued to grow in number and power.

From time immemorial, history has served as the quarry from which each side excavates the stones it uses to construct its myths and to hurl at its opponents. Hence it is fitting to regard historical analyses as expressions of political imperatives, worldviews, ideological issues, or calls to arms, and the "scientific" disputes between "old" and "new" historians are no exception. It is possible to draw some unexpected conclusions from, of all places, the "mobilized" version of history propounded by settlers and other defenders of the bastions of Zionism.

Every Israeli child learns that the War of Independence broke out in the wake of "an invasion by the armies of the Arab world." The preceding, and perhaps decisive, stage—bloody combat between the Yishuv and the Palestinians—has been suppressed. It is significant that the number of Palestinians displaced from areas that became Israel—seven hundred thousand—is larger than the entire Jewish population of Mandatory Palestine at the beginning of the 1948 war—slightly more than six hundred thousand. The Israelis are endeavoring to expunge this embarrassing chapter of their history: warfare against a community whose cities and land they had previously shared, a community that was subsequently defeated and exiled. Yet the Palestinians, instead of being perceived as phantoms from the past, have achieved recognition as a real, present-day enemy, which poses nothing less than an existential threat. The al-Aqsa Intifada followed on the heels of four earlier wars. The Palestinians were thoroughly trounced in all of them, but the Jews did not triumph; and the pseudo-heroic pronouncement that "we are destined to live by the sword" only goes to show that the Palestinians have remained unvanquished.

The settlers' self-serving history is wonderfully similar to that of the Palestinians—where 1948 is regarded as only one in a succession of acts of Zionist aggression, beginning with the establishment of the Zionist enterprise, and the Intifada is viewed as the final battle for Palestinian independence. Since history is a quarry for slingshot ammunition, the question is who will take more hits?

The events portrayed below are, in my opinion, the most traumatic to have taken place thus far in the current round of violence. On 1 June 2001, a summer Sabbath eve, a suicide bomber blew himself up while standing in the midst of a group of young Israelis outside a seaside discotheque in Tel Aviv. Many of the twenty-one dead were natives of the former Soviet Union.

A RUSSIAN TRAGEDY

The nighttime attack on the Tel Aviv beachfront, while Israelis turned their backs on the bloody conflict, abandoning themselves to the "Mediterranean" cult of zest for life and seeking only enjoyment in the moment, struck at the soft underbelly of the country. The murderer could not have been blind to the youthful exuberance of the girls in whose midst he placed himself; and only he knew that in just a moment their lives would end before they had really begun. He knew nothing about Mariana and Raisa, Yelena and Yulia, Anya and Maria, or their friends, Aleksei and Roman, Diaz and Jan. He simply wanted to kill Jews; but in doing so, he visited a catastrophe upon a wonderful tribe of kind-hearted men and women, diligent individuals steeped in culture, who had come to this country to avail their children of a better life than that offered by their homeland, but who had gained neither security nor the affection and appreciation of the country that absorbed them.

And the names, the names—as if plucked from the pages of Dostoyevsky, Turgenev, and Pasternak. The lament for youthful lives cut short was accompanied by an upwelling of grief among those who had become acquainted with the greatness of the Russian soul in their own youth— many with aunts and grandmothers named Sonia, Mania, or Fania. Who could remain unmoved at the sound of the Kaddish recited in a soft Russian accent by a father who did not understand its words or at the sight of the lone grave in the section to which "doubtful Jews" are relegated? The killer had certainly had no doubts.

And among those who eulogized the victims were politicians who harbored no doubts as to their right to nationalize the tragedy, nor did they hesitate to exploit the murder victims, enlisting them for their own debatable political ends. The declarations of hatred, the calls for vengeance, and the utilization of the tragedy in the service of one's personal political agenda, and to bolster the claim that "Kiryat Arba and Tel Aviv are one and the same" all call to mind "The Sonnet against Those Who Speak for Spilled Blood" written in 1986 by Meir Wieseltier: "If I should die . . . / in a bomb blast while gaping at the price of cucumbers at a stall in the market, do not dare say that my blood provides proof of the rightness of your claims / . . . / that my spilled guts testify that with 'them' one cannot speak or strive toward settlement / Let the blood soak into the dust; blood is blood, not words. Terrible is the vision of dominion in evil hearts."

Apparently, the leaders of the warring communities—Arafat and Sharon—felt the immensity of the tragedy more than those with the temerity to "speak for the spilt blood" with outpourings of hatred: Arafat declared a truce; Sharon finally realized that "restraint is strength."

The attack served not only as an occasion for emotional outbursts, however; it also provided a pretext for the revival of the "Separation Wall plan," the demarcation line defining the psychological space within which Israelis can hope to find a sense of security and keep the barbarians outside the gates of civilization.

Meanwhile, "separation" is being employed as a means of collective punishment. The West Bank has been divided into eight cantons, Gaza into three, and it has again become commonplace to see pregnant women trudging heavily along stony paths between roadblocks. Of course they must pay for the blood spilt on the Tel Aviv beachfront; they are Arabs, aren't they?[1]

Between the fourth and eleventh of April 2002, battles raged between Palestinian resistance fighters and the Israeli Army in Jenin Refugee Camp on the West Bank, in the course of which fifty-two Palestinians and twenty-three Israelis were killed and most of the homes in the camp were demolished.

BETWEEN JENIN AND DEIR YASIN

Exactly fifty-four years have gone by since the Deir Yasin massacre, and now the Jenin catastrophe has been added to the tragedy-filled Palestinian commemorative calendar. There are signs indicating that Jenin will assume a place beside Deir Yasin in the canon of national myths. Most of the occasions circled on the Palestinian calendar mark national defeats and disasters—an accurate reflection of the sorry lot of this downtrodden people. There is nothing unique in this; other peoples, too, regard catastrophes as more effective than victories in enlisting public support for their national cause. What transpired in Jenin appears to wield extraordinary power—even in comparison with the Sabra and Chatilla massacre in the Lebanon war, the battle of Karama in 1968, or the Temple Mount massacre of 1991—which places Jenin in the same class as the tragic symbol of the 1948 Nakba [cataclysm]. And indeed, several Palestinian spokesmen have employed the hallowed term *nakba* to describe the events of April 2002 as well.

Some would maintain that there is no call to draw parallels between a savage massacre carried out by a gang of Jewish terrorists against defenseless Arab villagers in 1948 and a military operation that resulted in widespread destruction and civilian deaths in the course of clashes between the Israeli Army and Palestinian guerilla forces. But it is not "the facts"—which will forever remain the object of controversy—that are responsible for the construction of a myth, but the context into which fragments of facts and a continuum of cause and effect are selectively inserted. And the context that the Palestinians have identified—which makes Jenin and Deir Yasin comparable—is the intention, in both instances, to destroy the infrastructure of Palestinian society.

It is not what took place in Jenin—in all its horrifying particulars—that is the main issue as far as the Palestinians are concerned, but the fact that they regard these events as symbolic of the Israelis' true intentions. These—in their opinion—deviate from rational military objectives such as control, deterrence, and prevention, and instead have the aim of fragmenting Palestinian society and setting it back two generations, to the conditions that prevailed in the aftermath of Deir Yasin. The mounds of ruins in Jenin Refugee Camp not only became a memorial to the tragedy that created them, but also perpetuate the memory of the thousand-year-old buildings demolished in Nablus, Bethlehem's broken-up streets, and the computers and masses of accumulated data stored in the Palestinian National Archives in Ramallah destroyed at the same time by the Israeli army fighting "terrorist infrastructure."

The Palestinians are not alone in comparing Jenin with Deir Yasin; there are Israelis who, far from being disgusted by the comparison, also see a direct link between April 2002 and April 1948 and would be delighted were the Palestinians again to react in panic, as in the case of Deir Yasin, and flee in the wake of Jenin. On the other hand, there are also Israelis who agree with their leaders that one should not make a distinction between the "terrorist infrastructure" and the collective infrastructure of the Palestinian nation, since in their eyes the Palestinian body politic, as represented by its elected governing bodies, is itself a terrorist organization, and therefore the destruction of its archives serves the objectives of the "war on terrorism."

Any attempt to erase the fifty-four years between Deir Yasin and Jenin reinforces the apprehensions of those who suspect that implementation of the rationalistic and optimistic model portraying the Israeli-Palestinian conflict as a national-ethnic struggle whose resolution lies in "two states for two peoples" was never feasible, even from the outset, or that alternatively, powerful forces have succeeded in thwarting it. The fundamental animosity between the settlers who have put down roots and the natives who were expelled or subjugated does not, apparently, allow them to aspire to mutual recognition of their respective rights, and therefore a solution based on the dictum of "separate but equal" is not feasible. The existing bi-ethnic entity—which encompasses the entire territory of Mandatory Palestine—became all the more entrenched in the wake of April 2002.[2]

Jenin as Allegory

A few months after the battle in Jenin, a large advertisement appeared announcing a seminar on "Israel's communications strategy: Jenin as allegory." The event was not open to the public—entry was by invitation only—but the ad's publication showed that the organizers deemed it important that the public be aware of the academic effort "to learn lessons" from the events in Jenin. The fact that a seminar bearing such a title took place at all prompts gloomy reflections regarding the nature of the academic contribution to public discourse. The designation of the events in Jenin as "allegory" revealed a profound sense of alienation, and the public relations orientation of the discussions ensured that their essential concern would be with image, rather than substance.

Israeli public discourse did not completely ignore the destruction, the suffering, the loss of human life, and the violence, but all of these were seen as the fault of the suicide terrorists who made Jenin their "capital" and its civilian population "human shields." What concerned the Israeli public was how to cope with the negative media coverage, which it viewed as being hostile and one-sided. The fate of the human beings for whom Jenin was not an "allegory" but a terrible disaster was put out of mind by defining it as a mass of exaggerations, by arguments over the question of whether there had or had not been a "massacre" in Jenin, and by learned disquisitions about the diplomatic price of an operation that was "forced upon us."

The critical examination of violations of the rules of war and breaches of international humanitarian law, of collective punishment, and of the very choice of a power-oriented strategy had been left to "marginal leftist elements," whose activities are defined as "political" and, therefore, as having no place in an academic framework and certainly no access to research funding. Descriptions of atrocities—such as the story of the bulldozer operator who razed homes in Jenin Refugee Camp in an orgy of drunken destruction—were not viewed as matters that called forth a shamed silence at any learned discussion of "communications strategy." On the contrary: they were merely an additional hurdle to overcome in the struggle against the hostile media that dared to publish such stories.

The "Jenin allegory" also served as a means of cultivating the esprit de corps and patriotism of the soldiers, who earned medals for their part in the courageous battles. In this way, it influenced operations on the West Bank and drew a veil of "image" and communications strategy over acts that should have been examined substantively according to moral or universal-legal criteria. But the patriotic and public relations contexts overshadowed the criticism, and if it was heard at all, it was limited to questions of operational efficiency and image building—or else presented as quoting the words or opinions of others, to ensure distance and demonstrate lack of involvement.

The few objections that have been raised have largely been confined to questions of efficacy and risk: will terrorism increase, will attacks be foiled, will there be food riots? Only the "lunatic fringe" mounted protests against the immorality, cruelty, and illegality of these acts, and academics organized seminars where researchers helped army officers devise "communications strategies" to cope with the "diplomatic and public relations fallout." About the moral implications, no one said a word.

"Rainbow" in Rafah

In May 2004 Palestinians ambushed and killed thirteen Israeli soldiers in the Gaza Strip. In revenge, the military launched Operation Rainbow against the southern Gaza Strip city of Rafah and neighboring refugee camps.

The scenes of Rafah were too painful to watch—lines of refugees strung out along the roadway beside carts laden with bedding and the meager contents of their homes; children dragging suitcases larger than themselves; black-clad women on their knees in the rubble of their homes, wailing mournfully. And in the memories of some of us—whose number is dwindling—arise similar scenes, which have returned to haunt us time and again for over half a century, in a kind of refrain that stabs at the heart and the conscience: refugees wending their way from Lydda to Ramallah in the heat of July 1948; processions of the banished villagers from Yalu, Beit Nuba, and Emmaus; in June 1967, refugees from Jericho clambering onto the ruins of the Allenby Bridge after the Six-Day War. And, perhaps most shocking of all, the parents and grandparents of the Rafah refugees abandoning the houses in Yibna (a village inside Israel proper) in which they had been born for fear of the approaching Israeli Army on 5 June 1948. "At dawn," reported the AP correspondent, "it was possible to see the civilians fleeing from the town [Yibna] and heading towards the coast, without intervention from the Israeli forces." Fifty-six years had gone by, and they were again fleeing in fear from their Israeli assailants.

And the assailants used the same tactics now as then: they spread rumors and fired shots in the air to frighten the people away. They claimed—when the residents fled in terror—that they were not responsible for the flight. But then they destroyed the empty homes, for "after all, they've been abandoned." All this was cloaked in unctuous self-righteousness and justified with atrocity stories and with biased and incomplete information. Laundered language and sterile military terms camouflaged a primitive lust for vengeance and the uninhibited use of force. Slogans such as "combat heritage," "the righteousness of our path," and "the most moral army in the world" shielded the soldiers and their commanders from the necessity of coming to terms with the humanitarian catastrophe they were creating. The political leaders, who were supposed to set the moral standards for the IDF, have revealed an even greater bent for extremism and brutality than the army's own commanders. All that interests them is safeguarding Israel's "image" and denouncing the "hostile media."

Back in 1949, referring to the IDF's expulsion of the residents of Khirbat Khiza'a (some of whom now lived in a refugee camp in Rafah), S. Yizhar described us as "knowingly led astray, unthinkingly joining the big, common throng of liars—replete with ignorance, expedient apathy, and just plain shameless selfishness—and exchanging one great truth for the know-it-all shrug of the hardened criminal."[3]

Those who craved revenge and "the appropriate response" responded angrily and with abusive language: "How can you show empathy for a bunch of degraded murderers, desert savages led by corrupt gangsters?" But one had a sneaking suspicion that this was Israel's "combat heritage" again coming to the fore: using the Palestinians' murderousness as a pretext for "punishing" them, uprooting them from their homes, "laying bare" their fields and then "redeeming" the abandoned land for Israeli use.

We have forced generation after generation to abandon their homes; then we moved in and, later on, when the opportunity presented itself, we took over their places of refuge and drove them out of there as well. Generation after generation, we have nourished the "refugee consciousness," reproducing the original pain of displacement and exposing yet another generation to the powerless rage of the displaced. And then—feeling scared and threatened—we are confronted by the specter of "the return," the fondest hope of every refugee, but a burden on our conscience.

Something is fundamentally wrong here. If military commanders, the sons of those who fought for Israel's independence in 1948, send the grandchildren of that generation of fighters to "widen the axis"—which means expelling the grandchildren of the refugees of 1948—on the pretext of a threat to our survival, then the founding fathers' vision must have been flawed. If the survival of their enterprise is still under threat after half a century, this can only mean that they unwittingly sentenced it to a future of everlasting enmity; and no community can survive a violent war for survival for years on end. On the other hand, if the contention that Israel's survival was threatened is merely a pretext—and Operation Rainbow (in Rafah) was the kind of instinctive response that has become second nature to us—we must seriously ponder the accountability of an enterprise that started out as the embodiment of so many exalted ideals. Is there a "tragic flaw" at the foundation of the Zionist enterprise? Those who launched the Rafah operation—and those who carried it out—should have known that this question would inevitably arise as a consequence of their actions.[4]

• • •

The curtain of words that has descended on the violence and killing has multiple objectives: to cover up the all-pervading fear people feel, bestow meaning on random deaths, incite Israelis against the enemy, inspire patriotic emotions, furnish the country's leaders with an opening that will allow them to escape the consequences of their tragic mistakes, envelope atavistic acts of vengeance in a cloak of rationality, contend with the moral burden inherent in the taking of human life, and foster the development of a positive image for propaganda purposes. One could cite many examples from the abundant supply that comprises the "word-curtain"; however, it seems that the thread by which it is suspended essentially consists of the two words that define the ongoing violence, "war" and "terrorism." There is scarcely an Israeli commentator who does not depict the situation in which the Israeli nation finds itself as "war." Opinion is divided as to whether this is a "limited war," a "war for survival," a "continuation of the War of Independence," or a "struggle that has been forced upon us"; but as to the definition of Palestinian violence, there is no disagreement. It is terrorism.

Self-Defense and Terrorism

The distinction between Israeli and Palestinian violence has no analytical significance, but it bespeaks a value judgment: war, and particularly defensive war, is a legitimate form of violence, whereas terrorism is a criminal act with illegitimate objectives. By defining the violence that they initiate as "war," the Israelis are striving to retain their monopoly on legitimate violence, since to their way of thinking, only their national objectives are just; they are the only ones that should be using force and the only ones to which the imperative of "self-defense" applies. Palestinian violence, on the other hand, is a "terrorist crime," since its aim is the achievement of criminal objectives such as the destruction of the Zionist enterprise or murder for its own sake.

The Palestinians, of course, cannot be expected to leave it to the Israelis to define when violence is legitimate and when it is not, and they put forth an opposing definition: that it is they who have been plunged into a war against a brutal power that seeks to impose upon them a cruel and oppressive regime, and the fact that the violence is being carried out by the army of a sovereign state makes Israel a terrorist state. This mutual delegitimation thwarted what had appeared to be a historic achievement by Yitzhak Rabin and Yasir Arafat, who believed that by their 1993 signing of the Declaration of Principals, they were defining each other as legitimate enemies—a crucial stage in the process of moving toward mutual recognition, culminating in coexistence.

The return to employing the language of "war versus terrorism" signals the disintegration of the Oslo process even more than did the outbreak of violence in late 2000, and those who subscribe to this distinction sabotage the chances for peace, since it is possible to craft a peace agreement only with a legitimate enemy, not with terrorists.

Israelis' definition of "war," which they claim the exclusive right to determine, is arbitrary from an additional point of view: a party that claims it is "at war" acknowledges the authority of rules of engagement and laws of war laid out in international law and accepted throughout the civilized world. These prohibit harm to private property and to civilians, collective punishment, population transfer, starvation of the populace, and indiscriminate killing. Israel's "war" activity is not consistent with these laws. The initiators of "preventative measures," "fitting responses," and "maintenance of deterrence" know they are violating the laws of war, but choose to apply them to suit their own convenience. This is the real reason for Israel's opposition to the stationing of international observers in Palestinian areas. The last thing Israel wants to see happen is the establishment of a foreign body charged with examining its "military actions" according to accepted standards.

No one has ever been able to predict exactly when opposition to war and bloodshed ceases to be regarded as treachery and becomes accepted as a legitimate, indeed proper, attitude; when moral condemnation of war crimes becomes politically correct, and slogans like "a war for our homes" go from being a resounding battle cry to being recognized as blathering nonsense. Nobody has ever foreseen it beforehand, but experience teaches us that the moment inevitably arrives when the "patriotic" herd mentality is replaced by a critical skepticism—sometimes in a matter of weeks or months, and sometimes after years or generations.

Past experience also proves that the influence of international censure, of revelations regarding atrocities, of demonstrations and political protests is cumulative. This is counterbalanced, however, by a sense of tribal unity, moral superiority, and self-righteousness. One would expect that the price in blood exacted by the continuing violence would lead to rational consideration of the value of human life versus that of the goals in whose name people are dying. But communities that have become accustomed to evaluating their actions in terms of absolutes seldom subject them to a cost-benefit analysis. The very act of comparing the cost in human lives with the benefit derived from this sacrifice is problematic: The high cost in loss of human life—and the need to justify it—necessitates inflation of the value attributed to the ideals on behalf of which this heavy price was paid.

Leaders who have embroiled their nation in a situation producing numerous casualties cannot allow themselves to let everyone know that they erred in their assumptions, so they make of their objectives absolutes: victory in "a war for our homes" or winning "a war for our survival"—objectives the cost of whose achievement is infinite. The actual relationship between the goal and its cost is decried as irrelevant, and to bring up rational considerations is tantamount to blasphemy—attempting to quantify something that is beyond price.

Nonetheless, experience teaches that inflating the worth of what is being fought for in order to justify the sacrifice of human life cannot succeed in the long run, because the survival instinct is stronger than any manipulation, and the cynicism behind counterfeit patriotism quickly becomes apparent, as it did in Lebanon following the invasion of 1982.

Nobody can foresee when the tide will turn and all the experts and commentators will start squabbling over who was the first to expose the real cost of the "war" against the Palestinians: the misguided strategy, the lack of vision, the illusions, the political stupidity, the surrender to a lust for vengeance, and the brutality. But the manipulators should not delude themselves; that moment will come.

When the time comes, and the curtain is pulled away from the phony patriotism, it will turn out that the fifth Israel-Palestine war (after the Arab Revolt, the 1948 war, the Lebanon war, and the first Intifada) will truly have been another battle in the War of Independence—though not Israel's, as Ariel Sharon claimed, but that of the Palestinians. And nobody—neither side—will win that war, because in conflicts between communities there are no victors, only losers. All that will remain will be the horrific memories, the profound hatred, the calls for vengeance, and the bitter taste of missed opportunities, since it almost, just almost, could have been different.

Patterns of Commemoration

Sadly, the chain of bereavement and mourning has not come to an end, and with its continuation, highly meaningful patterns of commemoration, which convey controversial political and educational messages, have been making deeper inroads and are becoming increasingly entrenched and firmly rooted in Israeli society.

These messages are infused with a sense of spiritual union with the fallen. They are, however, not entirely innocent of declarations of hatred and the assignment of collective blame—or even the politicization of victims of terrorism and their enlistment in the service of a political culture that advocates the perpetuation of the conflict and continuous provocation, which labels any attempt at reconciliation as evidence of being "soft" or even of treason.

Some years ago, a memorial to the victims of hostilities and terrorism was dedicated on Mount Herzl (site of Israel's principal military cemetery and the burial ground of Israel's revered leaders), and it was decided that the Remembrance Day for the IDF's fallen would become, as well, a day of commemoration for all the civilians who had been killed in violent incidents going back to "the beginning of Zionist settlement 140 years ago"—arbitrarily setting the date of that event as 1860. In the official publicity for the expanded Remembrance Day, IDF soldiers are lumped together with civilians killed both before and after the establishment of the state, the total number of dead cited in these publications (by 2005) being in excess of 21,000. The IDF casualties are buried in military cemeteries, whereas the civilian victims are scattered among civilian burial grounds, and only a small percentage of their names are engraved on the black marble slabs of the monument, which has been erected between the military cemetery and the grave of Yitzhak Rabin—a location unequalled in symbolic meaning.

The definition of "fallen soldiers of the IDF and the other security forces" (including members of the pre-state Jewish underground) is quite straightforward: anyone who fell in the line of duty while engaged in wartime or other service required by his or her sovereign state's government or pre-state Yishuv leadership. By contrast, the definition of "civilian casualties" is somewhat unclear: one version has it to be "everyone who was killed because of being a Jew," or, in formal language, anyone killed in an incident defined as a "hostile act" by the National Insurance Institute—which apparently regards itself as qualified to determine the status of all those who have perished since 1860.

The list of names adorning the walls of the monument for victims of terrorism has provoked numerous bewildered reactions; for example, who is responsible for the inscription bearing the name of Avraham Shlomo Zalman Tsoref, head of the Solomon family who was murdered in 1851 by Arabs seeking vengeance for his having evicted them when he received permission from the Ottoman authorities to rebuild the ancient Hurvah Synagogue in the Jewish Quarter of Jerusalem's Old City. Is he, too, to be numbered in the ranks of the heroes of the Zionist enterprise—by virtue of an action taken fifty years prior to the First Zionist Congress?

And who is responsible for including the names of some of the Jewish victims of the 1946 King David Hotel bombing? Is that explosion—carried out by the Irgun—to be defined as "a terrorist act," or perhaps as "hostilities"? The name of the retired general Rechav'am Ze'evi (an outspokenly racist government minister who was killed by Palestinians in 2001), of all people, is there, although he would undoubtedly be insulted if he knew that his name appears among those of people who met their deaths by happenstance when they chanced upon the site of a terrorist attack on a city street; the bullet that hit Ze'evi clearly bore his name.

It would seem, however, that a scholarly critique of the inclusion or exclusion of names of those who have perished "since 1860" is not relevant, and that in-depth discussion of what constituted "a hostile act" in the conditions that prevailed in nineteenth-century Eretz Israel was of no importance to the monument's designers—whose whole objective was to blur the distinction between combatants and innocent victims and the difference between the pre-state era and that following the Jewish people's attainment of sovereignty and independence.

The monument builders were not interested in the long list of dead, but in their enlistment in the eternal struggle "for the realization of Zionism" and the display of their victimization "because of being Jewish." They and the IDF soldiers appear side by side in the ranks of those who "have fallen in Israel's campaigns," as if all of them were victims of Arab animosity, murdered "by the iniquitous enemy." Of course, in the all-out intercommunal struggle being waged between Israelis and Palestinians, the distinction between uniformed combatants and civilians is blurred. Even so, there is a crucial difference between one who risks his or her life in battle and one who perishes by chance; between a passive victim and someone killed while participating in an assault on a fortified target. At least the families of fallen soldiers are entitled to feel thus; and that is what the educational system should convey on the subject, and not the message that all of the dead are "martyrs."

If there truly is no difference and everything is "Israel's campaigns," then the attitude held by the most extremist of the Palestinians has been adopted—that there is no distinction between civilian and soldier, and all Israelis are legitimate targets. Along with all the sorrow and mourning over the murder of innocent men and women, those responsible for molding the nation's collective memory perpetuate the cycle of animosity by turning a commemoration into a call for revenge.

NEGOTIATIONS: OSLO AND BEYOND

The assassination of Yitzhak Rabin did not halt the implementation of the Oslo II agreement, signed in September 1995, under the terms of which all the Palestinian cities on the West Bank, with the exception of Hebron, were to be transferred to Palestinian control. The negotiations over the areas to be handed over to the Palestinians bring up a tantalizing question: What part does territory play in the Palestinians' conception of nation building?

Land and the Human Element

Imagine how the Jewish Yishuv would have reacted to a political arrangement that transferred to its control only those areas actually populated with Jews, leaving the remainder of the homeland for discussion "some time in the future." The Yishuv would have rejected any such arrangement out of hand, believing that Eretz Israel would never be Jewish unless Jews were deemed the owners of the land, regardless of the number living on it.

Many seek to draw an analogy between Zionist nation building and the corresponding Palestinian process. In this context it is important to note that all nation building is based upon a fundamental assumption regarding the factor most vital to its advancement. From the Zionist perspective, territory was the most critical factor and an absolute prerequisite for building the nation; whereas to the Palestinians, it may be that the most vital component in the process is the human element.

Yasir Arafat drew strength from the sea of humanity cheering him in the squares of the liberated cities, and he was not particularly troubled by the pathetic boundaries of the enclaves that comprised Free Palestine. The human contact was more meaningful to him than physical contact with the soil of the homeland. Only after a thorough perusal of the hundreds of pages of text of the Oslo II agreement did Arafat take the time to peek at the maps delineating the geographical boundaries of his jurisdiction. The Palestinians had spent many long hours in debate with the Israelis over the former's access to Rachel's Tomb once it passed into their (Palestinian) control, but it was only after the fact that they discovered that the shrine had "mistakenly" been left in Israeli hands—not having taken the trouble to look at the map before it was finalized.

The Zionist "redeemers of the soil of the homeland"—the Hankins, the Weitzes, and their colleagues among the leaders of the Yishuv— would not have operated in that way. They wore out their eyes in the dimly lit land registry offices and the soles of their shoes climbing boulder-strewn hills. It was not the wording of every little clause in the documents granting power over human beings that preoccupied them, but the "blocks and parcels" charted on surveyors' maps. Only empty territory attracted the land redeemers' attention: once a Jewish community had been established on redeemed land, they lost interest in it. The Jews would be able to take care of themselves. "We shall make sure that there will be room for more Jews," they proclaimed.

They knew that any form of control over land—be it through purchase, the draining of swamps, a human presence, afforestation, or agriculture—constituted the grounds for a successful claim to sovereignty. Thus, when offered a state half of whose inhabitants would be Arabs in 1947, they received the proposal with open arms. The land would endure forever, whereas human beings were transient, and if they would not move on under their own volition, they could always be moved by force. This was an attitude typical of settler societies with ample human resources at their disposal in search of land for settlement. The attitudes of the heirs of the Zionist land redeemers toward the soil of the homeland, however, reflected a fundamental change of mind-set; for the majority of them, it had become no more than a commodity, whereas a minority regarded it with almost pagan reverence. But the allure of the remaining shreds of unoccupied land never faded. Thus, nearly all Israelis are united in their willingness to hand over heavily populated areas, so long as the rest remains in the hands of the settler population that has struck roots there. For these Israelis, a division of the land that leaves the Arabs with less than 11 percent of the territory that was in their possession prior to the arrival of the Jews in Eretz Israel / Palestine constitutes a generous and morally acceptable, if painful, compromise.

The attitude of the Palestinians toward the relationship between the land, the people, and the nation-building process is, like that of their Israeli counterparts, embedded in the past and influenced by the long history of conflict in Eretz Israel / Palestine. Theirs is a fundamentally native and primeval relationship with the soil: an intimate, spiritual relationship with an actual piece of land—which forms a concrete basis for their personal and collective identity—and not with an abstract concept like a geographically defined national "homeland."

The Arab citizens of Israel do not dream of immigrating to an independent Palestinian state, because their ancestral heritage is concretely here; and this is, therefore, their true homeland. Even the refugees in Gaza have organized their neighborhoods according to the villages inside Israel that they were forced to abandon in 1948. The Palestinians did not regard the soil as sacred until they lost it: it was simply theirs, and they could not fathom why they should compromise over it. However, it was precisely the Palestinians' individualistic (as opposed to communal or "nationalist") attitude toward the soil of the homeland that allowed the

Jews to "redeem" it in the first place. After all, had a number of large Arab landowners not sold their holdings to Jewish interests, the Zionist project would not have gained a foothold. The Palestinians did not perceive ownership of the land as being a prerequisite for the achievement of sovereignty, believing their dominion over the land to be a natural right and a claim whose moral force was such that its acceptance was a foregone conclusion. Now that they have realized that nation building is an evolutionary process, they are holding fast to their sole remaining resource, the masses of humanity at their disposal.

Who Gained from Oslo?

The Israeli participants in the Oslo process were driven by two contradictory expectations. For one group, the hope was that the process would create a confidence-building atmosphere that would foster the proper conditions for an end to the Israeli-Palestinian conflict. They did not delude themselves that the Oslo Accords had brought about peace, though they did not reprove the enthusiasts who regarded them as the harbinger of an era of lasting peace. But the peace seekers could not have developed their overblown expectations had they not been joined by individuals passionately pursuing a very different expectation: that the Oslo Accords would replace direct Israeli domination of the Palestinians—which had in any case collapsed during the first Intifada—with *indirect* domination via the Palestinian Authority. The evaluation of the situation, on which both groups of Israelis concurred, was that by signing the Declaration of Principles and Oslo I and II, Yasir Arafat had set himself on a course from which there was no turning back: the moment he gave up his revolutionary strategy and agreed to participate in an evolutionary process of achieving his objectives through negotiations, he enabled Israel to fully exploit its decidedly more powerful position.

All of these expectations persisted only so long as a balance existed between those Israelis who were fostering a confidence-building political climate and those who were using Israel's superior power to tighten its indirect control. The essential contradiction between these two approaches repeatedly put the entire process at risk. The Oslo partners evolved a mutual dependency that persisted until Israeli expectations were ultimately frustrated when Arafat ceased to play his role. When he realized that the Israelis were not allowing him achieve his own political objectives through participation in the Oslo process, there was no escaping the conclusion that this process was dead.

Who gained and who lost? Supposedly the strong side, the one with the power to dictate expectations, gained. What had the Palestinians to show for the Oslo process? A few enclaves, cut off from one another and lacking in economic viability; the continuation of direct Israeli control of most of the territory on the West Bank; a Palestinian Authority that is totally dependent on the generosity of donor nations and on political assistance from the Arab states (which is impossible to rely on); inability to change the one-sided policies of the sole world power, the United States; and especially, loss of the most effective weapon in their pre-Oslo arsenal: the power to grant legitimacy to the "Zionist enemy" or to withhold it.

The Palestinians, however, only appear to be the losers. It was actually they who gained the most from the Oslo process. This process—with all its contradictions and twists and turns—reestablished the center of Palestinian power in their homeland and created conditions that have allowed Palestinian nation building to proceed. Rarely does history grant a second chance to a perennially downtrodden community. A second chance for the Palestinians is what the Oslo Accords were all about, and Arafat understood this when he relinquished the revolutionary option and pinned his hopes on the evolutionary process. During the al-Aqsa Intifada, he returned to a strategy of violence, but even the termination of the Oslo process cannot eradicate what was already achieved. Historical processes are not human beings that die and are buried; they are flows of events whose continuity cannot be halted at a word. Even if the Oslo process is dead, its consequences live on.

"The Return"

The two shoals of contention upon which the ship of negotiations repeatedly ran aground were Jerusalem and the right of return of Palestinian refugees. These two issues—and not security arrangements, borders, or settlements—are regarded as so crucial that obstinacy regarding them is considered to be worth the price of forfeiting the opportunity for peace. The difference between the Jerusalem issue and that of the right of return is that the former is more of an internal Israeli matter, whereas the latter reaches down to the very roots of the Israeli-Palestinian dispute, with the entire spectrum of the Israeli-Jewish public united in its opinion of it. Even the most vigorous opponents of divided sovereignty over Jerusalem know that a mutually acceptable plan is achievable, given a rational approach and some creative ideas for solutions. By contrast, virtually everyone in Israel agrees that implementation of the right of return can be equated with the destruction of the state.

A host of arguments are employed to discredit the right of return; including the invocation of historical parallels supposedly demonstrating that population exchanges in the aftermath of war are the accepted norm. One of the commonly cited examples is the expulsion of millions of ethnic Germans from Czechoslovakia following World War II. The example of the ejection of the Sudeten Germans by the Czechs was cited by Israelis as early as 1948 and is again being alluded to, since a liberal-democratic government implemented it, with the approval of the Western powers. This is an excellent example; however, those who cite it neglect to specify how the Czechs and Germans went about ridding their relationship of the obstacle presented by the past and the effort they made to "break out of the vicious cycle of mutual recriminations," as former chancellor Helmut Kohl put it, adding, "It is forbidden for us to remain prisoners of the past, for if we do so, the past will have triumphed."

It is worth quoting the relevant passages of the German-Czech Declaration on Mutual Relations and their Future Development signed in January 1997:

> Convinced that injustice inflicted in the past cannot be undone but at best alleviated, and that in doing so no new injustice must arise . . . both sides are aware that their common path to the future requires a clear statement regarding their past which must not fail to recognize cause and effect in the sequence of events. . . . The German side acknowledges Germany's responsibility for its role in a historical development, which led to, the . . . breakup and occupation of the Czechoslovak Republic. It regrets the suffering and injustice inflicted upon the Czech people . . . by Germans. . . . [and] is also conscious of the fact that the National Socialist policy of violence toward the Czech people helped to prepare the ground for postwar flight, forcible expulsion and forced resettlement.
>
> The Czech side regrets that, by the forcible expulsion . . . of Sudeten Germans . . . after the war as well as by the expropriation and deprivation of citizenship, much suffering and injustice was inflicted upon innocent people, also in view of the fact that guilt was attributed collectively. . . .
>
> Both sides agree that injustice inflicted in the past belongs in the past, and will therefore orient their relations toward the future. Precisely because they remain conscious of the tragic chapters of their history, they are determined to continue to give priority to understanding and mutual agreement in the development of their relations.[5]

Among the issues meriting priority were reunification of families and other humanitarian considerations, the preservation of monuments and cemeteries, and equality for ethnic minorities.

Degrees of Self-Blame

Demands that the Israelis accept moral responsibility for the disaster that befell the Palestinians in 1948 became more vocal with the realization that an actual return of refugees would not be permitted. The official Israeli position has remained uncompromising, but there has been a precedent of sorts; Ehud Barak as prime minister issued a statement expressing regret for "the suffering that the conflict has caused not only us, but also all the nations of the Arab world who have fought against us, including the Palestinian people."[6] The statement deserves a place at very nearly the lowest position on the universal scale of apologies. Barak should have been aware of the fact that the apologies and requests for forgiveness regarding historic wrongs in vogue among world leaders (which Barak was attempting to copy) have generated honest, strongly worded documents, in comparison to which the Israeli prime minister's pronouncement appeared lackluster and uninspired. Anyone interested in adding an emotional dimension to a process of historic reconciliation—as a confidence-building measure—has to make a greater effort. The precedents require no less.

A person may rightly express regret for deeds done by his or her compatriots, whether unintentionally or with malice aforethought; but what is the meaning of regret for suffering "caused by the conflict"—as if the conflict were the reason for and not the result of sins of commission and omission for which one must apologize and take full or partial responsibility. Everyone knows that the Israeli-Arab "conflict" is over sovereignty in a common homeland, and that the Palestinians have endured the greater suffering as a result.

The Palestinians yearn for some indication of acceptance by the Israelis of moral responsibility, if only partial, for the catastrophe visited upon them. The clearer it becomes that "return" is not a realistic option and will never be accomplished, the stronger the demand for Israeli acknowledgment of the injustice done to the Palestinians grows. As the Palestinian-Israeli member of the Israeli Knesset Azmi Bishara wrote, "In order for a victim to forgive, he/she must be recognized as a victim; that is the difference between a historic compromise and a truce." A representative group of respected Palestinians who made an appeal to the

Israeli public believed that "Israel's recognition of its responsibility in the creation of [the problem of] the Palestinian refugees in 1948 is a prerequisite for resolution of the problem."[7]

In 1992, Shlomo Ben-Ami, then chair of the Israeli delegation to the Refugee Working Group (constituted as part of the follow-up to the Madrid Conference) stated: "The refugee problem was created when the country was partitioned by the sword, and not because of any prior intent of either Jews or Arabs. It was essentially the product of Jewish and Arab fears and of bitter and protracted fighting." The Palestinians regarded it as acknowledgment of "symmetry of responsibility."[8]

It is hard to voice regret for the suffering of the victims explicitly while at the same time demanding shared responsibility for the past. Apology for the past follows the culmination of a conflict, and if it deals only with acts committed in the past and not with present deeds, it is nothing but hypocrisy. One who expresses regret over suffering that was caused in the past because of "the conflict" must refrain from causing additional suffering, because the conflict is apparently not yet over. Expressions of regret and the assumption of responsibility for the past have no meaning in isolation. The leaders who chose this path—such as those of the Germans, Czechs, and South Africans—did so with the intention of demonstrating that they had transcended the reprehensible norms of the past. Anyone wishing to follow these precedents needs to appreciate the courage required to formulate such forthright statements as these; doubtless the choice of words has immense significance. But neither the Palestinians' demand nor the regret expressed by an Israeli prime minister is sufficient: the former are demanding acknowledgment of Israel's responsibility only, but not of their own, for the outbreak of the war that "prepared the ground" for the creation of the refugee problem and for refugees' manipulation as pawns in a political game. Meanwhile, the Israelis have been incapable of acknowledging any moral responsibility, even if only partial, for the Palestinian catastrophe.

The only way to be liberated from the obstacles presented by the past is via a mutual declaration wherein each side accepts responsibility for its actions and its shortcomings, even if there is no symmetry between them. Then it will be possible to seek practical solutions, such as the reunification of families or the return of refugees expelled in the aftermath of the 1948 war for reasons that had no connection with the hostilities. But first priority must be given to the internal refugees (or "present absentees")—Israeli citizens who were uprooted from their homes in Arab villages and mixed towns and cities, but who never left Israel—

especially those who have been prevented from returning to their homes in contravention of Israeli law, such as the former inhabitants of Bir'im and Iqrit (whose July 1951 High Court of Justice order allowing their return was pointedly disregarded by the then prime minister, Golda Meir). The past cannot be erased, but the dark deeds of the past must not rule the future.

THE CRISIS ON THE LEFT

Following the failure of the Camp David summit, an atmosphere of dejection pervaded the Israeli peace groups, which was exacerbated when the Israeli and American negotiators, with Ehud Barak in the lead, laid all the responsibility for the collapse of the talks on the shoulders of the Palestinians. It was natural and convenient to react by claiming that "there is no one to talk to" on the Palestinian side. The Palestinians' violence and its interpretation by many on the Israeli Left as "revealing their true face" tore the Israeli peace movement apart.

Disappointment

Amid the spate of militant and despairing reactions voiced in the wake of the recurrent acts of violence (and rational reactions were rare), that of the author David Grossman stands out: "Today I realize, with much sadness, that I shall not witness real peace in my lifetime. We may live in the twenty-first century and surf the Internet, but we continue to wage tribal wars." Although despair inspired a sense of powerlessness in this leftist author, his faith in a muse of history who would not disappoint him remained firm: "Ultimately, the solution that history will impose upon us is known. The question is only how much we shall pay on the way to it."[9]

Only one who recalls the peaks of euphoria at the time of the signing of the Oslo Accords can assess the depths of the depression of a man who believed that real peace was at hand; and only one who was the object of scorn and derision for his pessimism and skepticism is capable of understanding the hearts of those whose thwarted ambitions have filled them with depression and a powerless rage.

The discovery that we "are continuing to wage tribal wars" is difficult to bear for someone who believed that the Oslo process had freed Israelis and Palestinians from fighting ancient shepherds' wars and set them irreversibly on the path to an inevitable peace. This was how "the process" was presented to them, and they became ensnared by the illusion that what needed to take place was "necessitated by the situation" and would therefore—many predicted—surely come to pass. This illusion has not been dispelled, even though tribal warfare has not ceased for one moment.

The widespread perception that the Oslo Accords had broken through the walls of hostility obscured the fact that the accords themselves imposed a tribal framework and dictated terms of surrender to the Palestinian community that favored the Jewish tribe. Continuing land confiscation, settlement construction, curfews and other forms of collective punishment, the double standard toward those who shed the blood of innocents, depending on the tribal affiliation of those innocents, and other manifestations of Israeli tribalism were regarded as negligible and faded into obscurity in comparison with the uppermost objective, which was sure to be achieved. A course of inevitable progress had been set, and at the steering wheel were the very people who, through their part in Oslo, had brought salvation and a post-tribal era to the region.

Anyone who believed that they were living in a post-tribal era will not forgive those Israelis and Palestinians who disabused them of this illusion. Perhaps, however, the muse of history did them a favor when she forced upon them the reality they had ignored. The Oslo process was not, after all, a drive down a paved road leading inexorably to real peace, but a hesitant step in a protracted process of reconciliation between two warring tribes grasping at the same piece of land. This process included an important positive component: the mutual recognition of the two tribes' right to exist. However, Oslo did not possess sufficient energy to halt the spiral of violence. It was, in effect, an attempt to impose upon a tribal intercommunal conflict rules more suited to the solution of international confrontations. A conflict of this sort is simply not amenable to a solution that can guarantee a permanent, absolute, and stable peace.

One who bemoans the fact that "[he will] not witness real peace in [his] lifetime" between the Israeli tribe and the Palestinian tribe does not understand the truly endemic and organic character of the conflict between them. The Oslo process—often referred to as the "peace process"—has reached the end of its road. But it is only those who saw in it the prospect of "real peace" who sank into the depths of depression.

It was sad to observe the despair and to sense the rage and the mute disappointment of all the prophets of "an end to the conflict" who had promised that the longed-for "end" was surely within our grasp and instead found themselves facing Palestinian hostility and violence that had erupted "all of a sudden." Their despair and rage were directly proportional to the magnitude of the illusions shattered: the alchemists of "creative solutions" were unable to forgive the Palestinians for rejecting their "generous" once-in-a-lifetime offers and for defining for themselves their own national goals and ways of achieving them.

"There is no partner for peace," proclaimed those who had hoped for a low-cost "end to the conflict," only to discover that that sort of peace was perceived by the other side as perpetuation of the injustice. Anyone who states that there is no partner for peace is essentially saying that they are at war; and in a state of war, all is permissible. A few hundred Palestinians armed with Kalashnikovs imposed a mood of "war for survival" upon a powerful nation possessed of nuclear armaments and a mighty army, while its leaders promoted popular paranoia and "national unity in a time of emergency."

The Palestinians paid dearly for their uprising and for daring, once again, to use their pathetic weaponry: not only have thousands of them been killed or wounded, but they are also being subjected to collective punishment, humiliation, and economic hardships. Despite all of this, however, there is no more frustrating situation for the Israelis than one in which they win every armed confrontation, but can never enjoy their triumphs, which the Palestinians quickly turn into pyrrhic victories.

The Myth of Yasir Arafat's Culpability

The official Israeli interpretation of the circumstances, causes, and consequences of the failure of the peace process has gone almost entirely unchallenged, not only by the general public, but by professional historians as well. The version for which Ehud Barak and his cronies have succeeded in finding widespread acceptance goes something like this: Palestinian rejection of Israel's unprecedented generous offers at Camp David led to a wave of violence; the collapse of the Camp David and Taba talks proved that the Palestinians are not yet ready for an end to conflict; the violent confrontation that they initiated stems from their rejection in principle of Israel's very existence. The entire Oslo process was thus a tragic mistake, since the illusion upon which it was based provided Arafat with the wherewithal for continued terrorism against the Jewish state.

Various conclusions may be drawn from this analysis, but prominent spokespersons of both Left and Right are so completely in accord that they are all singing this refrain in unison, "with the exception of a small group of Israelis who will always blame their government." Hence, one particularly disastrous outcome of Barak's folly and the widespread acceptance of this version of events has been its crippling effect on the greater part of the Israeli peace movement. The success of "Barak's legacy" has been so impressive that it is no wonder that the Palestinians who participated in the negotiations are convinced that it was the Israeli negotiators' objective all along to demonstrate that they had "left no stone unturned," whereas the Palestinians had remained "recalcitrant."

Other participants and some observers paint a more complex picture, wherein each side bears a portion of the responsibility for the failure. Human failings, mistaken assessments of the vital interests of the opposing side, apprehensions regarding public reactions on both sides, contempt for emotional or religious concerns, reliance on the power imbalance, obsession with the past, lack of trust, and above all, the imposition of the agenda of "ending the conflict" when neither side was "ripe" for it—worked together to bring about the dismal outcome.

However, having become a unifying myth, the narrative suggesting that Barak offered Arafat the moon at Camp David, and that Arafat turned it down and then "pushed the button" and "chose the path of violence," is immune to all contrary facts and evidence; and like all myths, from the moment it was embraced by society, it became "truer" than reality. This myth serves a vital function in Israeli society, uniting all its factions and justifying all its deeds, cleansing its conscience, and, by defining the enemy as bloodthirsty, making it possible to deal with a difficult situation perceived as leaving "no alternative" to violence.

This narrative of Arafat's culpability belongs to a long line of formative myths created and promoted by Zionism in order to contend with the uncomfortable reality. Among these, to mention only a few, are the myth of Joseph Trumpeldor's death at Tel Hai, saying, "It is good to die for our country"; the myth of the voluntary flight of the Palestinian refugees in 1948; and the myth that the 1948 war was a defensive war that broke out following an invasion by the armies of several Arab states, and that it was a war of "the few against the many."

Myths are not figments of the imagination; rather, they are a hotchpotch of legend and fact created in the course of a society's attempts to construct an image to display to the world and to itself, and woe unto any who dare cast doubt on them. It is not surprising, then, that nearly every "learned" analysis of "the situation" takes as its points of departure the precise calculation of "the almost 100 percent of the occupied territories that Barak offered to Arafat" and the conviction that the 2000 Camp David summit involved "the shattering of the taboo regarding negotiations over Jerusalem," all of which ran up against "Palestinian obstinacy in the matter of the right of return and their terrorist campaign for the purpose of achieving by bloodshed what was not achieved by negotiations." Anyone who attempts to present a more complex and balanced picture that—while not absolving the Palestinians of blame—is critical of Barak for his conduct and of Clinton for his haste, and especially of the presumptuous notion of "an instant end to the conflict," is instantly denounced as aiding and abetting the enemy or written off as an "extreme leftist."

The implications of adherence to this myth are far-reaching: It is not the settlements that are an obstacle to peace—after all, to the Arabs, there is no difference between the settlement of P'sagot (near Ramallah / al-Bireh on the West Bank) and Netanya (a city on the Israeli coast). And it is not the occupation but the Palestinians' hereditary propensity for murder that is the root of the violence. There is thus no partner for peace, and the conflict is over Israel's very survival.

The trouble is, of course, that myths are a subjective creation of the society that requires them, and the myths of its opponents will reflect their opposing needs. Hence there is little chance that outside observers confronting the embattled protagonists with the objective facts will succeed in persuading them. Is it any wonder, in the circumstances, that the bulk of the Israeli peace movement was totally immobilized?

Arafat Gone

Yasir Arafat, the president of the Palestinian Authority, died in a French military hospital at the beginning of November 2004. The leader who for half a century embodied the wishes of an entire nation spent most of the last year of his life under house arrest imposed by the Israeli authorities. Ariel Sharon, whose treatment of Arafat was based on personal hatred, succeeded in convincing the entire world of Arafat's "irrelevance." Yet even those Israeli officials who did not hesitate to openly discuss his "targeted assassination" went all out to offer him medical and logistical assistance during his final illness. This was largely an attempt to remove any pretext for accusing Israel of standing in the way of efforts to save the ailing leader, but perhaps it was also an indication of a secretly held awe of the archenemy who was nearing his end, and a tacit recognition of his historical stature.

When all is said and done, Arafat was the shadow who followed the Israelis, and the stations of his life—from the Arab Revolt of 1936–39 to the al-Aqsa Intifada—mirrored the stations of their lives. Without him—and without the generation he led—there would be no meaning to Zionist history, to its sacrifices and victories. Anyone who scorns his enemy dwarfs his own victory and empties his history of meaning. Israelis walk, and with them walks their shadow—the Palestinian people; they beat the shadow with a big stick, but it doesn't leave them alone.

What will they do when the sun rises and they discover that the shadow, which was embodied in the figure of the "two-legged beast," as they called Arafat, has disappeared? Who will they cast in the role of the demonic villain? Nobody can fill Arafat's shoes. He played the part so perfectly. Now that he is no more, the Israelis have begun looking for an heir to fill the role, not of partner, but of the scapegoat who will bear away their sins, frustrations, and hatred and clear their consciences. Mahmoud Abbas (Abu Mazen), Arafat's successor, could not fill his shoes. He just does not look sufficiently demonic.

The person who best understood Arafat's role was Barak, who wove the myth of Arafat "the refusenik of Camp David": the man who was offered the moon, but refused it and began a war of terror to achieve through blood what was not achieved through negotiations. Who in Israel does not believe in this myth? And it's no wonder; otherwise, how would the Israelis be able to deal with the violent reality? They desperately needed a scapegoat.

The debacle of June 2000 was not the first time Arafat had served to salve Israeli consciences. The distress of the Palestinian people, and his personal distress, forced him, on the eve of the Oslo Accords, to relinquish the sharpest weapon in his arsenal—to grant legitimacy to the "Zionist entity." Although it is true that the Palestinians are an occupied and vanquished nation, only they, the victims of the Zionist enterprise, were capable of granting this legitimacy. Arafat—with the support of many of the activists of the first Intifada, and despite opposition from other quarters—decided to recognize Israel in return for Israel's recognition of the PLO. This recognition prompted a sigh of relief in Israeli leftist circles, since it saved them from feeling guilty over the fact that the realization of the Zionist dream had meant the destruction of the Palestinian nation: if Arafat recognized Israel, they were freed from the moral dilemmas imposed upon them by the conflict and their victories in it.

It did not take long for Arafat's historic move (in cooperation with the late prime minister Yitzhak Rabin) to be forgotten. New moral dilemmas caused by the new Intifada and its suppression made it necessary to revive the definition of Arafat as a terrorist and the PLO as a terrorist organization; the desire for recognition was replaced by "there's nobody to talk to," and the partner became a humiliated prisoner. Only a few understood that granting legitimacy to the Zionist entity was not an irreversible step. And in fact, although the retreat from "mutual recognition" unquestionably harmed Arafat and the Palestinians, it also harmed Israel, which had never before faced doubts about the legitimacy of its actions to the extent that it did then, after years of violence and oppression.

Arafat was fated to serve as a symbol both during his lifetime and after his death. Sharon apparently sensed this when, eager to humiliate the seriously ill Arafat, he declared that as long as he himself was alive, Arafat would not be buried in Jerusalem. The late Israeli prime minister thus vividly underscored a fate Arafat shared with many Palestinians: like them, he lacked both a homeland and a cemetery in which to repose with his ancestors. Arafat's "temporary" tomb in Ramallah has become a national shrine, and his successors are left to deal with his heritage.

New Hopes

Arafat's demise aroused new hopes for advancing the peace process. The feeling that "a window of opportunity" had opened became widespread among the Israeli public: Not only had Arafat's death launched a new chapter in relations with the Palestinians, but it seemed that the Arab world was changing its attitude toward Israel, "regardless of the Palestinian problem." The wave of optimism that swept the Israeli public as a result of the positive statements about Israel by Arab leaders was fed by the pendulum swings of the Arab states' positions, which oscillate between self-interest and ethnic solidarity. The complexity of the international system forces sovereign states to balance their own interests with loyalty to ethnic-nationalist affiliations. During severe crises, public opinion forces Arab leaders to take a hard line, straining relations with Israel to the verge of snapping, though never to the extent of harming their own interests. When the Israeli-Palestinian conflict shows even the faintest indication of moderating, however, the neighboring states' leaders are the first to jump at the opportunity to improve their bilateral relations with Israel—a move that is, of course, greatly advantageous for their relations with a U.S administration hungry for good news from the Middle East.

The Palestinian National Authority's presidential elections in 2005, declarations by its new leader, Mahmoud Abbas, regarding the need to cease the violence in the territories, Ariel Sharon's moderate statements, and above all, the disengagement from Gaza together created enough positive energy to swing the pendulum from ethnic solidarity back in the direction the Arab states' self-interest. The "positive" atmosphere also revived various "solutions" and "understandings" that had, not so long before, been regarded as pipe dreams and heretical ruminations that only served to undermine national unity in time of war.

It is a pity that my "Morning After" project (see chapter 5) was not better timed.

The Morning After

Only an inveterate pessimist or an absolute cynic could have failed to be moved by the signing of the Declaration of Principles on the White House lawn on 13 September 1993, an event that rekindled the hope of the majority of Israelis that the Middle East was on the threshold of a new era of peace and prosperity and obliged even those who had opposed the Oslo process from the outset to confront their future anew. This optimistic atmosphere was all too soon superseded by a pervasive sense of frustration as a consequence of the assassination of Yitzhak Rabin and the defeat of Shimon Peres in the 1996 elections. The new Netanyahu government's conduct and the obstacles it placed in the way of reconciliation and of implementation of the Oslo Accords intensified the gloom. Nonetheless, some members of the academic community responded to the impetus of Oslo by launching projects whose objective was to determine what awaited Israeli society in a peaceful future. The need to imagine "the morning after" the achievement of peace—which required one to examine questions that affected Israeli society internally—intensified when Ehud Barak became prime minister and announced his intent to bring about "an end" to the historic conflict between Israelis and Palestinians "within fifteen months."

Ehud Barak's directive that "the framework agreement should proclaim the end of the conflict between the two peoples" received minimal attention. Apparently, the inclusion of this solemn declaration in the preamble to the draft agreement was a foregone conclusion: the substantive sections of the agreement would define how the various issues contributing to the conflict were to be resolved. Closer scrutiny, however, revealed the pretentiousness both of this directive and of Barak's attitude: first of all, he perceived the conflict as merely the sum total of "the issues and positions" that are capable of being summarized in a printed document, while dismissing all the emotional baggage and hatred and sense of being discriminated against as unworthy of attention. It required considerable arrogance and presumptuousness to come up with a "directive" stating that an intergovernmental agreement based on an unequal power relationship must bring an end to a conflict between nations. Occasionally the signing of a peace treaty actually results in the intensification of a conflict, as in the case of the Treaty of Versailles, which bore within it the seeds of World War II.

One may safely assume that Barak was not so much interested in the historical significance of this "directive" as in its usefulness as a didactic tool: he wanted to make it clear to the Palestinians that he had made all the "painful concessions" that he was prepared to make (from a position of strength, of course), and that no additional demands would be entertained. And should the Palestinians not agree—since determination of "red lines" is the prerogative of the victor—it was they whom the world would regard as rejectionists.

This "directive," however, was a double-edged sword, and Barak must have understood its significance for Israeli policies, legislation, and attitudes. The agreement would have caused the collapse of the foundations of the conceptual system that has guided Israel since its establishment. Were the conflict to end, it would have necessitated cancellation of the state of emergency that has served to mask a regime of discrimination, emergency orders, authority to impose administrative detention (i.e., imprisonment without charge), land confiscation, and other deviations from the norms of democratic rule for which "Arab hostility" has provided the pretext. Or is the end of the conflict part of the victor's diktat, which the latter can conveniently interpret as placing obligations only on the Palestinians? If Barak understood the significance his declaration about the end of the conflict for the internal Israeli context, he ought to have invested as much effort in elaborating on its consequences in that respect as he did in stating his positions regarding the Palestinians. Simultaneously with preparing his case on the matter of the "red lines" (beyond which there will be no further concessions) for the negotiations, he ought likewise to have charged an Israeli peace team with the task of exploring the consequences for the home front, which would mean revising everything from textbooks to the Absentee Property Law. Israel has taken refuge in "the conflict" for far too long to be able to pronounce an end to it with a wave of the hand.

A "PEACE TEAM"

Seeing that there was no move to complement the peace negotiations with the Palestinians with a similar initiative to examine the internal Israeli ramifications, however, I came to the conclusion that I should organize an unofficial "peace team" myself, made up of relatively young Israelis whose approach to questions of war, peace, and society was different from that of my generation. My hope was that these young people would draw up a new agenda for the state of Israel on the "morning after" the outbreak of peace. Thus was conceived the Morning After Project, which ran from the summer of 2001 through the spring of 2002.

Ehud Barak's instructions regarding the declared objective of the negotiations for a permanent settlement with the Palestinians were unambiguous: the settlement had to be based on an agreement to "end the hundred-year-old conflict between Israel and the Palestinians." The Israeli prime minister flatly rejected the approach upon which the Oslo process was based, that of interim agreements, and even went so far as to decline to fulfill the commitment made by his predecessor, Benjamin Netanyahu, to withdraw from the territories agreed upon at Wye Plantation in October 1998. Barak's method of doing things—which he strove to impose at the Camp David Summit and subsequently—required a Palestinian commitment to ending the conflict. Only this, he felt, could put an end to what his partner on the Israeli negotiating team, Shlomo Ben-Ami, termed the Palestinians' strategy of "dragging us into a black hole of concession after concession, without it being at all clear where the finish line is."

When his attempt to get this condition (i.e., a commitment to ending the conflict) included in the draft agreement did not go well, Barak acted as if these concessions to the Palestinians had been proposed simply as an exercise, with the goal of exposing Arafat's "true face," charging that "it has been proven that he is not a partner for peace, but is a strategic threat imperiling the peace of the Middle East and the whole world." This conclusion was supposedly confirmed by the fact that the Palestinians had launched an armed uprising (the al-Aqsa Intifada) immediately following the collapse of the Camp David negotiations. The Israelis had no doubt that the full burden of blame for the failure of the permanent status talks lay with the Palestinians, and that no option remained but to conduct a "war to defend our home."

Since the signing of the Oslo Accords, public attention in Israel had focused on issues related to the "the peace process," the Palestinian Authority's conduct, and overcoming terrorism. Only in relatively narrow academic circles was any discussion devoted to the possible influence that "termination of the conflict" might have on Israeli society, its perceptions, its sociopolitical structure, and, especially, the identity it had fashioned for itself over the years of feeling under siege, dating back to the very beginnings of the state.

Starting in the optimistic days of the 1991 Madrid Conference, a number of studies and research projects were launched by members of the academic community to examine what Israeli society might expect should peace become a reality. In the process of designing these projects, it became clear that the time factor was key. Naturally, a project's timing strongly influences its character and underlying assumptions, as well as the manner of its execution and its results.

PEACE PROJECTS AND THE POLITICAL CLIMATE

There were two distinct waves of projects, the first in the years between 1993 and 1996 and the second between 1999 and 2001. The earlier projects were pervaded by a utopian vision of peace: a plethora of joint ceremonies with the Palestinians and with Jordan, rapid economic growth, the initiation of diplomatic relations with Muslim states, and the improvement in Israel's international standing together generated a sense that peace would usher in an era of bliss when all would be well. Hence, the tendency was to focus primarily on the positive changes that would follow—although there was also considerable reference to anticipated difficulties, particularly regarding the whole matter of the forging of a new collective Israeli identity. The second batch of projects were designed after Israeli society had endured several hard years of coping with terrorism from without and factionalism within, an experience that demonstrated that fulfillment of the dream was further off than anticipated, and that its achievement would be accompanied by more than a few rifts and other manifestations of social malaise.

The project that I initiated was among the efforts to depict or to prepare for the "morning after" the outbreak of peace. This initiative was in sharp contrast to my perception of the actual likelihood that an era of peace was in the offing. As mentioned elsewhere, from my pessimistic perspective, the Israeli-Palestinian conflict was not amenable to absolute resolution and would probably culminate, at best, in a political and military arrangement without intercommunal reconciliation. I maintained, therefore, that the most realistic objective would be to arrive at an arrangement—or series of arrangements—that would channel the conflict in such a manner as to promote a concomitant, ongoing process of reconciliation between the two sides. If this were to be the approach, then obviously the "normalization of intercommunal relations must be a gradual process fueled by complex internal dynamics rather than by a dramatic alterations in external conditions," as I put it in my (unpublished) research proposal for the project.

> Weariness with the conflict, an end to the era of the dominant ideologies, the striving for normalcy—all of these contribute to the perception of the "termination of the conflict" as a realistic option, and large segments of the population are prepared to pay a high price for its achievement. Under the conditions that have prevailed in the wake of the signing of the peace agreements with Egypt and Jordan, the withdrawal from southern Lebanon, the delineation of the subjects at issue with Syria, and the commencement of permanent status negotiations with the Palestinians, the termination of the conflict has become a matter whose discussion has moved beyond the ideological context, and deliberations regarding the realities of the era to follow the end of the conflict have come to merit in-depth consideration.
>
> Concern for the consequences of peace for Israeli society is directed primarily at providing guidelines for the changes to its structure that will be required by the ending of the ongoing "state of emergency" that has been in effect ever since 1948. These deliberations, however, have a clear objective over and above the design of a program for action and the analysis of alternatives, and that is to place a mirror before Israeli society in which the distortions and anomalies that the chronic state of violent conflict has imposed on its way of life, its self-image, its identity, and its values will be revealed.

THE CHICKEN OR THE EGG

Inevitably, the question of "Which came first, the chicken or the egg?" arises: is it the conflict that has prevented normalization or is it the absence of normalization that has prevented the resolution of the conflict? Even during the preparation of the project's programmatic platform, important questions of principle arose. Firstly, it was argued that the aim of ending the conflict was unrealistic, and that it made better sense to be content with a less ambitious goal, such as a declaration announcing the resolution of the bulk of the most contentious issues and an agreement to defer consideration of those subjects not yet ripe for resolution. Secondly, others contended that there is no such thing as a real "end" to a fundamental, deeply rooted, emotionally charged conflict like that between the Israelis and Palestinians, and that the way to deal with it was by means of a gradual reconciliation process that would eventually lead to a tolerable form of coexistence. There were also those in whose opinion the very setting of the goal of "termination of the conflict" was not only unrealistic but dangerous: Arab hostility toward Israel was a permanent fact of life, the Arabs harbored a fundamental unwillingness to regard the Jewish state as a legitimate entity, and the violent character of the region precluded the attainment of permanent peace, permitting only an armistice or, at best, an "armed peace." To this way of thinking, declaring an end to the conflict would endanger the state through lessening society's readiness to face threats to security and would undermine its Zionist destiny as a Jewish state bent on maintaining its unique character.

This attitude was diametrically opposed to that held by those who maintained that the struggle for survival that had placed Israel in constant peril of annihilation was over, and that a new era had begun. Israel would certainly have to deal with cultural and economic competition, and even with certain security risks, they felt, but such rivalry was not of a sort that would spill over into a war that would threaten the state's survival. Relations between Israel and its neighbors would not, of course, be like those prevailing among the member states of the European Union, but could instead be compared with relations between Greece and Turkey or, for that matter, the love-hate relationships among the Arab states themselves.

In addition to these opposing points of view—and other, less polarized observations based on a variety of scenarios for the future and appraisals of the situation—there is the argument that the debate itself is not free from psychological influences: that responses to the question of whether or not an "end to the conflict" is possible are not the product of sober evaluation but reflect the degree of trepidation felt in some circles when faced with the necessity of redefining their collective identity in the absence of an "enemy" whose chronic presence has permitted their self-definition in negative terms ("who we are not")—which is simpler than the positive formulation "who we are."

The claim can also be heard that the intensification of the debate between Peace Now and those who believe that the conflict will go on forever is evidence of a struggle over social, political, and cultural interests, as well as over the privileges that have accrued to certain Israelis in the course of a hundred years of conflict. Disadvantaged sectors of society, for example, look upon the very existence of this debate—and of the preference shown in influential circles toward those who advocate an end to the conflict—as a way of camouflaging the perpetuation of their marginalization. From their point of view, peace would improve the position of the wealthy while being detrimental to the poor.

WHEN, NOT IF, PEACE IS ACHIEVED

The "Morning After" project was guided by the working hypothesis that despite the difficulty of preventing intrusion by the outside world and of ignoring the actual character of the peace arrangements, the project should focus solely on issues related to the conditions that *will* be produced within Israeli society *when, and not if,* peace is achieved. The attempt to avoid external influences was put to the test even before commencement of the project, since the date it was scheduled to begin (late October 2000) was precisely when the upsurge of terrorism and violence heralding the start of the al-Aqsa Intifada took place. It appeared that the slogan "End the Conflict" had unintentionally led to its exact opposite: when it became clear that the goal was unattainable, the entire peace process collapsed, and its place was taken by a violent confrontation that some Israelis described as a state of emergency and others as a threat to survival. "We told you so," jeered those who had contended from the outset that the concept of "the morning after" was untenable, or even dangerous, and now saw that events had proved them right. At that point a number of participants withdrew from the project, viewing the very act of discussing "an end to the conflict" in the midst of a "war for survival" as somehow undermining the nation's invulnerability. One of these even charged that the whole project was just "propaganda" designed to promote the political interests of the left-wing parties.

It has become clear, with tragic regularity, that each time Israeli public debate has displayed openness to the consideration of a new national agenda, the imminence of major hostilities revives a sense of "threat to survival," which stifles all efforts to pursue such discussion. This is what happened on the eve of the 1967 war, just prior to the 1973 (Yom Kippur) war, at the time of the war in Lebanon (1982), and during the Gulf War of 1991. I, however, was of the opinion that the importance of our project not only did not decrease in the face of the current hostilities, but actually increased, since the craving for normalcy, weariness with the struggle, and the desire to form a stable civil society had not diminished, and they required serious attention—in the form of a response incorporating both an intellectual challenge and an expression of hope. I reasoned that the very fact that anyone dared to presume that there would be a "morning after" and was investigating its consequences would counterbalance the fatalistic attitude that the conflict would continue forever, which was back in vogue. Ultimately, a forecast that envisions a society in a chronic state of siege—perpetually surrounded by hostile forces—is not conducive to optimism, nor does it improve one's staying power; rather, it perpetuates the societal distortions that have taken root over the hundred years of conflict and is also liable to become a self-fulfilling prophesy.

The project got under way, was carried out as will be described below, and reached its conclusion. The participants in "The Morning After"—who, in the shadow of the al-Aqsa Intifada, were confronted with the reality that peace was far off—never ceased to ponder the degree of relevance of their work in light of the reality "on the ground." The emphasis was shifted, therefore, from consideration of the fruits of the anticipated peace to an examination of the difficulties that would likely arrive in its wake. The project thus concluded with a sense that no utopia awaited Israeli society, and that the problems attending peace would by no less severe than those brought about by its lack; and the goal of the project—as demanded by its name—was turned on its head, from envisioning the dream that would be fulfilled with the dawning of peace to the study of interim conditions and normalization processes taking place in the present, which were crying out for direction and care, here and now.

The opinion that "normalization is a gradual process fueled by complex internal dynamics rather than by dramatic external changes" was gaining acceptance. The participants' assumption was that the anticipated peace would be a "cold peace," following whose achievement the alterations to Israeli society would not be far-reaching and would primarily entail changes in emphasis, and that most of the modifications expected to occur on "the morning after" were already under way. As Daniel Levin wrote: "Israel, like every state, exists within a dynamic and ever-changing context; and, in and of itself, peace will not alter this agenda so much as enable the discussion of various issues that have not previously received the attention they deserve":[1] meaning that most of the relevant issues would sooner or later appear on the public/political agenda, even were the advent of peace delayed. What the "morning after" scenario did was permit the researchers to look beyond ongoing problems, enabling them to adopt a more comprehensive overview—in order to examine questions and subjects not currently on the agenda.

A PESSIMISTIC MOOD

The project's participants were well aware of the pessimistic mood pervading their deliberations. At the close of the group's first meeting, at which the participants had presented with the abstracts of their research proposals, one of them stated:

> What is perhaps most conspicuous here is the absence of the utopia that Zionism specializes in promoting—the vision of a utopian future, . . . and I think that behind everything that was said here today there is a certain amount of fear. From this I deduce that the prospect of the "day after" is so dismal that it's actually good that the state of war will continue a little while longer. . . . We have a kind of profound fear that the "day after" will arrive, and they will read what we've written and will see what nonsense it is.

Another member of the group attempted to downplay the significance of the pessimism, pointing out, "Now we're in a difficult period, so everyone is gloomy." Elsewhere, he elaborated:

> It's like in the Intelligence Branch of the IDF, all the thinking is directed toward perceived threats. . . . That means that in this profession, you have to be paranoid. . . . There is a problem in this way of thinking, because it leads to reactivity and a certain degree of pessimism: "It's going to come, and when it comes, I'll react." . . . [I say] that your job is to tell me about the threats, but also to tell me about the opportunities, and here in this project there is no effort at all to seek out the opportunities. We only speak about the threats. . . . They are real—I'm not arguing with that—but the opportunities also exist.

The generational context as well, was always in the background. "Today," said one participant, "when a group of academics like this one sits down together, it is an entirely different phenomenon than such a meeting would have been ten, twenty years ago—which would never would have come up with a picture like this."[2] This generational difference was, in fact, exactly what had guided my choice of the candidates to take part in the project: "Researchers with fresh and original thinking, whose views have not yet received enough public recognition; scholars sufficiently acknowledged in their fields of specialization, who are on the verge of breaking through to public awareness." I had sought to assemble relatively young scholars, in their late thirties and early forties, the age of my elder son, Eyal, whose employment as a professor of law did not permit him to take part in the project. In my view, these young scholars would represent the third generation of the Zionist enterprise, and I wished to set the picture that they would paint alongside those produced by my generation and my father's.

And so, in early February 2001, twenty-four men and women gathered for the first meeting in Jerusalem, the eighteen members of the project's research team plus six more mature participants who constituted a steering committee. Five of the participants had been born in the latter half of the 1950s and the rest during the 1960s; their ages ranged between 48 and 32. All but two of them were academics. They represented every university in the country and several colleges. Some were lecturers who had completed a period as postdoctoral fellows, whereas others had only recently completed their doctorates or were still writing their dissertations. Several were employed in their specialized professions rather than in teaching or research. The group included two Palestinian Israelis and four women, and almost all of them came from a socioeconomic background that could be described as middle-class. All but two were secular, and all but three were native-born. It was not possible to identify a specific set of political positions common to the group, even though the fact of their willingness to take part in a project dealing with peace suggested affiliation with the political camp referred to as "center-left"—or at least not with the ideological Right.

This latter bias had not escaped the notice of several of those who had been invited to join the steering committee and had declined; and also of two potential participants in the research end of the project, who argued that the platform of the project promoted leftist positions. They perceived the very fact that our working hypothesis dealt with peace with the Palestinians as "a concession to terrorism," since in their view, any work based on the assumption of "revoking the state of emergency" would lead to serious (and undesirable) consequences—in both theory and practice—for Israeli society. Local financial sponsors who had helped make the project a reality also leveled the charge of a leftist bias; for example, regarding our invitations to lecturers who were experts on South Africa or Northern Ireland. Our inviting them to speak under the auspices of the project was seen as tantamount to adopting a position supportive of "the characterization of the Israeli-Palestinian conflict in a manner that was subject to controversy."

"AN ASHKENAZI AGENDA"

In the course of the group's deliberations, however, criticism from the Left became evident as well; for instance, that voiced by a participant (who withdrew after the opening meeting) who viewed involvement with "the conflict," not to mention "peace," as "the agenda of the secular Ashkenazi establishment and its hangers-on." The departing participant stated:

> Every group in Israeli society has its own agenda, and it is not solely political. The groups that I mean are Haredim [ultra-Orthodox Jews], Israeli Arabs, Mizrahim, Russians; altogether they are some four million people, the majority of this society. What's left are the Ashkenazi establishment and its hangers-on. This group's affiliates, from Meretz leftward and from Moledet rightward, still regard the conflict as an essential aspect of life: actually the conflict is what gives their lives meaning, one way or another.

Another participant responded:

> Try the following exercise. Think of Peace Now [the major center-left peace organization in Israel, which is overwhelmingly Ashkenazi and middle-class in membership] as a group identified by its ethnic and class makeup and not by its politics, Right versus Left. That could be interesting.

Many researchers have, in fact, analyzed the sociocultural makeup of Israeli peace groups: "That portion of the Ashkenazi elite that affiliates itself with the peace movement has noted that the war [sic] and the escalation of violence have begun to constitute an obstacle to the realization of its interests, but it hasn't figured out how to make its demands more universal, in order to draw in other Israeli social groupings," one says.[3] Left-wing pundits, too, join in the critique of involvement in peace issues as diverting attention from the appalling social conditions that exist in Israel. Zeev Sternhell writes:

> When one asks spokespersons of the Left what needs to be done in the present catastrophic situation, the answer is that we must make peace, because only an end to the war of occupation and to settlement activity will bring about prosperity. . . . The powerless do not believe the Left, because they think that the Left does not have their interests at heart. In their eyes, the Left is more involved with the Palestinians than with those who live in [the public subsidized housing of] the Amidar projects, who can barely pay their rent.

"For them," says Sternhell, "there is no time to wait for a peace that perhaps will come and perhaps will not."[4]

The issue of the centrality to the Israeli agenda of the struggle for peace—as opposed to a social program and efforts to correct the inequities and other distortions that plague Israeli society—was not conclusively resolved in the course of the project's deliberations, just as it has not been conclusively resolved within Israeli public discourse as a whole. The discussion that did take place, however—and even more so, the hints that were dropped when specific subjects were broached—demonstrated what a drain on energy the preoccupation with an elusive "peace" had become. As well, they illustrated the degree to which these very deliberations served as a means of settling old scores between the "center" and the "periphery" of Israeli society and as a way to precipitate the decline of "old elites" and the rise of new ones. Israeli discourse concerns itself with the monetary cost of holding on to the occupied territories and establishing new settlements. It does not, however, devote attention to the heavy price being exacted by the debate over "the future of the territories"—in terms of energy diverted from efforts to temper the contradictions within Israeli society.

The project's participants were virtually all members of the generation that came of age in a divided Israeli society that had awakened from the "melting pot" illusions of the state's early years. In the main, they subscribed to the near universally held perception of Israeli society as being subdivided into six principal sociocultural groupings: *Haredi*, Mizrahi-traditional, Russian, religious-nationalist, Israeli-Arab, and the secular-Jewish successors to the founders of the state. Like other observers, they debated the veracity of the reported decline of the ruling elite, the "heirs of the founding fathers": had the time finally come to acknowledge the fall from supremacy of the cultural and socioeconomic stratum that had established the state and had long retained absolute control over all of its internal workings? In that vein, one participant depicted the power struggle that would ensue on "the day after" as "a sociological class struggle and a sociocultural battle over how the cards will be dealt . . . : who takes how much, who receives, who rules?"

Baruch Kimmerling, in proclaiming the "end of the hegemony" of the heirs of the founding generation, states that Ariel Sharon's February 2001 victory in the general elections—when the Labour party (the obvious political representative of the heirs of the founders' generation) joined the National Unity Government as a junior partner—rang down the curtain, both symbolically and politically, on the saga of the old-time socialists and secular-nationalist Ashkenazim. Some participants in the project—which had begun at precisely that time—agreed with the claim that the eclipse of the "founding clique" as a dominant elite was indeed complete. Others, however, maintained that not only had Israel's "Mayflower generation" not disappeared as an elite, it was, in fact, increasing in power. Oren Yiftahel stated at a February 2001 session:

> Perhaps the most impressive success story in the annals of Zionism is that of this small nucleus of Ashkenazim . . . which succeeded in maintaining its dominance in Israeli society and the pre-state Yishuv for eighty years. . . . In politics, one counts heads, one counts hands, but if we look at other arenas of Israeli society—for instance the law, the media, the world of art, academia, or economics—we find this same group there . . . and very, very dominant.

This group has grown and expanded because, Yiftahel continued, "many other groups want to become a part of it."

Despite the continuing vigor of the old elite, it is worth noting one important phenomenon that may serve as a basis for the claim that this dominance is coming to an end. In one key sphere, that of party politics, both local and national, the sabra elite has, indeed, lost control. The years since 1977—and particularly since the mid 1980s—have seen new sectors of society take over both the centers of political power and the apparatus of government and public rule that had previously been the exclusive province of the secular Ashkenazi elites. The ascendancy of the social strata represented by the parties that constitute the right-wing political alliance known as the Likud in the political arena, at both the municipal and national levels, has brought control over the allocation of public resources (the granting of budgets, patronage appointments, and other favors) to new sectors of the population, thereby generating substantial socioeconomic mobility.

It seems, however, that this takeover was not much of a struggle, since the founders' heirs did not put up a real fight. Most of them had lost interest in politics and readily relinquished the perks of political power. Two generations of all-but-absolute control over the institutions of state, local government, the Histadrut (the principal trade union federation), and financial bodies—along with economic, social, and cultural dominance—had given the founders' heirs such an unshakable socioeconomic base that they no longer had any need to squabble over a slice of the pie. On the contrary, many of them were interested in reducing the role and power of the governmental apparatus. They therefore began to work determinedly for privatization, installing a market economy that would essentially destroy the welfare state they themselves had established in the 1950s and 1960s. The system they had set

up at a time when they found it advantageous to control the distribution
of resources to massive numbers of new immigrants did not interest
them now; it was even perceived as a burden, since it no longer bene-
fited them and, moreover, they were still paying most of its operating
expenses.

The ideology of globalization undergirding the privatization of much
of Israel's public sector, and the consequent brutal exposure of the population to the laws of the marketplace, depicted peace as the cure for all
of society's ills. In the process, the old-guard secular-Ashkenazi "peace
camp" succeeded in turning its struggle into a marginalized lost cause
that alienated large segments of the population. Firstly, by dissociating
themselves from the political fray, they also effectively distanced themselves from positions of political influence. Secondly, the best and bright-
est of the "heirs of the founders" withdrew from the corrupt political
arena, leaving it in the hands of others who were less able, and whose
honesty could not always be relied upon. Thirdly, the ever-widening
socioeconomic disparities amongst various sectors of the Israeli public
served to increase the power of populist and xenophobic ideologies and
fostered a violent and uncompromising attitude. Fourthly, as already
mentioned, "peace" had come to be perceived as the slogan of the "well-
fed Left," and was therefore despised in many circles—whose members
maintained that they were "for peace" but hated those who spoke on its
behalf. They viewed the pursuit of peace as a strategy for maintaining the
dominance of the arrogant chattering classes. Involvement with peace
issues and advocacy for peace became marginalized activities, which—
although not ceasing to keep many groups of Israelis occupied and even
producing the occasional glittering media event—were limited to
"preaching to the converted." The Morning After project was no exception; hence it, too, failed to achieve its primary objective.

From the very outset, I had striven to move the project outside the
exclusively academic context and to make its findings available to the
general public. It was thus planned to include a series of open discussions that would be publicized in newspapers and weekend supplements
and on the Internet. However, the Intifada, the atmosphere of hostility
toward any attempt "to talk peace during a war for survival," and lack
of experience with the media resulted in the audience for the Morning
After project being confined to the narrow academic world. The publications it produced had no impact. Other, comparable projects embarked upon at that time suffered a similar fate and likewise failed to
stimulate public interest.

Surprisingly, the only place where the project I directed did garner attention, and where people sought to learn from it, was actually outside of Israel, in Northern Ireland. There, they took an interest both in the basic concept of attempting to envisage the morning after the end of a violent conflict and in other subjects that seemed relevant to their own situation: the army and armed forces, ecology, land-use and planning, emergency regulations, intercommunal relations, and ethnic symbols. These subjects, and others, were among those treated in the fourteen pieces of research prepared for the Morning After project (the fifteenth, on the psychology of the conflict, having been disqualified).

THE THIRD GENERATION'S WORLDVIEW

A brief overview of the project's written and oral submissions may contribute to an understanding of the aforementioned "third generation's" worldview, and the picture they paint is not an optimistic one. Indeed, some participants based their papers on the words with which I had summed up the situation: "As in Northern Ireland, we can at most arrive at a settlement without reconciliation. The conflict is unresolvable . . . although in the best case it may be channeled in ways that make it manageable, albeit without . . . a process of true reconciliation between the two sides. This is not a cold peace; it is not peace at all: it is twilight." The members of our research team, however, did not accept these words as prescriptive, but came to their own independent conclusions. Michael Feige wrote, for example:

> The conflict will come to an end with the two sides still holding fast to their positions and still believing that they are right. . . . Since the conflict will not end with a solution that the sides define as being just, reconciliation [will] involve forgetfulness and not remembrance. Reconciliation will be possible only if the dark past is relinquished, not resolved or hushed up. Each side must forget the deeds of war and terrorism committed by its opponents, . . . which is an emotionally complex thing to do. . . . For Palestinians and Israelis alike, the construction of one side's narrative has entailed the negation of the other's. Both the Israelis and the Palestinians will have to give up their opposing narratives, whose persistence has made the conflict endemic and not readily resolvable. . . . *The nature of the "morning after" is dependent above all, not on the ability to forgive, but on the ability to forget, or at least to place one's memories in parentheses.*[5]

Feige acknowledges that it will be difficult (and perhaps impossible) for Palestinians to wipe 1948 and "the right of return" from their collective memory, and that it will be similarly impossible for many among the hundreds of thousands of Israeli settlers and their supporters to obliterate the memory of the trauma of their eviction from the occupied territories, without which no peace settlement can be achieved. It may even be, he cautions, that the settlers' eviction will be perceived as heralding a disastrous dismemberment of the state of Israel, itself, and will lead to a destructive generalized desperation. "Crisis lies in wait for the post-Zionist, post-conflict utopia at every turn, at every moment," he concludes.

Ilan Saban asks:

> To what degree . . . is the future concealed within the past? . . . [Even] a deterministic view of human history requires acceptance of one generalization . . . that the future is somewhat "open," since it . . . is only partially determined by the past. . . . For "futurists," these reassurances regarding the absence of a predetermined fate are, of course, encouraging. . . . We are endeavoring to assemble a puzzle some pieces of which are as yet blank: What additional crimes, mutual atrocities, internal rifts, messianic visions, emotions, disillusionments, compromises—will accompany us on the way to the new dawn? . . . What precise form will "the morning after" take, and to what degree have the seeds of violence sown in the past been uprooted? A third troubling difficulty remains: what assurance do we have that a new dawn will actually break through, even an ashen dawn?[6]

COLD PEACE

Saban's answer to his own question paints a far from rosy picture of the approaching daybreak:

> There is no question of a reconciliation agreement between the two peoples. The agreement is not going to heal the past. From the Palestinian point of view, any healing of the past can only be partial. What this means is lingering hostility—on the part of a significant proportion of Palestinians in diaspora, in the territories, and even within Israel—toward the agreement. . . . We can expect their determined and violent opposition to the peace agreement, which will detract greatly from its power for Israel and Israelis. . . . The supposedly concrete fact that the abovementioned agreement will not secure a reconciliation between Israel and Palestine will strengthen Jewish opposition to the agreement, since the shadow of "the PLO's program of [taking over Israel in] stages" will not have been lifted. . . . Thus, significant segments of Israeli-Jewish society will be left confronting a sense of impending doom on the "morning after." And some of these will constitute a civilian support-base for Jewish underground groups. The sense of threat to Israel's survival will certainly dimin-

ish after the signing of a peace agreement. There will, however, remain a
not inconsequential degree of anxiety regarding security, which will furnish the motivation for retaining the vast majority of the state's security-
related legislation. This anxiety will not be entirely groundless.[7]

Daniel Levin states:

> I have chosen as my point of departure the assumption that a "cold
> peace" will reign in our region; that is, that there will be continued appre-
> hensiveness concerning the outbreak of a regional war. This does not
> mean that there will not be warm relations and cooperation between the
> peoples and/or the governments. The conditions prevailing at the outset
> are not the only reason that we can expect a cold peace. In the academic
> literature there is an overwhelming consensus regarding the "coldness" of
> the peace anticipated in the Middle East on the "morning after." We live
> in an exceedingly violent "neighborhood." . . . Even following the
> achievement of a comprehensive peace between Israel and the Arab
> World, the region will continue to be rife with tensions and violence.[8]

Sufian Kabaha, one of the project's Palestinian Israeli participants,
writes:

> My basic assumption is that a cold peace will prevail between Israel and
> Palestine, not that there will be acts of violence between the two states;
> however, the balance of power and trade will be asymmetrical. The state
> of Israel will retain its position of superiority, particularly as regards the
> economy and the realm of formal politics and will manipulate its trade
> relations with the Palestinian state in such a way as to place the latter in
> a position of dependence. . . .
>
> Even in an era of peace, it is difficult to envision a situation wherein the
> internal rifts and tensions of Israeli society will vanish. . . . In the various
> religious-nationalistic and ethno-cultural groups, people will continue to
> follow their own agendas and will not alter their positions or their belief
> and value systems. . . . The transition to peace will [also] not bring about
> qualitative or far-reaching changes in the sociopolitical structure of Pales-
> tinian society. . . . The geopolitical division of the population will continue
> to be a central factor in Palestinian politics. . . . The Palestinian Authority
> will find itself between the Israeli hammer and the Islamic anvil. . . . The
> instability of the sociopolitical structure will impact the Palestinian
> agenda, preventing the development of democracy. . . . The Israelis will
> continue to control Palestinian and Israeli-Arab natural and human
> resources in whatever way best serves their revised security strategy. . . .
>
> . . . Relations between majority and minority in the state of Israel will
> continue to follow the model of an unequal pluralism. The members of
> the Arab minority will not have the access to the centers of the regime's
> power and strength that the Jewish majority enjoys. . . . Israel will not
> relinquish its identity as a Jewish state or the Jewish majority's dominance

in every domain . . . or its ethno-national character. . . . The state of Israel
will continue to treat the Israeli Arabs as a security threat—and as a
demographic threat whose electoral strength is ever-increasing and is nib-
bling away at the governing power and cultural hegemony of the "state of
the Jewish people."[9]

Erez Tzfadia concludes:

In light of reality as it has been portrayed since the Oslo Accords—and
even more so since the outbreak of the al-Aqsa Intifada—the option of a
"warm" peace appears to be an unrealizable vision. However, discussion
of this alternative is of great theoretical value. . . . A warm peace would
allow the state to act primarily in the economic interests of the more powerful sectors of the population. . . . And because of the prevailing inequality in the accumulation of capital . . . , this holds the potential for a conflagration the very moment that the conflict reaches an end. . . . The "cold
peace" option hints of a peace process attended by violent incidents, thus
not fulfilling the vision that "the wolf shall dwell with the lamb." . . . In
general terms, we can predict that in an era of "cold peace," the disparities among sectors of Israeli society will continue to grow, albeit at a more
moderate pace than in an era of "warm peace."[10]

A NARROW NATIONALISTIC CURRICULUM

Other participants also voiced pessimistic views and sketched bleak scenarios of what awaits Israeli society on "the morning after." Sigal Ben-
Porat, for instance, described the civics curriculum currently in use as
teaching "a narrow and one-dimensionally nationalistic version of citizenship." In her summary of the objectives of Israel's formal educational
system, she wrote: "The demand that schools prepare members of the
younger generation for good citizenship is interpreted in a significant
proportion of localities as meaning preparation for military service (and
the moral and social values derived from this assumption) and the promotion of the beliefs required to enable civilians to cope with the conflict."[11] She went on to unwittingly pinpoint my father's two favorite
spheres of activity: organizing holiday ceremonies in the schools and the
activities of the Jewish National Fund's Teachers' Council:

Even with very young children, the Israeli educational system emphasizes
the military aspects found in most of the holidays and does not deal mean-
ingfully with universal themes. The holidays . . . provide a vehicle for the
transmission of a nationalist message—Jewry as a nation in a state of perpetual warfare, which, time after time throughout its history, has celebrated its victory over one enemy or another.

I am reminded of my father conducting choirs of schoolchildren declaiming heroic texts recounting the wars of the Maccabees (at Hanukah), Bar Kochba's revolt against the Romans (on the eve of Lag B'Omer), or Joseph Trumpledor's dying words (at ceremonies marking Tel Hai Day, the 11th of Adar), and I ask myself whether the pedagogue and educator David Benvenisti did not foresee the educational consequences of this activity. His active participation in the JNF's Teachers' Council went on for more than sixty years, and a few days before his death, he took part in an educational excursion organized by the council (which Ben-Porat describes as "having played a central role in the shaping of educational policy in the early days of the state"). In the words of one of the council's founding members, Baruch Ben-Yehuda:

> It is incumbent upon us to suppress any tendency toward self-isolation or avoidance of involvement in public life and to develop the sense—atrophied during [our] exile—of civic responsibility to the state. We are obligated to inculcate a sense of civic duty, discipline, and patriotism—even to the point of the sacrifice of one's life on the altar of national freedom and political independence.

The council's educational programs emphasized the key importance of military service, "pioneering" settlement, and excursions promoting familiarity with the countryside "in molding a citizenry that will be able to assume the burden of maintaining the security of the young state and attending to its development."

Did my father ask himself what price Israeli society had paid for its attitude that education was just one element in the struggle for national survival, and that its goal was "to develop the traits and viewpoints required by a society engaged in a protracted conflict"? "The ideal graduate of the Israeli educational system," states Ben-Porat, in summing up, "is not evaluated (or only marginally so) in terms of the degree of his/her commitment to democracy, proficiency in critical thinking, or of his or her pluralistic attitude."

The fruits of this form of education are recognizable in the generation of leaders, both military and civilian, who were born in the early years of Israel's statehood and came to power at the end of the second millennium. They are shrinking segment of the population, which recent waves of immigration have transformed into an insignificant minority. A typical representative of this generation is the man who became the IDF's chief of staff in 2002, Major General Moshe "Bogi" Ya'alon, born in 1950.

Ya'alon belongs to the Ashkenazi elite of the "sons of the founding fathers," and his roots are in the conceptual world, myths, and educational agenda of what is referred to as "the labor movement." Of all people, however, this product of the social stratum that made peace an indicator of class affiliation does not believe that a peace based upon negotiation and compromise is possible, but rather that he is engaged in a struggle for survival that can only end with the capitulation of the enemy. In August 2002, Ya'alon told an interviewer:

> [The Palestinians] feel that they have the backing of a quarter of a billion Arabs, and they believe that time is on their side and that, through a combination of terrorism and demography [i.e., greater numbers and higher birthrate], they will exhaust us, wear us down . . . I do not think that there is a threat to Palestinian survival. There is a threat to *our* survival. . . . Israel's objective is to bring about a profound realization on the part of the Palestinians that we will not be defeated by terrorism and violence. . . . If this does not become engraved upon the Palestinian consciousness, there will be no end to their demands upon us. Despite our military might, the perception of the surrounding nations will be that we are weaker. . . . This is the most important confrontation since the War of Independence.[12]

In Ya'alon's opinion, "Israel is regarded as a foreign body in the region, and its right to exist as a Jewish state is rejected in many quarters." The reasons for this are ideological, religious, and cultural; this therefore suggests that peace initiatives are a waste of time, and that in their place it is necessary to devote ourselves to "engraving upon the Palestinian consciousness" that Israel is invincible.

When the recently appointed chief of staff came under fire because of such blunt and strident statements, a number of respected men rose to testify to his upright character. One likened him to "a kind of precious metal, a 'nature reserve' of Israeliness." Another, the former prime minister Ehud Barak, praised his character and his perception of history, saying: "His integrity is unblemished. His diagnoses of the nature of the conflict and the roots and essence of the confrontation are correct."

But Ya'alon arguably had no need for character witnesses. Who would dare challenge the credibility of this typical scion of moderate, pragmatic, secular, working-class Israel by calling him a right-wing settler or a "revisionist"? Every aspect of his life—working-class background in the socialist stronghold of Kiryat Haim (a suburb of Haifa), active participation in a "pioneering" youth movement, "realization" of his Zionist aspirations in a kibbutz in the Arava (the arid southern portion of the

Negev), distinguished service record in the paratroopers and in an elite reconnaissance unit; "Zionism, egalitarianism, and humanitarianism—and holding on to the land"— testified to his being an authentic specimen of the mythical sabra, a being whose existence the combined efforts of all the "new historians" have been unable to disprove.

The perspectives and positions of Ya'alon's peers have never been homogeneous, but the Israeli system of education and inculcation of national myths undoubtedly succeeded in imbuing this generation with a sense of the formative experience of the War of Independence, which became etched upon their consciousness. This is the story that became the sacred national myth, whose deniers were denounced as traitors and blasphemers: The Jews agreed to the partition of Eretz Israel in 1947, but the Arabs rejected this historic compromise and embarked upon a bloody war. The Jews battled the invading armies of the Arab world, "few against many," were victorious, and extended their hand in peace, only to be repeatedly rebuffed.

This myth has defined what is called "the righteousness of the way" and has been a cornerstone of the Zionist effort ever since it was formulated. Woe unto any who even whisper that, from the Arab point of view, it was not possible to agree to the partition of the Land; that "few against many" is an unsubstantiated slogan whose objective is to convey a sense of Israel's being a victim fighting for its life; and that the canard that "the war was forced upon us" masks "war fever"—since war and the employment of power serve strategic objectives such as ethnic cleansing and control of territory, and peace can wait. This conceptual-mythological infrastructure is so firmly established that it has been possible to project it—unmodified—onto reality over half a century after 1948, as if history were a cyclical process and what has been is what will be.

"The Palestinians have taken us back to the days of the War of Independence," said Ya'alon. Now, as then, "Israel offered a specific proposal that was supposed to solve the problem via territorial compromise (at Camp David and Taba), and the Palestinian response was war." Thus, Ya'alon deduces, what is at issue is not "[Israel's] occupation of Palestinian territory" but "[Palestinian] nonrecognition of Israel's right to exist as Jewish state." True, Israel is ten times more powerful than its enemies, but nevertheless, this is a war of "few against many," since we're speaking of some "quarter of a billion Arabs," and "a combination of terrorism and demography."

There is now conclusive evidence that, in the first months of the al-Aqsa Intifada, the army that Ya'alon commanded deliberately escalated the violence in the occupied territories and sabotaged every attempt to reach a cease-fire or to achieve a relaxation of tensions by political means—all with the express aim of defeating the Palestinians, since "if we did not do so, there would be no end to their demands upon us."

What would the "founding fathers"—those who designed the system of indoctrination under which the consciousness of the archetypal sabra Ya'alon and the perceptions shared by most members of the elite "state generation" were shaped—have thought if they could have foreseen that half a century after 1948, people would still be making self-righteous claims that "our hand is extended in peace and they are stabbing us in the back"? Perhaps if they knew that the myth of the War of Independence had become an instrument employed by "classic sabras" to perpetuate and justify subjugation, humiliation, and violence, they would recognize the folly of continuing to embrace this myth. I would like to believe that my father, too, would come to see that his dream had gone awry, but of that I am not at all sure.

"The expectation of peace is not a part of the worldview of graduates of the Israeli educational system," Sigal Ben-Porat writes.

> One does not associate "the enemy" in any clear fashion with "the dream of peace," and in an imaginary age when there will be no more wars, one can still dimly make out those "bloodthirsty nations" and "inflamed mobs" who "rise up against us to destroy us" as in the past. In the Israeli educational system, no attention is given to the way to achieve peace, the compromises required, the need to learn sympathetically (rather than for "intelligence" purposes) about former enemies, and vice versa.[13]

My father would not be pleased, it is safe to assume, with the prediction that his great-grandchildren will have to continue the "War of Independence," and that perhaps even their children will not enjoy "the morning after." But there is no doubt that he would be pleased to read the following words spoken by Bogi Ya'alon:

> I was active in the Working Youth movement [an organization that educated its members for settlement in kibbutzim], and it was clear to me that I must go after fulfillment of its aims. Settling the Arava was an integral part of Zionism, from my point of view. I took the whole matter of egalitarianism and humanitarianism very seriously—and making the desert bloom, and getting a hold of and hanging on to land. I take all of this seriously even today. . . . I am a kibbutznik and I am very proud of it.[14]

My father would be proud of this product of his educational system, the youth movement, with its stated goals of "*halutziut*, the kibbutz, egalitarianism, and humanitarianism." This sums up the story of my own youth—nearly a generation before Ya'alon—and on into my late thirties, though not into the sixth decade of life, as in the case of the IDF chief of staff.

The resilience of the Zionist ethos is truly wondrous to behold, given the collapse of the kibbutzim and the transformation of "hanging on to land" into the theft of national property via the privatization of agricultural landholdings belonging to some of the earliest-established communities of the "labor settlement movement" and their sale to speculators. In the eyes of the IDF chief of staff and of a large number of Israeli Jews, neither the new meaning of "making the desert bloom"—that is, the destruction of open spaces and their desertification by paving them over with asphalt and concrete—nor the identification of Zionism with settlement of the occupied territories by dispossessing the local population has detracted from the force of the old Zionist values. Nor has the credibility of those values been marred by changes in objective circumstances since the Zionist myths first took shape. On the contrary, the success of the Zionist enterprise has provided everlasting proof of the merit of these values. And there is a connection between the endurance of the "Zionist revolution" and the perception of a perpetual threat to Israel's survival and of undying Arab enmity. The perceived threat has not changed since early days of the Zionist enterprise; hence, the response has remained identical: settlement and self-defense. And anyone who dares demand that the ideology be adapted to the changing reality is regarded as attacking Israel's collective identity—indeed, as guilty of treason.

THE DEMISE OF THE PIONEERING ETHOS

Erez Tzfadia, who wrote about "the Israeli 'space' in the era of peace" as a part of the Morning After project, would undoubtedly have aroused my father's utmost ire, because he did not hesitate to slaughter all my dad's sacred cows in one fell swoop, albeit in a restrained and businesslike manner:

> The establishment of new cities and *moshavim* [sing., *moshav*, smallholders' cooperative settlements] in the 1950s and 1960s contributed to the creation of social and geographic segregation and isolation within Israeli society. Most of the newly established immigrant communities suffered from economic backwardness and deprivation. . . . Thus—via the push for settlement of the periphery [where the range of economic and social opportunities was severely limited]—the dispersal of the immigrant pop-

ulation [i.e., away from the "central" cities] became the principal vehicle
for the preservation of ethno-class stratification within Israeli settler society and for its replication. This ethno-class stratification was to serve in
the future as one of the most important principles in the distribution of
capital, both geographically and socially. . . .

For 120 years, agriculture was integral to the cultural and social way
of life of an Israel that was in the process of being built up and of developing. . . . The Israeli ethos is intimately bound up with the myth of
halutzic settlement and working the land. . . . Yet some fifty years after
the establishment of the state, almost nothing remains of all this. . . .
Agriculture is essentially dead . . . Alongside the plummeting economic
and mythic value of agriculture in Israel and the trend toward privatization of capital and of public assets, members of kibbutzim and moshavim
began to demand rights over state-owned land that had been turned over
to these settlements in the past for agricultural use. Business interests,
which joined ranks with the agricultural lobby in the Israeli Knesset in
order primarily—though not exclusively—to advance the interests of the
members of the "founding group" [i.e., the social stratum to which the
state's founders had belonged], backed these demands for the right to
modify the purposes to which the land was put. . . . In sum, there was created a space that was segregated and distributed in an unegalitarian
manner—along both geographic and ethnic lines [i.e., with both certain
ethnic groups and certain geographic locations being discriminated
against].[15]

Of the coastal plain, my father wrote: "Cornfields, gardens, citrus
groves, carob trees, and mighty oaks; settlements standing cheek by
jowl, surrounded by an abundance of greenery, rows of young trees,
roads humming with the profusion of cars and trucks traveling to and
fro, full of passengers or loaded with produce from the many farming
communities."[16] However, to quote project participant Tamar Achiron-
Frumkin's gloomy forecast:

It is almost certain that the red loam and sandstone vistas of the Sharon,
the views of coastal sands and of the valleys between those ranges of sandstone hills that still remain are destined to be buried beneath roads and
other infrastructure, creeping suburbs, and a world of shopping malls.
Stream banks will become, at best, narrow parks amid urban and suburban sprawl stretching throughout central Israel. . . . With the increased
pollution of soil and water, the coastal aquifer will become totally unus-
able, and the need for desalinated water will become all the more
urgent.[17]

My father had seen for himself the ecological disaster that had befallen
the idyllic coastal valley, but even so, he enthused over "the develop-

ment" he witnessed. Mercifully, he was spared the anguish of the sight of the almost complete devastation wrought by his children and grandchildren's generations and never read their lamentations.

POSITIVE SCENARIOS

There were of course other voices, more "positive" than those of our project participants, though not so much in their depiction of present and current trends as in their sanguine portrayal of the future. An interesting experiment was carried out under the auspices of the German Friedrich Ebert Foundation, which wanted to repeat a "bridging" project it had sponsored on the eve of the dramatic changes in South Africa a decade earlier. There, they had put together a group representing all of the major political tendencies and religious and racial groupings, which discussed their respective scenarios for the future. Rather than arriving at a single, shared conception of a desirable future, they agreed on several possible "futures," hoping thereby to acknowledge the fact that the scenario advanced by any one of them was precisely as achievable as those proposed by the others. Once their scenarios were formulated, they were presented to decision makers and shapers of public opinion from throughout South Africa; and indeed, the project's initiators report that its research exerted an influence on Nelson Mandela's first actions as president.

The Ebert Foundation's project in Israel was based on a similar premise. The participants in "Israel 2025" were chosen with the aim that "they would represent most of the groups and sectors of Israeli society" and that, therefore, any conclusions reached would be meaningful on a national level. The project's participants shared a common concern that "continuation of the status quo entails real danger to the survival of the state of Israel"—differing only when it came to specifying whether the danger was to Israel's survival "as a democratic state," as "one state," or "as a Jewish state." They also declared that, "there is no need to come up with a solution this very moment," but that the "wakeup call" they had issued regarding the danger constituted a serious warning, which they hoped would stimulate a national effort to create conditions that would avert any such outcome. It had been "relatively easy" for the Israel 2025 participants to agree on these "daunting" scenarios, but difficult to settle on an optimal picture of the future. Nonetheless, they felt a need "not to be satisfied with the warning alone, but also to propose a solution." There were apparently no differences of opinion among them as to the principal characteristics of the current situation: "societal rifts, disparate attitudes toward the proper place of religion and religious tradition in running the state, increasing inequality in the distribution of wealth, and the intensification of efforts by Arabs in Israel to effect a change in their rights that would allow the reinforcement of indicators of their separate identity," as well as the fact that struggles among groups [within Israeli society] presented a challenge to the legitimacy of the regime, and that Israel was "a state that invested a large proportion of its resources . . . in the problem of its permanent relations with its neighbors." In light of this analysis, the Israel 2025 team members warned that Israeli society "is like a boat . . . that is liable to be shipwrecked if steps are not taken."[18]

On the basis of the above analysis, three scenarios for the year 2025 were advanced, all of which were focused on the political plane. The first portrayed "a dictatorship in which the Jewish majority imposes its will by force as well as by virtue of its majority in the Knesset"; the second, "rule by a Jewish-Arab coalition desirous of considerably reducing the Jewish identity of the state"; and the third depicted the dramatic breakup of the state "into three separate entities, each with its own exclusive, ethnically and religiously defined, identity": secular Jewish, ultra-Orthodox Jewish, and Arab. Because they found all three scenarios so hard to stomach, the project's participants felt obliged to add an optimistic fourth, wherein the state of Israel would achieve an improved standard of living, increased identification with the state by its population, egalitarian distribution of capital, assimilation of the Arab minority, and the firming up of relations with the Diaspora. This perfect world would be realized following the signing of peace agreements "between Israel and its neighbors" and an internal Israeli dialogue concerning the basis in principle for mutual concessions—leading to a new social contract.

The Ebert Foundation's project concluded its work only a few months before the outbreak of the al-Aqsa Intifada. Thus, the immediate "scenario"—including the events of October 2000 and the killing of thirteen Palestinian-Israeli citizens, suicide bombings, the economic crisis, the "closure" of the territories, targeted assassinations, and the rest of the events that radically altered the realities of intercommunal life—effectively rendered it irrelevant. Despite this, attempts to sketch a "normative" version of Israel's future—namely, how it "ought" to be—continued to be made by various groups, taking the form of "declarations of reconciliation" and joint manifestos. The majority of these initiatives were intended as a way of both creating "consensus" and fostering national unity—in the face of what was perceived as a "war for [Israel's] survival" imposed by the Palestinians—as well as a response (albeit belated) to the murder of Yitzhak Rabin. This promotion of joint initiatives inevitably resulted in the obfuscation of the issues, and discussion became, perforce, shallow and apolitical.

One typical initiative from that period, the Kinneret Pact (October 2001), received widespread publicity because its sixty authors included Haredim, secular Jews, leftists, military officers, settlers, intellectuals, academics, and businesspeople—but not one Arab. The signatories to the Kinneret Pact, like the participants in the Israel 2025 project before them, were full of "deep concern for the future of Israel and for the form its society [would assume]." The articles of the pact reiterate all the old Zionist clichés, as if the state of Israel had yet to be founded: "We believe that it is of utmost importance to the survival of the Jewish people, and fully justified morally, that they have a national home of their own; that is, the state of Israel." "The demographic problem" associated with the threatened emergence of a non-Jewish majority west of the Jordan River is handled as follows: "In order to guarantee the continued existence of a democratic Jewish Israel, a significant Jewish majority must continue to be maintained there. This shall be achieved by ethical means only." The preponderance of settlers and right-wing leaders amongst the signatories of the Kinneret Pact is indicative of the fact that, in their opinion, the solution to the "demographic problem" would not be found in withdrawal from the territory of the West Bank and Gaza Strip but in other approaches—apparently to be based upon ethnocentric Jewish moral principles and not universal ethical norms.

The worse the situation became, and the more profound the economic crisis, the wider grew the gap between rich and poor and the stronger the sense of having reached a dead end. Initiatives preaching "togetherness" proliferated, devoid of any commitment to concrete action, whether political or extraparliamentary; and the gulf between realistic forecasts and fanciful projections of a "virtual future" continued to widen.

"Separation" became the magic formula offered to resolve the endemic conflict, and at the same time to serve as an ideology unifying Left and Right.

CHAPTER 6

Separation and Disengagement

For many years, I have been following the changing incarnations in Israel/Palestine of the concept of "separation," which has become a supermarket of contradictory meanings and perceptions. It adorns the banners leading the Left into battle for an end to the occupation, whereas for the extreme Right, "separation" is a politically correct term for expulsion of the Palestinians or their imprisonment in enormous concentration camps. A decade ago, I dealt elsewhere at length with the different forms of separation—spatial, functional, economic, legal, conceptual, horizontal, and vertical—a veritable galaxy of measures, generally radical and involving the employment of force, which are supposedly meant to bring an end to intercommunal strife once and for all.[1] It is the weaker, "separated" side that always bears the whole cost, while the stronger party placates its conscience by fooling itself into thinking it is creating "separate but equal" conditions—something that has never really existed. The worse the distress grows and the more the violence mounts, the greater the preoccupation with attempts at "separation" and the more fantastical and cruel these become. And the self-righteousness accompanying these measures becomes increasingly pronounced.

In the violent decade since Oslo, "separation" had been at the center of public discourse in Israel—culminating monstrously in the "separation wall" and the "disengagement" from the Gaza Strip (see below). The debate and the plans to enforce physical, political, and cultural "separation" within Israel/Palestine have exposed the patent absurdity, cruelty, and injustice of the urge to separate from the Other.

The policies and actions of successive Israeli governments were designed to eradicate any chance of real disengagement from the Palestinians in the guise of implementing policies of "unilateral separation." All of them have acted energetically to transform "separation" from a formula for creating the conditions for arriving at an agreed-upon solution into a recipe for domination and oppression

CONCEPTUAL AND EMPIRICAL "TRANSFER"

Restrictions placed by the Jordanian government on movement into that country by Palestinian residents of the territories aroused considerable interest in Israel. This was not because Israelis care what happens to the Palestinians but because someone had dared to sabotage the hope—or illusion—of many that "the problem" had been solved, that the Palestinians were once again fleeing. "Knowledgeable people" were optimistically noting that an estimated 150,000 had abandoned their besieged and starving towns and villages during the Intifada and had, as in 1948 and 1967, pulled up stakes and crossed the Jordan River. The intensification of Israeli punitive measures did not lead to a decisive military victory for Israel but encouraged some Israelis to believe that "voluntary transfer" of Palestinians was indeed taking place.

The Jordanians had gone and spoiled this illusion; they would no longer tolerate the export of the Israeli-Palestinian conflict to their country and the resulting amplification of its prevailing instability. Reports of efforts to rescind the restrictions on movement gave new impetus to the hope for "voluntary transfer"—since, after all, this hope does not depend on actual conditions but on a deep-seated desire to bring an end to this prolonged period of violent intercommunal strife with one stroke of the surgeon's knife.

Few advocated outright ethnic cleansing; it was obvious to most that the world, having learned from the outrages of Rwanda, Bosnia, and Kosovo, would not countenance the implementation of this "solution" in Israel/Palestine. But there are other ways to "disappear" the Others. If not by removing them bodily, this can be done by confining them beyond "the wall" and roadblocks, "cleansing" Israeli living space of their presence; if not by their physical expulsion, then at least by their obliteration from the collective consciousness of the dominant group: their conceptual externalization.

There is no need to revisit the events of 1948 to find descriptions of a process that began with the conceptual externalization of the Palestinians, reflected in the slogan "a land without a people for a people without a land," continued through their empirical externalization—their expulsion from the territory of the Jewish state and the prevention of their return—and culminated in their obliteration from the national consciousness.

The post-1967 movement to establish settlements in the occupied territories replicated this process, but with differences arising from altered circumstances. First, Jewish "islands" were "planted," while millions of Arabs were conceptually externalized by settlers who planned to live their lives among them, but separate from them, regarding the "locals" as no more than a collection of exotic riffraff, incapable of disrupting the Zionist settlement project.

When this illusion faded, another was promoted—of Arabs hidden from view, who would not be visible to those traveling the bypass roads and underground tunnels, and who would themselves somehow not see "the Others" driving to and fro between Jewish enclaves. When this, too, proved illusory, a system of "native reserves" was devised. The first phase of this was the creation of "islands of independent Palestinian rule," followed by closures to make the roads crisscrossing the territories effectively Arab-free. When this failed as well, the cry for all-out war again went up, in the mistaken belief that this would create the conditions necessary for the "disappearance" of at least a fraction of the locals. Some, aspiring to be less brutal, still nurtured the fantasy that enforced separation was a less risky approach to gratifying their desire for the disappearance of the Others. Sadly, those Others are similarly deluded about their ability to cause the disappearance of *their* Others— the Jews—first from the settlements and then perhaps from the entire Palestinian homeland, if not as individuals, then at least as "a Zionist collectivity." All of these desires for "disappearance" of the Others are, after all, nothing but dreams, the product of deep distress.

The proliferation of statements advocating "transfer" and of public-opinion polls showing broad-based support for the expulsion of Arabs provoked enraged responses from those who reject the concept in principle and regard its implementation as contrary to the basic precepts of civilized society. The advocates of transfer argue—in their own defense—that they only mean "voluntary transfer," claiming that there is nothing undemocratic about transfer. On the contrary, they assert, separation, like surgery, aids the healing process. Those who abhor the idea of such a brutal "solution," on the other hand, point out that there is not—and never was—such a thing as voluntary transfer, and that population relocation has always been accomplished by force and accompanied by extreme violence. Even the 1923 exchange of populations between Turkey and Greece by mutual agreement (trotted out by the transferists as the ultimate pro-transfer argument) was nothing more than a fig leaf concealing a great humanitarian tragedy—one that fueled hatreds that endured for generations. The Convention Concerning the Exchange of Greek and Turkish Populations was put in place to deal retroactively with the problems that had arisen in the wake of the terrified flight of entire populations from their home communities over the preceding decade.

Some suspect that the Israeli army's brutal behavior and the human suffering caused thereby are purposely aimed at making life in the occupied territories unbearable and creating conditions that promote "voluntary" transfer. Closer scrutiny of the concept of transfer and the possibility of its implementation, however, will make it obvious that the call for "transfer" is an empty slogan calculated to stir up hatred, fear, and a politically motivated desire for revenge. In fact, the option of expelling a large portion of the Palestinian population from Israel/Palestine does not exist: the Palestinians will not leave their homes, no matter how unbearable the living conditions; more to the point, the neighboring states will not permit large-scale population movement into their jurisdictions. Anyone who preaches the doctrine of transfer knows that it would involve civil war (in Israel) and international intervention. He or she also knows that Israeli society, despite a growing moral insensitivity, will not permit the employment of the degree of force that would be required in order for transfer to be carried out. The most vehement opponents of transfer, too, are aware that this is not a real option; nonetheless, it is important to them that they express their opposition, because that is what allows them to define themselves as being affiliated with the "enlightened" camp. As such, they preach what seems to them to be a more humane—or even peace-seeking—alternative: "unilateral disengagement." Indeed, those who consign transfer to the realm of concepts labeled "separation or disengagement" are not mistaken.

Violent intercommunal strife leads to efforts to effect its eradication either by physically separating the warring parties or by eliminating "the Others." And if the brutal alternatives of annihilation of the other side or its expulsion seem excessively cruel, there exist less drastic measures, ones perceived as more humane or even as morally acceptable.

One could describe a whole spectrum of methods of unilaterally imposing separation, the most radical being genocide, followed by forcible cross-border transfer, relocation of communities within the country, spatial and functional separation (i.e., apartheid), conceptual externalization (i.e., "There is no Palestinian people"), buffer zones, and Bantustans (native homelands). There is also, of course, the option of voluntary separation in a context of equality and mutual respect—but this does not fall into the category of "imposed separation" forced upon the weaker side.

Measures touted as security imperatives are often actually methods of enforcing separation in disguise. The "containment" policy (i.e., restrictions on vehicular travel) applied to the Palestinian cities on the West Bank is supposed to keep settlers and Palestinians separated and the roads "clean" of Arabs, so that the space will "belong to the Jews." Placing the inhabitants of Palestinian cities under curfew creates the illusion that "the market square is empty"—a kind of "transfer by the hour" that hides the mass of Arab humanity from view, sometimes for days at a time, but does not apply to Jews. "Buffer zones" are intended to "divide" settlers from the locals, whose presence in those areas is prohibited "for reasons of security." All of these methods of "separation" are perceived as reasonable and humane—at least as compared to transfer—and unilateral separation as a positive, liberal concept is gathering moral acceptance. This regime of "separation" that serves the interests of the strong alone is regarded as neither a moral nor a political mistake. Supporters of "unilateral separation" consider themselves to be "the good guys." After all, have they not raised their voices against the brutal transfer of an entire population? In comparison to that, the "mini-transfer" being carried out day by day is nothing at all. Or is it?

SATAF AND HEBRON

Only a few dozen kilometers separate Hebron's Kasbah (old city) from what's left of the Arab village of Sataf, abandoned in 1948, but there is no comparison between the narrow and convoluted alleyways of the Kasbah and Sataf's verdant olive groves and reconstructed hillside terraces and remnants of the mountain village's irrigation system. The crowds of visitors who chose one site or the other for a "day of fun" during a recent Sukkot holiday also differed greatly in terms of cultural background. Hebron was toured by men sporting knitted *kippot* (sing., *kippah,* the skullcap worn by observant Jewish men) and militant right-wingers. Sataf's visitors, on the other hand, were secular Jews bent on a carefree day of olive picking in a pastoral setting.

Despite the differences, both sites provided their visitors with the identical experience: that of a homeland "cleansed" of Arabs; in Sataf, it was the past that had been cleansed and sterilized, whereas in Hebron, it was the present. In Sataf, the Jewish National Fund invited the public to experience "the flavor of the past," not mentioning that in the past, the olive trees of Sataf belonged to people now living in refugee camps only a few kilometers away. In Hebron, the government took pains to give the participants in "the traditional Sukkot celebrations" the intoxicating feeling that the city had become purely Jewish, with nary an Arab to be seen in the streets: almost 100,000 people were placed under curfew for the duration.

Much has been said about the brutality, closed-mindedness, and racist arrogance of the decision to impose a curfew on an entire city in order to allow a group of extremists to revel in their dominance and spread their message of hate and expulsion. But perhaps the repressed side of the curfew has not received adequate emphasis: it is none other than the desire to keep the fact of an entire people's existence concealed from consciousness, along with the aspiration that a transfer measured in hours and days become full-fledged transfer.

The celebrating that went on in the shadow of the curfew in Hebron was an expression of power-drunk racist chauvinism; but the rape of the past manifested in the olive-picking festivities at Sataf is violence of another sort: historical provocation is also a form of violence. There is a direct line joining the rewriting of history with the senseless brutality of the present.

"THE RETURN"

One cannot understand the depth and urgency of the urge to "separate" without realizing how much Israelis fear the return of Palestinian refugees, which would destroy the Jewish character of their state and their society. The nightmare of the Palestinian return—which has haunted Israelis for more than fifty years and is made up, in equal parts, of legitimate fears, paranoia, and a guilty conscience—was revived during the al-Aqsa Intifada. Nightmares are, by nature, impervious to rational argument, and those who suffer from them will always mistake the shadow for the real thing. Anyone who thinks that the right of return is a Palestinian plot aimed at Israel's destruction will find it difficult to believe that many Palestinians have long since come to the conclusion that "return" to their abandoned homes in Israel would mean a shift in the location of their wretched conditions and no more. As one Palestinian scholar has pointed out, "The refugees would exchange their unequal status as refugees for unequal status as citizens of a country that is not theirs." Official Palestinian spokespersons acknowledge that it is impossible to fully realize the right of return in practical terms within the borders of Israel, and that it will have to be implemented principally within the Palestinian state.

If the notion of "the return" induces nightmares of Palestinian hordes inundating the Jewish state in a human flood, one would do well to examine the Palestinian Authority's official forecast regarding the number of refugees who would actually return to the territories if peace were achieved. The prediction is that the number of persons would total no more than 500,000, if allowed, of course. This forecast is described as "very pessimistic"; but any forecast is predicated upon implicit political assumptions, and this one certainly is. This number is of only marginal significance when the anticipated demographic developments in Israel/ Palestine are taken into account. To those for whom predictions of an imminent Arab majority in Israel/Palestine are the stuff of nightmares, the expected return of half a million refugees need not be cause for additional concern; even without them, the Arabs will attain a majority sometime between 2007 and 2010. Nor should these figures frighten those who stubbornly cling to the illusion that there would be a qualitative difference between the absorption of the returnees into the Palestinian state and their incorporation into the state of Israel (ignoring the porosity of the border between Israel and the territories); they would constitute no more than 10 to 15 percent of the population of the Palestinian territories. That is to say, the nightmare of the return is situated, not in the realm of demography, but in that of psychology.

In his speeches commemorating the *Nakba* of 1948 (the disaster of the Palestinian defeat and expulsion), the late Yasir Arafat never missed an opportunity to stress the centrality of "the right of return" to the Palestinian political program, thereby reinforcing the widespread Israeli perception that *Nakba* Day (15 May) is yet another manifestation of the Palestinians' desire for Israel's destruction, inherent in their "mourning over the establishment of Israel." The observance of *Nakba* Day, while Israelis and Palestinians are trapped in a cycle of bloodshed portrayed as the final battle of the 1948 war, reinforces the sense that the Palestinians are indeed intent on turning back the clock. This cyclical perception of events not only precludes a real understanding of Palestinian grief, it prevents one from discerning that *Nakba* Day is not simply the commemoration of a historical event from a bygone era but one aspect of an ongoing historical and emotional dynamic that assumes various forms.

When Israeli real-estate developers, working under cover of darkness, demolish all traces of a mosque that was impeding construction of a new residential estate; when Jewish "mystics" appropriate the tomb of a sheikh and declare it a Jewish holy place; when a Muslim cemetery is razed and a Jewish educational institution built on its site—actions that are taking place all the time—one cannot simply invoke the routine excuse that references to such things are just so much post-Zionist slander or take refuge in claims that "They started it," "It's only a matter of right versus right," or "That's how it is in war." Admitting the inequities and promising to build a sewage system in the Palestinian Israeli town of Umm al-Fahm also does not address the issue.

The nearly quarter of a million internal refugees who commemorate the *Nakba* are doing so not so much to mark the historical event as to articulate their present-day emotional distress at seeing their ancestors' graves used as garbage dumps. Okay, you say, they're being punished for a war they forced on us. But for how long? Okay, it is not possible to turn back the clock and let them return to their villages (some 400 of which have been wiped off the map), but why do Israeli Jews get so agitated over the activities of a few Palestinian Israelis who are restoring mosques, sheikhs' tombs, and other relics of their past? "This is not the innocent activity of people searching for their roots," some will maintain, "but a deliberate campaign to utilize their heritage as a means for establishing a precedent upon which to base the right of return." From whom did the Arabs learn the use of "Knowing the Land" as a device for furthering their national cause? Popular support for the concept of *Nakba* Day grew in reaction to celebrations marking Israel's Jubilee Year (in 1998), and excursions to the ruins of Palestinian historical sites regularly cross paths with columns of Jewish hikers exploring the remnants of their past. The Palestinian Israelis' journey back to their roots symbolized by *Nakba* Day is actually a typical expression of their Israeliness and not of their Palestinian nationalism. It is no coincidence that it was the Israeli Arabs who taught the residents of the territories to commemorate *Nakba* Day. Palestinian heritage (even in the form of negative Jewish reaction and hostility) will remain a permanent feature of the mosaic of traditions and ethnicities that is Israeli society, and there must be a way to live with it in peace.

. . .

In 1999, I ridiculed the new ingenious new device of *vertical* separation in an essay published in *Ha'aretz*.

BIRDS AND MOLES

In Eretz Israel, the first attempt at peaceful separation of tribes related by blood took place more than 3,500 years ago. Abram the Hebrew [later renamed Abraham], upon observing that "the land was not able to bear them, that they might dwell together," suggested to his nephew, Lot: "Let there be no strife . . . between me and thee. . . . Separate thyself, I pray thee, from me: if thou wilt take the left hand, then I will go to the right; or if thou depart to the right hand, I will go to the left" (Genesis 13:6–10).

The descendents of Abraham, sophisticates that they are, are not bound by the primitive perceptions of their sheep-herding ancestors. They know the world is not two-dimensional, so there is no need to divide up the surface, they can divide the volume. Separation to the right or the left—"we here and they there"—can also take the form of "you above and I below." One need only take advantage of the wonders of technology and raise funds for the realization of the vision of a three-dimensional partition that will finally bring about peace between the children of Abraham, whom "the land is not able to bear . . . that they might dwell together."

Proponents of this revolutionary approach have gradually grown in number. Naturally, the experiment was begun in Jerusalem, which, as everyone knows "will never again be divided"—though only in the sense of plane geometry. Who ever said it was not possible to divide the volume of your and my strata of habitation and governance? What's going on in subterranean Jerusalem demonstrates an understanding of how to execute the three-dimensional division of space: a whole subterranean universe has been created underneath the Western Wall. In this case, the Arabs are on top and the Jews underneath. This physical division is reproduced in the two-tier political realm as well: my "sovereignty" and your "sub-municipal control." All that remains is to construct a tunnel (or a bridge) joining Palestinian Abu Dis [a town on the outskirts of East Jerusalem that has been proposed as the capital of the putative Palestinian state] with the Temple Mount / Haram al-Sharif, and the problem of Jerusalem will be solved.

Then there is the "Tunnel Highway" between Jerusalem and the Jewish settlements of the Etzion Block, which demonstrates how three-dimensional separation could be achieved between large Palestinian population centers and Jewish settlers roaming among the enclaves of their countrymen. The assignment of who would be above and who below was done in an egalitarian manner: the longest tunnel in Israel was built under the feet of the Palestinians, but the longest bridge in Israel reaches over their heads. Primitive thinkers are still preoccupied with laying down old-fashioned bypass roads, but already plans for the Ramallah Tunnel and the Hebron Bridge are being executed—exactly the way they dug the Mount Scopus Tunnel, which "bypasses" the Arab neighborhoods of Jerusalem from below.

It is just a small step from there to the construction of subterranean settlements or the erection of a gigantic dome over el-Bireh upon which to build a new neighborhood of the next-door settlement of P'sagot. Would Israel not, in so doing, be within its rights as regards control of the airspace and underground resources of the territories ruled by the Palestinian Authority?

The Palestinians, too, are finding creative solutions to the problems of separation. They have strung fiber-optic connections between Ramallah and Bethlehem and Hebron to connect their virtual populations and have set up an "independent" cellular phone network.

Three-dimensional separation is a breathtaking feat of engineering, but the revolution will not be limited to the realm of technology. Whole new fields of theoretical and applied science will undoubtedly blossom: experts in international law will invent theories to regulate the reciprocal responsibilities of Israel and Palestine on the three-dimensional plane; geographers will reexamine the meaning of the physical space; environmentalists will seek a new balance in the ecological system; esthetes will debate the nature of beauty and ugliness in the "new world"; political scientists will develop new models of three-dimensional sovereignty. And the world will stand in awe: how is it that such a creative solution to intercommunal strife never occurred to anybody before now?

Only our father Abraham, from his place beside the Throne of the Most High, will shake his old head; after all, even birds need somewhere to touch down, and even moles bore breathing holes in the earth. When Israelis and Palestinians emerge from their tunnels and descend from their bridges, they will inevitably meet—all attempts to keep them apart must fail. Even Abraham's attempt at separation culminated in the fall of Sodom and Gomorrah. What has happened to the simple logic of our sheep-herding ancestors? [2]

A MEDITERRANEAN GREEN LINE?

There have also been other, no less creative attempts at separation. One such sought to divert Israelis' gaze westward to the waves of the Mediterranean, and away from the occupied territories in the east, suggesting that Israel should logically be attached to Greece or Italy, and that the location of the Mediterranean is a sort of geographical aberration—the sea should really be located at the Green Line, thus literally separating "Greater Israel" from its "overseas" colony on the West Bank.

In the late 1990s, it became fashionable in Israel to be "Mediterranean." This attitude was promoted by academics with the support of philanthropies funded by northern European countries aiming to reduce the volume of immigration from the Mediterranean basin. Israel, of course, has been among the beneficiaries of this philanthropy. A group of intellectuals, artists, authors and architects have banded together in a forum whose objective has been defined thus: "Toward an Understanding of the Encounter between East and West within the Israeli Identity." At well-attended conferences, scholars in many fields—from Israel and abroad—have been cultivating the fiction of "the Mediterranean identity," a kind of lowest common denominator uniting all the countries of the Mediterranean basin, which supposedly possess a shared historical tradition and more openness, ability to merge cultures, and joie de vivre, and less zealotry and national self-absorption than are to be found elsewhere.

This pastime is especially attractive to the Israeli participants, since it permits them to dream of connecting with their geographical region to foster a cultural heritage that is "local" rather than European, while indulging in the regional culinary and musical delights. And all this without becoming entangled in painful relations with their Arab neighbors, especially the Palestinians; such relations are perceived in their political context and therefore are supposedly irrelevant to culture. In words of the Forum's chairperson, all Mediterranean ports are similar: "In Marseilles, Tangiers, Beirut, Tel Aviv, Cyprus, Palermo, and Piraeus you will see what they have in common: life in the out-of-doors, the atmosphere of the sidewalk cafés, a greater openness, less patriotic zeal and national self-absorption." The Mediterranean Sea, with its rich heritage "dating back to Hellenistic times," is a symbol of openness and the ability to combine the best of several cultures.

The notion that the Israeli identity is essentially "Mediterranean" speaks to the hearts of many Israelis and exerts a special charm for those whose forebears never left the shores of the Mediterranean Sea, including the writer of these lines. But these latter, in particular, must know that this cultural identity is a fiction and that the torrid climate, the sidewalk cafés, the archaeological remains, the regional music, and the exotic natives making up this huge and varied hotchpotch do not constitute "some sort of cultural entity blending several cultures." Hiding behind the pretext of "connecting with our local and regional roots" is an attempt to resurrect a cultural attitude that is aloof, arrogant, and cut off from the local experience and culture—in short, an effort to revert to Levantinism. It is no coincidence that the academic director of the Forum portrays a forgotten Jewish Egyptian author, Jacqueline Kahanoff, as an exemplary figure "who was ahead of her time." The atmosphere of Lawrence Durrell's *Alexandria Quartet*—which immortalized the life of a "cosmopolitan" community moving in its own insular circles amid a sea of "natives" with whom it had neither social nor cultural ties—is touted as an inspiration for this new Israeli cultural identity.

The Levantine Jacqueline Kahanoff is lumped together with another Mediterranean, Albert Camus. Alongside passages from Kahanoff's writings, beautiful though worthless words of the young Camus concerning "things Mediterranean" are quoted. Michael Walzer, in his brilliant essay on Camus, says the following about the revered philosopher and author: "The sole authentic example of Camusian nonsense appears in the many pages that he wrote (most of them in his early period) about the Mediterranean culture—an imaginary world of classical moral attributes, which neither his countrymen (the European settlers) nor the Algerian Arabs gave any indication that they were living in."[3] The reference to Camus brings us to the main point. The message of "Mediterranean culture" is that of flight from the only real option, the one championed by the mature Camus—for which he fought and whose elimination broke his heart—coexistence of the disparate communities inhabiting one land, Algeria (in Camus's case); an option in which cultural ties and cross-fertilization, intimate coexistence, and a sense of belonging to a common homeland were stronger than militant tribalism and the impulse toward seclusion in national ghettos.

The fact that the "Mediterranean" vogue gathered momentum at a time when the Palestinian population of the occupied territories was under strict closure is instructive; it is no coincidence that many of the participants in the Mediterranean movement are supporters of "separation" between Israel and the Palestinians, not as a temporary measure, but in principle. It's easier to construct a "Mediterranean" culture with the inhabitants of the Maghreb than to come to terms with the unresolved Israeli-Palestinian conflict, which could give rise to a creative cultural tension. Virtual separation is inherently escapist.

A long series of confrontations between Israeli Jews and Arab Israelis—in many places, but primarily in areas where the two populations live side by side—has underscored the pernicious effects of the "separation" slogan. In all these cases, the Jews complain that the Arabs "are filling the parks, hogging the play equipment, making a mess, being provocative, and making passes at girls." Border Police were called in to eject Arab children who were playing in the public park in Pisgat Ze'ev, a Jewish neighborhood adjacent to Jerusalem. In Jewish French Hill (another Jerusalem neighborhood built on confiscated Palestinian land), there has been grumbling in the local paper about how the police are not kicking out the Arabs and the Jerusalem municipality is not setting up a park just for them. Meanwhile, French Hill has considered following the example of the municipality of Ra'anana, which has already decided to collect "entrance fees" from "outsiders," that is, people from the nearby Israeli-Arab towns of Tira and Qalansawa, with the claim that the purpose is "to prevent certain persons from entering the park." If they weren't ashamed, they would just pass a bylaw prohibiting entry by "outsiders," and the specter of apartheid South Africa would arise. These are the rotten fruits of the pro-separation slogan "Us here and them there," which exploits xenophobia while purporting to recruit support for "the peace process" and actually legitimizes racist tendencies.

ISRAEL AND SOUTH AFRICA

The comparison to South Africa is used frequently in Israeli public discourse.

For the past twenty years there has been an ongoing stream of learned academic discussions and newspaper articles on the similarities and differences between Israel and South Africa (as well as Northern Ireland). And of course, much has been made of the South African–Zionist analogy, which nourishes the anti-Zionist and anti-Semitic discourse.

The very use of this terminology has become a mark of leftist radicalism, and the angry denial of the validity of such a comparison purports to testify to Zionist patriotism. It's unnecessary to add that an objective comparison or a discussion on the feasibility of comparing two such different phenomena is nearly impossible to find, and if anyone dares go into those issues, he is judged by his conclusions: if he finds points of similarity he will be pegged as an anti-Semite, and if he emphasizes the differences, he will be defined as a fascist.

The radical immorality of the apartheid regime and the injustices of the Israeli occupation serve as easy targets for hostile description and condemnation, and the comparison between them—especially since the end of apartheid—seems to imbue radical criticism of Israel with authenticity and reinforce the hope that the occupation will be obliterated, just as apartheid was. But those who indiscriminately use this radical term are interested, not in analysis or in drawing conclusions, but in ideological mobilization—which inevitably radicalizes the argument, blurs nuances, and makes it easier for the person on the other side of the dispute to avoid dealing with the issue.

The careless and tendentious use of the Israel–South Africa comparison blurs the major differences between the two societies and political cultures, which make the comparison irrelevant. For instance, the mutual economic dependence of blacks and whites in South Africa bears no relation to the Palestinians' one-sided dependence on Israel. This interdependence made it impossible to create a true territorial division in South Africa. In addition, the existence of a significant black majority in South Africa contrasts with the demographic near-parity that prevails west of the river Jordan. In South Africa, blacks and whites share the same faith; even if some racist statements were made in the name of religion, there were still common values that allowed for the post-apartheid reconciliation process. In Israel, though, Jewish-Muslim clashes are becoming more virulent.

The apartheid regime was completely isolated, considered a pariah by the international community. But Israel receives massive, unshakable support from a unified Diaspora Jewry and American aid, and—as a result of guilt over the Holocaust and past anti-Semitism—is not the object of effective sanctions. In South Africa, blacks and whites believed that they shared a homeland, and the black struggle was for civil and political equality. In contrast, the desire for national self-determination and separation dominates the Israeli-Palestinian conflict.

A study by Heribert Adam and Kogila Moodlay comparing South Africa and Israel points out that the personal connection between blacks and whites in South Africa was much more intimate than the connection between Israelis and Palestinians.[4] Although this relationship was effectively that between a horse and its rider, these connections nonetheless moderated people's stances, prevented demonization, and allowed for a successful transition to a multiracial society. This study also notes that the South African government supported the creation of the governing institutions of the Bantustans, funded them, and subsidized their economies—in contrast to Israel, which destroyed the institutions of the Palestinian Authority, smashed the economy in the territories, and placed the financial burden on the international community.

The apartheid regime imploded in large part because the ruling Afrikaner elite could no longer face the huge international pressure and cultural isolation to which it was subjected, not to speak perhaps of a gnawing sense of guilt. In Israel—with the exception of a minority thought of as borderline traitors—there is no sense of guilt, and the cracks that occasionally appear in the "national consensus" are effectively plastered over with alarmist statements warning of "the threat to Israel's existence."

SPATIAL SEPARATION

As violence escalated in the wake of the outbreak of the al-Aqsa Intifada, the security establishment pandered to the Israeli public's fears and promoted the establishment of a physical barrier between Israel within the Green Line and the territories on the West Bank. This brought great satisfaction to supporters of "unilateral separation," a curious mixture of leftist supporters of partition and rightist "defense activists." How important it was for enlightened, liberal people that separation be understood as a positive concept, leading to "separating in peace," even if it perpetuates the indirect occupation and imposes the entire cost of the separation on the other side. The Palestinians "had" to understand the basic difference between "positive" separation, whose aim is to fight terrorism without harming the civilian population, and aggressive "insulation," which is designed to permanently divide the West Bank into "reservations." And if the Palestinians unsophisticatedly insist that there is no difference between the positions of the Israeli Right and Left, and are not interested in the benign intentions of conscience-stricken Israelis, just in the destructive outcome of the separation schemes, "there is nobody to talk to."

For a long time, one could take the various plans for "separation" lightly, because they were all wasteful, impossible to implement, and politically unacceptable. Due to the deterioration of the situation, however, absurd plans that required huge investments have been actually implemented. The most prominent of these plans has been the barrier wall (see also chapter 3).

The construction and route of the "separation wall" were never a rational matter, but were dictated by a psychological need that politicians and generals were avid to fulfill in an attempt to assuage their sense of helplessness. This fearsome wall—which is brutally ravaging the countryside and turning the lives of tens of thousands of human beings into hell on earth—is first and foremost a psychological boundary line whose purpose is to divide the world in two: on one side is the protected "home" space, where people are supposed to be living normal, peaceful lives; and on the other side lurks the threat of death.

The earliest proponents and supporters of the idea of a "separation barrier" were members of the Israeli Left; that is, champions of "territorial compromise" as an ideological principle—without defining the extent of the "compromise." They regarded the erection of the barrier as indicative of the restoration of the function of the Green Line—which had been blurred by the placement of new settlements and bypass roads along or straddling it—as the boundary between the state of Israel and a Palestinian state. However, it was the security argument that spurred the aggressive campaign for the wall's construction: the erection of a physical barrier would reduce the danger of infiltration by terrorists into Israeli territory. Military opinion was divided, whereas the settlers and the rest of the Right—including Ariel Sharon at first—opposed it out of considerations that were precisely the opposite of those of the Left: in their opinion, the installation of such a barrier was liable to give the impression that they were willing to retreat to the Green Line and abandon the settlers who lived "beyond the barrier."

The Israeli government eventually gave in to the pressure of the majority of the public and invested many millions of dollars in a cure for the "geography of fear" syndrome. The true significance of this magic potion is obscured by the argument over whether the wall is a "security measure" or is "political." This national project has captured a place of honor for itself in the front ranks of similar ventures—all of them cynical and populist, grossly wasteful and destructive—which at the time of their implementation were touted as crowning achievements of Zionism and model feats of security-oriented construction, but whose originators later denied having had anything to do with initiating them—white elephants that have sunk into oblivion. And as usual, no one is about to call the witch doctors to account. The nation's morale has no price tag, and the wall's effectiveness will never be put to the test, since it will always be claimed that were it not there, the number of terrorist attacks would have been ten times greater.

CHECKPOINTS

The "separation wall" has required an elaborate system of checkpoints, which have become the main points of contact and friction between the occupying power and the rebellious population. Their function has been defined as one of security, but their real purpose is to convey a sense of force and authority, to inspire fear, and to accentuate the downtrodden state and inferior position of the population under occupation.

The large blocks of cement, the fortified positions, and the half-dozen or so frightened and arrogant soldiers at a checkpoint are nothing but a display case whose purpose is to show who has the power to rule the lives of those under occupation—even to the point of causing their deaths. Often this is done without the use of real force, exploiting the anxiety of the occupied, who have been coerced into behaving in accordance with the rules dictated by the agents of power. Scorn for the Palestinians and an arrogant reliance on the mentality of subservience are expressed not only by the very existence of the checkpoints, but also by the fact that they have been placed in populated areas, with total disregard for the dignity and needs of the Palestinians, who are expected to wait patiently and obsequiously in line. It would not occur to the occupiers that the occupied might use checkpoints for demonstrations of active rebellion.

Colonial regimes have always been based on the arrogance of a few soldiers controlling the lives of millions of subjects through minimal use of force and a "deterrence" that perpetuates the inferior status of those under their rule. Such regimes can last as long as their subjects agree to behave in accordance with the dictates from above. But the moment the rules of the game are broken and the checkpoints turn from showcases of control into barricades of revolt, the soldiers do not have a chance.

The lesson learned by the British in India (and by all the other arrogant colonialists) is dismissed as irrelevant by Israelis, because the checkpoints in Palestine are intimately connected to the settlements, and the security of the settlements and their access roads must be guaranteed at all costs. The colonialist mentality of those who introduced the checkpoints is the same mentality that established the settlements in the belief that the Palestinians would forever accept their inferior position uncomplainingly.

The blocks of colored concrete that have been "sown" throughout the length and breadth of the West Bank are more than an attempt to impose a "containment" preventing the movement of vehicular traffic out of each of the "islands" ruled by the Palestinian Authority. They signify the Israeli intent to institutionalize the expropriation of the physical space and public infrastructure of the West Bank and their transfer to the exclusive use of Jews. The concrete blocks have already proven ineffective at accomplishing the purpose for which they were put in place: no one can prevail against the improvisational skills and knowledge of local terrain possessed by the beleaguered populace. But these blocks of concrete were not intended simply to serve security purposes, and of course those who decided on their placement were aware that their practical value would be minimal. "Containment" is also more than a form of collective punishment; a crucial factor in this decision by the security apparatus ("with the approval of the political echelon") was the need to placate enraged settlers and to respond to their demands "that the IDF be allowed to triumph" or they would take the law into their own hands.

The settlers' lives have been disrupted beyond recognition since the outbreak of hostilities. With the settlements in danger of becoming besieged enclaves, their classic Zionist fantasy of "a land without a people for a people without a land" has disintegrated. In the past, this illusion was sustained by means of bypass roads connecting Jewish settlements, where one could travel without encountering any signs of a Palestinian presence, but then it was discovered that the Palestinians were using these roads too. The settlers chose then, absurdly, "not to see" the Palestinians, penning them in their enclaves. The rest of the area is at the disposal of the Jewish settlers, who thus are able to go about their daily routine of "group activities, visits to friends, leisure-time pursuits, movies, and the like" undisturbed. It has become clear to anyone who once thought of the "settlement project" as a collection of discrete communities that it is really a scheme for control of the entire countryside, and that the settlements themselves were just the tip of the iceberg. A complex network of roads and other infrastructure, army camps, holy places, nature preserves, and officially designated "state land," together with the activities of the Civil Administration, solidify continuing Israeli control over most of the territory of the West Bank. The Israeli government has actively reasserted its control via "containment," thereby legitimizing the "routine life" enjoyed by 10 percent of the West Bank's inhabitants (the Jews) at the price of hell for the other 90 percent (the Palestinians).

Two related slogans have gained currency: "The ideology of 'Greater Israel' has had its day" and "There is no military solution to the current violence, only a political one." The hypocrisy of these slogans is laid bare by the colorfully painted concrete blocks of the roadblocks: the expropriation of physical space that they symbolize is proof that the concept of Greater Israel has not faded away but has merely been prettified by the addition of "reservations" for the "natives." Moreover, the "military" decision regarding containment demonstrates that the distinction between a military solution and a political one is artificial. What a "political solution" means is that the Palestinians will capitulate to military pressure and will agree to the expropriation of their remaining land reserves, which is necessary since "it has already been proven that any territory given to them will only become a base for terrorists."

WALL AND WITHDRAWAL

The years 2003–5 saw the emergence of a strategic initiative aimed at imposing a unilateral, quasi-permanent "solution" to the conflict. A series of major actions devised and implemented by Ariel Sharon have been perceived by most observers as separate and unrelated but were actually part of a plan to fragment the Palestinian territories by creating isolated cantons on the West Bank and in the Gaza Strip. In fact, there was nothing new in these plans, which had been on the Israeli agenda—though unrealized—since the 1990s, except that now they were actually being acted on.

In compliance with Sharon's orders, the line to be followed by the barrier wall was drawn in such a way as to precisely define the boundaries of the Palestinian cantons, leaving some 50 percent of the occupied area in Israel's hands. The route of the separation barrier—snaking deep into the West Bank to encompass what are referred to as "Jewish settlement blocks" and their access roads—has made the nature of the Palestinian areas remaining between the fences and walls that constitute that barrier abundantly clear: small spaces cut off from one another and from access to the outside world, lacking the wherewithal to develop a physical infrastructure, and utterly dependent on Israel for everything having to do with the economy, employment, trade, and communications.

In accordance with Israeli plans, a separate road network for Palestinians has been built, consisting of fifty-two road projects, with total length of more than 500 kilometers, and sixteen underpasses and bridges, which separate the Palestinian roads from "sterile thoroughfares" for Jews only, thus creating "transportation continuity" for the Palestinians rather than territorial continuity. A system of sophisticated "border crossings" has been erected, not only on the roads leading to Israel, but also deep on the West Bank (e.g., at Hawara on the municipal boundary of Nablus, as well as between Jerusalem and Ramallah and between Jerusalem and Bethlehem). The Israelis had the chutzpah to ask the international community for funds to construct the expensive checkpoints, "because they will facilitate the flow of Palestinian traffic."

By constant humiliation of the occupied, shows of arbitrary force, and ability to harass, the crossings and checkpoints manifest Israeli domination. The Bethlehem Crossing, alias Rachel's Crossing, is a prime example of their absurdity and arbitrariness. Two opposing places have symbolized Bethlehem since 2005—the Church of the Nativity and Rachel's Crossing. The first symbolizes the hope that emerged with the birth of the baby Jesus, and the second represents alienation, hostility, and aggression. Calling something as functional as a border crossing a symbol might seem an exaggeration to the reader, but it is impossible to treat Rachel's Crossing as anything other than a provocative monument, because the practical, supposedly security reasons that dictated its position are totally unfounded. Anyone interested in entering or exiting Bethlehem can do so easily by well-known paths. Rachel's Crossing is meant for people with travel permits, tourists, and VIPs. It's primary purpose is to create the image of Israeli control over the "natives."

A lot of architectural input, engineering, security know-how, and especially many millions of dollars were invested in building this monument to Israeli arbitrariness. The "corrals"—revolving steel doors, electric gates, exposed concrete corridors supervised from above, and x-ray installations—exude horror. Bethlehem's mayor has characterized his town, which is reached through a huge iron door, as "an open-air prison." There were complaints about the chaos at the former primitive, dusty crossing that was improvised up the road, which quickly became a kind of bazaar. Everyone knew that it was easily bypassed, and it exuded a temporariness that communicated hope that the walls of hatred would disappear. The new crossing sends a message of concrete permanence, with stylized roofs, environmental design, orderly parking lots, and electric gates. "The crossing was built according to standards at border crossings in the country and around the world," a police officer in an Israeli TV show at the time said proudly.

A border crossing between Bethlehem and Jerusalem? What kind of perverse geography seeks to establish a frontier between these twin cities? Winding its way through olive groves and past abandoned houses, the "separation fence" demonstrates its own absurdity, dividing Palestinian lands to satisfy Israel annexation desires. The crossing named for the matriarch Rachel is not on any geopolitical border but on a cultural one: it strengthens the feeling that Israel is closing itself in behind the ghetto walls it has created for itself. True, there are similar "crossings" elsewhere on the West Bank, but this one on the route into Bethlehem, which is mostly used by tourists, emphasizes that Israelis are losing their ties to the western European culture to which they claim to belong.

A CARICATURE OF A STATE

Ariel Sharon did not object to conferring the exalted title of "a Palestinian state" on the Palestinian cantons he planned to create. The "state" that he envisaged will be of a totally new sort: its "sovereignty" will be scattered, lacking any physical infrastructure, without direct connection to the outside world, and restricted in the height of its residential buildings and the depth of its graves: the airspace and the water resources will remain under Israeli control. Helicopter patrols, the airwaves, the hands on the water pumps and the electrical switches, the registration of residents and issuing of identity cards, as well as passes to enter and leave, will all be controlled (directly or indirectly) by the Israelis, with American approval.

Indeed, this is a unique Israeli contribution to political science, and to the definition of national sovereignty and the partition of the Holy Land. For devising the cantons, Sharon won high praise from President George W. Bush "for his leadership and commitment to build a better future for the Palestinians." And it is all to come about, of course, on the condition that the Palestinians appreciate Israel's generosity and pay for it accordingly. This ridiculous caricature of a Palestinian state, headless and without feet, future, or any chance for development, is presented as the fulfillment of the goal of symmetry and equality embodied in the old slogan "Two states for two peoples."

Sharon's plan for unilateral disengagement from the Gaza Strip was designed as a sort of "pilot project" for the fragmentation model he envisioned for all of the occupied territories. The main objective of the Gaza withdrawal was to relieve Israel of responsibility for the fate of some one and a half million Palestinians by pulling Israeli forces and settlers out of the Strip, surrounding it with fortifications, and declaring the occupation over. At the same time, however, Israel would continue to exercise control over the outer perimeter of the strip—on land, sea, and air—and over the Palestinians' access to physical infrastructure and the resources necessary for running the economy, providing employment, and operating communications. The same grand plan is envisaged for the West Bank cantons.

Sharon was very close to the goal he had been aiming at ever since he became an adult: to remove the Arab demographic threat unilaterally.

He was a junior partner in the removal of the demographic threat in 1948 by expelling hundreds of thousands of Palestinians. And later, when he climbed the rungs of power, his wish to initiate major historic moves grew. His "big plan," which led to the 1981–82 war in Lebanon, attempted to solve the demographic problem by turning Jordan into Palestine, deporting the refugees from Lebanon, transferring them from the West Bank, and destroying the Hashemite kingdom. After this plan failed disastrously, Sharon drafted his canton plan and strove to implement it in every post he filled. For many years, he had to resort to underhanded, even illegal means, but he did not tire and filled the territories with settlements and outposts.

Becoming prime minister enabled him to pursue his plan to "remove the demographic threat." Pulling out of Gaza would subtract one and a half million Palestinians from the demographic balance sheet. The "separation wall" made it possible to fictitiously "lose" hundreds of thousands more. Setting up a separate transportation system, "border passes," and "closures" shattered the Palestinian community.

DIVIDE AND RULE

The classical colonial policy of divide and rule is being implemented in the occupied territories by geographical fragmentation, with each fragment subject to different security, legal, and economic measures. And to cope with the challenges of the regime and its dictates, each of these fragments is compelled to create an agenda of its own, and even to develop a distinct subculture and lifestyle.

The first partition of Palestine, in 1948, created the community of the "1948 Arabs," citizens of Israel, who during the course of more than fifty years have developed an identity, a political, economic, and social agenda, and even a unique dialect and culture different from those of the territories and the Palestinian diaspora. The events of 1967 created the community of inhabitants of the territories, which gradually distinguished itself from the diaspora community (which was itself split into the Jordanian fragment and the Lebanese fragment, among others). This community, which was given the sobriquet "1967 Arabs," split into the Arabs of East Jerusalem, the Gaza community, and the West Bank community. The 1967 Arabs have been profoundly affected by the Israeli occupation and have developed political and cultural mechanisms that are different from those, for example, of the Palestinian citizens of Jordan.

When this overall strategy is fully implemented, Palestinian fragmentation will be complete. The almost five million Palestinians living in the area of what used to be Mandatory Palestine will be divided into four separate entities, each with its own particular characteristics: The first will consist of Palestinians holding Israeli citizenship ("Israeli Arabs"), who define their political objective in terms of "Israel as a state of all its citizens, not a Jewish state," and who do not wish to be part of a Palestinian state. The second fragment will be the inhabitants of separate northern and southern West Bank cantons, lacking territorial contiguity. They will be subject to weak, autonomous Palestinian rule, combined with terrorism perpetrated by local gangs, Jewish settlers' militias, and raids by the Israeli army. In the third fragment, Gaza, a semi-sovereign Palestinian regime will be characterized by attempts to develop a normal state despite efforts by Israel to hinder its progress. The last fragment will consist of the Palestinian residents of "East" Jerusalem, who enjoy some benefits of Israeli citizenship and the right to reside in Israel and are therefore not keen to lose their privileges through transfer to Palestinian rule. The fragmentation scheme will enhance particularism, submissiveness, inter-clan tensions, chaos, and violence.

The smashing of the Palestinian community might well have won the Israeli regime the colonial club prize in the imperialist era, but that is long gone, and in the twenty-first century, "divide and rule" is considered a policy worthy of condemnation and deserving of economic sanctions. At best, the existence in "real time" of a process that belongs to a bygone era presents opportunities for sociopolitical research.

EVACUATION OF SETTLEMENTS

The point that was most strongly emphasized in the plan for disengagement from Gaza—and hence received especially vehement reactions—was Sharon's about-face in proposing the evacuation of settlements in Gaza and on the West Bank. The closer the date of the disengagement, the clearer became the real meaning of "the historic event of epic dimensions" being staged by Sharon and his assistants, with the enthusiastic participation of supporters and opponents of the disengagement. In reality it was an internal, limited, intratribal, Jewish-Zionist struggle between two camps split over the evacuation Jewish settlements but united in their attitudes toward the sanctity of "settlement"—the Jewish tree, the Jewish house, the Jewish kindergarten—as an object of supreme value, as if possessed of a soul.

One camp aspired to apply the sanctity attributed to the Zionist house and tree to all the settlements and outposts in Israel/Palestine, whereas the other reserved such exalted value and political significance only for the settlements that had been established by its own parties or at least shared its geopolitical outlook. This "family spat" was endowed with a supposedly "fateful" character only by virtue of the fact that although both sides accepted the myth of the sanctity of "Jewish settlement," they drew opposing conclusions as to its meaning in practice. In Zionist eyes, the clash over the preservation or destruction of any Jewish settlement is perceived as tantamount to civil war, pitting brother against brother, or by some, even equivalent to "the destruction of the Third Temple." Anyone who remains on the fence is accused of not doing his Zionist duty.

The majority of the population remained indifferent, despite the heart-rending scenes of the evacuation that were broadcast incessantly on Israeli television. The apathy of most Israelis drew criticism from both camps, because it ostensibly showed that they were not prepared to come to the rescue of the Jewish people by supporting the demolition—or, alternatively, the preservation—of the Gaza settlements. And woe betide anyone who dared to say, at that crucial hour for Zionism and the settlement ethos, that the whole business was an anachronism, everything long ago having been turned into bargaining over fat compensation.

If anyone needed proof that maintaining the tribal Jewish-Zionist paradigm was the chief concern of both sides in the dispute, the common core in their attitudes toward the evacuation of the Jewish settlers could provide it. All unquestioningly accepted the maxim that every Jew in Eretz Israel is a pioneer, an active participant in the collective struggle, and never just a plain civilian. Therefore, every settler everywhere sees him- or herself as having been "sent" there by the Israeli government, whatever party is in control and irrespective of whether he or she has chosen to live in a flourishing suburb near a major Israeli city or in a remote outpost. And because they are pioneers who have been "sent" to settle, the government is obligated to look after them, protect their children, and, of course, compensate them generously should they be evacuated.

This same Zionist common denominator made it inconceivable, even in a whisper, to consider the Algerian model of disengagement. There, when General Charles de Gaulle made a decision no less traumatic than that of the withdrawal from Gaza, he did not hesitate to privatize the evacuation: any colonist who wished to remain in Algeria could do so at his own risk, and anyone who chose to leave would receive a small stipend and a relocation loan. No European settler remained in Algeria, and there was no need to employ tens of thousands of soldiers in the evacuation.

If anyone in Israel had tried to suggest a similar approach, he would have been silenced immediately, because "it is forbidden to abandon a Jew," and offering to leave settlers behind without IDF protection would have been seen as abandonment, pure and simple. Actually, the total compensation paid to a few thousand settlers plus the other expenses of the evacuation amounted to close to U.S.$2.5 billion. Furthermore, employment of de Gaulle's method would have avoided the spectacle, which garnered widespread media coverage in Israel and abroad from journalists eager to showcase the "tragic uprooting," which "must not be repeated on the West Bank." To top it off, to underscore the symbolism of the Jewish home, the houses were demolished, because, although Jews may boast of living in an Arab house, an Arab must not inhabit a house infused with a Jewish soul.

Israelis often invoke the Algerian model: Algeria—a colony distinct from France, the mother country—is equated with the Gaza Strip, and Israel with France. In the absence of a sea dividing them, where does the border between the colony and the mother country run? Has Israel at any time defined the borders of "the mother country"? What happens when part of the capital of the mother country, the seat of its government (i.e., Jerusalem), is in the colony and part in the mother country? And how do those who invoke the Algerian model define the Ma'aleh Adumim, Gush Etzion, and Ariel settlement blocks, which are part of the Israeli polity—as belonging to an annexed colony or to the mother country? Algeria cannot be employed as a model for analyzing the case of Gaza, but those who seek optimistic precedents are fond of using the metaphor, hoping that just as the occupation ended there, it will also lapse here.

THE "DISENGAGEMENT" PROCESS

To understand the narrow, "family quarrel" character of the debate over disengagement, one need only be cognizant of the fact that it focused exclusively on the few thousand Israelis in the Gaza Strip and did not relate at all to 1.5 million Palestinians living there. Virtually nobody in Israel troubled themselves about what would happen to the Palestinians of Gaza after the evacuation. Questions regarding relations between Israel and the Palestinian Authority, including contact with the outside world, free passage to the West Bank, and economic arrangements, among others, have been absent from the public debate, amid a plethora of discussions about the disengagement (read evacuation of settlers and withdrawal of Israeli troops). The Israeli public had been united behind the perception that this was a unilateral step taken by Israel in the name of protecting its own interests, and the Palestinians could go to hell for all they cared. The world was invited to wring its hands at the drama or to applaud the Israeli sacrifice—on condition that it covered the financial cost of the disengagement and made no political demands. This myopic attitude would backfire when the Hamas Islamist party won a decisive victory in the 2006 Palestinian general elections (see below).

This narrow internal spat about the settlement removal—blown up into "a historic event of epic proportions"—was scarcely worth all the violent uproar. In the space of six days, and with minimal resistance, the entire operation was completed. Only one month after the "tragic" events, the issue had totally vanished from the public discourse. A sure sign of the internal-tribal character of the event were the calls for "reconciliation," the pride expressed in the way the security forces had "sympathized" with the settlers, and the calls "to dress the wounds and knit together that which was torn asunder," which were heard from all sides.

There was something touching, albeit predictable, about the enthusiastic reactions and the rosy forecasts voiced by spokespersons of the Israeli Left with regard to the disengagement and its aftermath. Touching, because the need to celebrate the defeat of the Right and prove that the settlements and the occupation are reversible was so great that caution and skepticism were thrown to the winds, and in their stead an infectious optimism held sway. Wishful thinking was presented as realistic forecast. The common sentiment was: "This was only the first evacuation; there will be more."

The congratulations heaped upon Sharon by the Left were reminiscent of their unconditional support for Yitzhak Shamir, who in 1991 went to the Madrid Peace Conference as if he were being frog-marched. "Do it your way, with your own tactics; the authority is all yours. Just bring peace now," they told him. Indications that the disengagement from Gaza might bring about the expansion of settlements and the further entrenchment of Israeli control over the West Bank were swept under the carpet as irrelevant. And, indeed, the instant the evacuation of the Gaza settlers was complete, the government announced the inclusion of the settlement city of Ma'aleh Adumim within the perimeter of the wall surrounding Jerusalem and the construction of the first structure (not surprisingly, a police station) in "area E1," which connects Ma'aleh Adumim to Jerusalem, thereby cutting off the Palestinian areas in the north and south of the West Bank from each other. These developments and the renewed violence did not affect the optimistic feeling that the "disengagement" process—and the improvement of Israel's international standing in its wake—had once again set it on the right track, with Sharon at the helm, moving along with "his own tactics." As the Israeli general elections of March 2006 approached, Sharon capitalized on that attitude and launched a new party called "Kadima" (Forward).

The Israeli Left congratulated itself that Sharon was acting in accordance with its ideology—and failed to realize that the waning of Sharon's commitment to the settlement enterprise was actually a reflection of his understanding that settlements were no longer as meaningful as they once had been: that their significance had passed from this world, like that of other obsolete twentieth-century paradigms.

In the new paradigm, the settlements no longer have importance as instruments of spatial control. The barrier wall and its gates, the "sterile roads," and a myriad military regulations have taken the place of the settlements as symbols of Zionism.

"NEW REALITIES ON THE GROUND"

In the 1970s and 1980s, the very fact of building and populating a settlement at any given spot in the territories had played a vital role in the creation of political faits accomplis. Those who planted the settlements in the Katif Block (Gush Katif) or in the heart of Samaria and northern Judea assumed the Palestinians would forever remain submissive; otherwise, how could one explain the logic of establishing Jewish islands in the heart of Arab populations? The settlers have argued that from the very beginning, Zionism flew in the face of reality. It succeeded, they say, precisely because it ignored reality and never surrendered to a rationale that considered the possibility of failure. The demographic and geographic arguments used against the settlers thus evaporated in the fervor of their visions.

But it turned out that others, too, could alter reality through the power of commitment to a nationalist ideology; and the attempt to claim a monopoly on ideals, in the false belief that the Others would not and could not rebel, led to disaster. The Palestinians became the ones who were rising up against reality, refusing to surrender to rational perceptions of the balance of power that predicted their failure. Sometime in the late 1980s, the settlements crossed the critical threshold beyond which continued demographic and urban growth were assured. Settler leaders had successfully set up a powerful lobby that straddled the Green Line; the legal and physical infrastructure making possible the de facto annexation of the territories was firmly in place. From that point on, the number of settlements, and even the size of their population, became immaterial, because the apparatus of Israeli rule had been perfected to such a degree that the distinction between Israel proper and the occupied territories—and between settlements on the West Bank and in the Gaza Strip and Jewish communities inside Israel—was totally blurred. Similarly, takeover of land ceased to be chiefly for the purpose of settlement construction and became primarily a means of constricting the movements of the Palestinian populace and of appropriating the physical space.

Nevertheless, most settlements, large and small alike, have continued squandering public resources on a colossal scale, while falsely claiming to be "foci of Zionist ideological endeavor" and necessary for security. Almost forty years after the establishment of the first settlement, "the settlement"—like the kibbutz and the moshav and like the tower-and-stockade colonies of the pre-state era—has become just another exhibit in the museum of Zionist antiquities. The age of ideology has, alas, passed; and erecting settlements, as well as dismantling them, has become an outdated pastime without real impact on political developments, except as a symbol and a recruiting device for both Right and Left.

The historical process that commenced in the early 1970s has yielded both territorial and political fruits and has reached the point of ripeness; the time has come to harvest its bounty. The barrier wall marks the limits of the Jewish community's territorial expansion. Anything beyond this is liable to undermine the "demographic balance," leaving Israel responsible for the fate of millions more Palestinians. It is best, therefore, to exhibit magnanimity and "give back" to the Palestinians the territory they are actually living on—while retaining absolute control over the barriers and gates that demarcate these "native reservations." To his delight, Sharon discovered that, when couched in terms of Israel's security needs, his cantonization "vision" was received enthusiastically, not only in Israeli leftist circles, but also by the nations of the world, including the Arab states.

The unilateral separation scheme's transformative effect in the realm of politics and diplomacy was immediate and perhaps even worthy of being called revolutionary. U.S. President Bush not only wholeheartedly embraced Sharon's plan, he fully comprehended its true significance, commenting that "in light of new realities on the ground, including existing major Israeli population centers, it is unrealistic to expect that the outcome of final status negotiations will be a full and complete return to the armistice lines of 1949."

The downhill journey that began in the 1970s with the American declaration that "settlements are an obstacle to peace," followed by the statement some time later that "settlements do not contribute to peace," had now reached its final destination, and "new realities on the ground," along with American agreement to the route of the separation barrier wall, defined the new boundaries. This was all, of course, expressed by President Bush in politically correct language: "[The] barrier . . . should be a security rather than a political barrier, should be temporary rather than permanent." That the wall determined reality for those in the cantons behind it and made it impossible to establish a viable Palestinian state was conveniently ignored.

American officials said self-servingly that there had been no alteration in the U.S. position; after all, the Clinton Parameters, too, spoke of border adjustments to include blocks of settlement. However, the Clinton Parameters had been articulated in the context of a permanent status agreement, in which adjustments would be made as part of the give-and-take of Israeli-Palestinian negotiations, whereas here these things were being said in reference to a unilateral interim measure that might or might not be implemented. Sharon's chief of staff, Dov Weisglass, who had negotiated with the White House regarding the Disengagement Plan, said candidly in an October 2004 interview: "What I effectively agreed to with the Americans was that a portion of the settlements would not be dealt with at all, and the rest would not be dealt with until the Palestinians turned into Finns."[5]

THE ROADMAP

The so-called Roadmap sponsored by the "quartet" of the United States, the European Union, United Nations, and Russia, which was made public with much fanfare in early May 2003, stated its objective to be the establishment of "an independent, democratic, and viable Palestinian state living side by side in peace and security with Israel and its other neighbors," based on President Bush's vision of two states, Israel and Palestine.[6] However, although it appeared to resurrect the partition of what had been Mandatory Palestine and to enshrine the principles of national sovereignty and "two states for two peoples," in actuality, it carried the principle of the connection between territory and ethnic identity (on which the idea of partition was based) to its absurd extreme. What was actually proposed was a regime of ethnic cantons within a geopolitical unit where a meaningful connection between land and ethnicity would be safeguarded for the dominant Jewish ethnic group alone, leaving the Palestinian community fragmented and marginalized.

But even this "vision" was hazy. President Bush stressed that he had no intention of setting a rigid timetable for the establishment of a Palestinian state. He said that he continued to adhere to his vision of two states living side by side in peace and to believe that the Palestinians are "closer to realizing" this goal, but declined to promise that statehood would come about before the end of his term. "I believe that two democratic states living side-by-side in peace is possible," he declared in October 2005, but added: "I can't tell you when it's going to happen. . . . if it happens before I get out of office, I'll be there to witness the ceremony. And if it hadn't—if it doesn't, we will work hard to lay that foundation so that the process becomes irreversible."[7] This indefinite postponement of the president's "vision" has proved that Sharon's advisor Dov Weisglass knew what he was talking about: "Effectively, this whole package called a Palestinian state, with all that it entails, has been removed indefinitely from our agenda."[8]

UNILATERALISM

The evacuation of settlements was widely perceived as a dramatic change of policy on the part of the "father of the settlements," but the most significant aspect of the disengagement plan lay in its unilateral nature. The unilateral aspect was not a minor matter; rather, it was an attempt to return to the tried-and-true route taken by Israel (and the Jewish Yishuv before the establishment of the state) for almost ninety years, from which it deviated for a short and tragic period—the Oslo era and its aftermath.

The Oslo process—the signing of the Declaration of Principles and the announcement of mutual recognition—had legitimized the PLO and the Palestinian national movement as a whole and had made it the independent agent for a collectivity entitled to assert control over its own future. Prior to that, Israel had for many years successfully denied the Palestinians this status. Then, in Geneva in December 1988, Yasir Arafat—reading a statement dictated to him by the Americans—officially announced the recognition of Israel by the PLO, and in return obtained recognition of the PLO by the Reagan administration, to the bitter disappointment of the Israeli government. Five years later (and after a number of failed attempts to prevent this outcome), Israel, too, recognized the PLO as a legitimate independent actor, and this recognition became the basis for relations between the two peoples.

Sharon was now seeking to turn the clock back a generation and to determine the Palestinians' future for them without taking into consideration their desires and aspirations. "My plan is hard for the Palestinians," he declared, "a mortal blow. With unilateral disengagement there is no Palestinian state."[9] Weisglass had revealed the prime minister's true intentions when he stated: "The significance of our [unilateral] disengagement plan is the freezing of the peace process. . . . When you freeze the process, you prevent the establishment of a Palestinian state."[10]

A people that is not considered to be a legitimate national collectivity is not entitled to demand the right to represent itself and certainly not the right to self-determination. It can be dealt with unilaterally in negotiations through a third party, such as the Americans or Egyptians. The Americans, it should be emphasized, accepted these arguments, along with Israel's demand that there be no progress on the Roadmap until terrorism halted. It quite soon became clear that these provisions applied solely to contacts with Arafat and had to be revised after his demise. The election of Mahmoud Abbas (Abu Mazen) as Arafat's successor compelled the Israelis to modify "unilateralism" and disguise negotiations by calling them "tactical coordination." However, the decisive victory of Hamas in the 2006 elections reinforced the strategy of unilateralism. After all, since Hamas's charter calls for the destruction of Israel, it is "a terrorist organization" and cannot be a partner in peace. Thus Israel has returned to its positions before 1990. Unilateralism has, of course, been a sham, because it could be presented as such only with the cooperation of third parties. It was impossible to enforce it without the vital involvement of additional parties—the United States, in particular, but also the Egyptians, who would accept some responsibility for security. The UN, aid organizations, and the institutions of the European Community would have to pay to maintain an impoverished populace lacking means of livelihood.

Ariel Sharon stressed the "unilateral" aspect of his actions, for in this way he destroyed the last vestige of the Oslo process. But why is it that liberal-leftist groups who were not partners to Sharon's attitude toward the Palestinians agreed to this unilateralism, which precludes any effort to conduct normal dialogue between the sides to the conflict? The accepted explanation is that the collapse of the peace process, the "rejection of the outstretched hand," and the war on terror have proven that there is no partner for peace, or at least that the Palestinian leadership is not yet ripe for such a role. But it seems more likely that the slogan of "unilateralism" based on the "lack of a partner" was a convenient way to free the Israelis from the need to wrestle with the legitimate claims of the other side and to justify their use of immeasurably greater force against the Palestinians.

This was not the first time that moderate Israelis professing support for dialogue and peace had surrendered to the aggressive concept of Zionism that rejects the necessity to hold a dialogue with the Palestinians and promotes "unilateral" steps that reflect the disparity in power (and Israeli arrogance). Arthur Rupin, a leader of the moderate Brit Shalom who supported Jewish-Arab rapprochement and abhorred Zionist belligerency, is a well-known example of a supporter of compromise who succumbed to despondency and ideological breakdown because of violence. The Arab Revolt in the late 1930s led Rupin to despair of any negotiations with the Arabs and to adopt a "unilateral" policy. "What we can get is not what we need, and what we need we cannot get," he said. Moshe Dayan liked to quote Rupin, whose remarks jibed with his own worldview—although he did not share in the ideological crisis they reflected—and would paraphrase them in his own style: "I am against concessions in any area, and if the Arabs want a war because of that, I don't object."

And after much soul-searching, Dayan's great patron, David Ben-Gurion, reached the conclusion that negotiations with the Arabs were not important, since obviously it was military might that would decide things. For that reason, he did not attach importance to negotiating with the Arabs, but instead directed his efforts toward creating a Jewish military force, as well as influencing the Mandatory government to act favorably toward the Jews. After the 1948–49 war, he did not hesitate to state that "peace is vital, but not at any price," and "if we chase after peace, the Arabs will demand a price of us—borders, or refugees, or both. We'll wait a few years."[11]

Sharon represented classic unilateralism, and he drew upon the long history of aggressive Zionism for the legitimacy that permitted him to enjoy the support of a domestic peace movement that had lost heart and returned to the warm bosom of the old Zionist consensus. The direct link between unilateralism and aggressiveness leading to violence did not deter Sharon. On the contrary, and he was not inventing anything new here either. As the historian Motti Golani writes: "It was convenient for the Israeli leadership to take the route of war, and it was the way of peace that caused it great difficulties. . . . In many senses, it is easier to go to war than the alternative of restraint and concessions of various kinds."[12]

THE DEVALUATION OF PARTITION

Most Israelis felt that the withdrawal from Gaza actually diminished the "demographic problem" by virtue of the fact that it removed the one and a half million Palestinian inhabitants of Gaza from the equation. Moreover, the evacuation of the Gaza settlements supposedly prefigures the solution for the West Bank as well and sets a precedent for a "historic return to the 1967 borders." The peg on which supporters of partition opposed to "Greater Israel" ideology hang the wings of history is the magical phrase "the partition of Eretz Israel." No importance is ascribed to the circumstances under which partition of the country was suggested in the past, let alone to the historical contexts within which the debate over partition has been conducted. Nor is there any need to calculate the relative size of the portions allocated to each side by those "partitions." The world is simply divided between supporters of partition—those who advocate a compromise "of historic proportions"—and its opponents, who preach eternal enmity. "Partition," like "separation," "settlements," "security," and "terrorism," is an absolute concept behind which to rally—and that is how one's position on the roster of "good guys" versus "bad guys" is determined.

The concession called "partitioning the land" (in which Gaza is supposedly the first step) has always served as a measure of peace and compromise, and anyone who supports it, particularly anyone who initiates and implements the partition, is considered a seeker of peace and reconciliation. The chronicles of partitioning Israel/Palestine exemplify the devaluation of the concept from a historic compromise to a humiliating diktat, and the correct calculation must not be, as is generally understood, how much is returned, but rather, how much remains with each side. According to the partition resolution of 1947, the Palestinian territory was supposed to comprise about half of Mandatory Palestine, but the armistice lines reduced the area to about 22 percent. The Allon Plan, devised by Foreign Minister Yigal Allon after the June 1967 Six-Day War, left 14 percent of it. Sharon's partition along the route of the barrier wall, incorporating the settlement blocks into the Israeli enclave and cutting the Palestinians off from the Jordan Valley, leaves in the hands of the Palestinians no more than 2,900 square kilometers, or 11 percent of the former territory of Mandatory Palestine. Both the plan that included 50 percent and the one that includes 11 percent of the territory are defined as "partition plans," and though the latter can only be implemented unilaterally by force, it is seen by many as praiseworthy and is depicted as a historic compromise.

TURNING POINTS?

It is extremely difficult to sort out—from the stream of dramatic events that comprise the blood-drenched Israeli-Palestinian struggle—those moments that will be regarded as turning points from the perspective of decades in the future. It does seem, though, that three events that took place in the winter of 2005–6 were potentially such turning points: Ariel Sharon's massive brain stroke at the beginning of January 2006; the overwhelming victory of Hamas in the Palestinian general election at the end of the month; and the Israeli elections in March 2006.

Prime Minister Sharon was hospitalized a few days before he finished launching his new party, Kadima, which the polls predicted would win a landslide victory in the general election. On the eve of his hospitalization, Sharon might have surveyed his achievements with satisfaction. His moves to deal with the Palestinian "demographic threat" unilaterally had brought him unprecedented popularity, leading him to believe he would be able to create a Peronist-presidential regime in Israel and silence any criticism of his establishment of a cantonized, apartheid-style "Palestinian state" in the occupied territories. The United States, entangled in Iraq, has signaled that the canton plan could be regarded as implementing a Palestinian state, and the Israeli peace camp also agreed enthusiastically, crowning Sharon as its leader.

In addition to determining the size and borders of the cantons in keeping with Israeli interests and ensuring a Jewish demographic majority, someone had to be found to manage the relinquished Palestinian-populated areas. Unless there is basic physical, economic, and political control of those areas, Israel will not be able to shake off responsibility for the fate of the millions of people inhabiting them, and its objective of ridding itself of a demographic threat will be undermined. This is the role that Israel envisages for the Palestinian Authority, and the reason why the PA is being portrayed as a sovereign state electing a parliament and a government. It is common knowledge that the PA is a community council devoid of governmental powers, managing an area devoid of sovereignty; but it is useful to hint that this is only a preliminary stage before Israel, out of the goodness of its heart, unilaterally disengages from areas in which it has no interest. Then the PA will become a government with sovereignty over the liberated territories of the Palestinian nation-state.

The irony is boundless: Israel, which during the Oslo process rejected any use of terminology suggestive of Palestinian sovereignty, such as "government," "parliament," "president," and "prime minister," has suddenly began emphasizing them to nurture the illusion of the existence of a Palestinian government—not one that is a partner, but one that will wait at the ready to pick up the scraps that Israel leaves behind after satisfying its demographic interests. No wonder Israeli politicians have become the prophets of "two nation-states—Israeli and Palestinian," while the Palestinians are the ones who are opposed to declaring an independent state under the current conditions.

There is another reason for Israel's distinct interest in nurturing the illusion of the Palestinian government and its pretensions of sovereignty: absent such a government, the sources of foreign aid will dry up, exposing the fact that Israel's occupation—both direct and indirect—is funded in its entirety by the budgets of "donor states." Some 150,000 people, who provide a livelihood for around half a million individuals, receive their wages directly from the PA, while a similar number live off the charity of foreign organizations. Were Israel required to live up to its obligations as an occupying power, it would have to cough up approximately U.S.$1 billion a year just to maintain services to the West Bank population.

Unprecedentedly, however, the occupation is funded entirely by the international community, and the Palestinian elite, the Israelis, and the international community share a common interest in perpetuating this charitable state of affairs. The Palestinian establishment can thus continue to maintain the corrupt system that oversees the distribution of foreign handouts; Israel can perpetuate the occupation without spending a cent; and the international community can preserve the illusion that there's no alternative, because the collapse of the PA and the destitution of its population would rule out any hope of peace.

EXIT SHARON

The intense emotions of shock, orphanhood, and fear elicited by Ariel Sharon's exit from the political arena evoked expressions bordering on kitsch, even from observers otherwise known for their sober approach. "Parting from him is like parting from a father: expected, but always frightening and sad," said one commentator.[13] Parallels between Sharon and Yitzhak Rabin—and between the two of them and Moses on Mount Nebo—were inevitable: "From Moses to Sharon, they all saw the land from afar, but none succeeded in bringing the train to a safe haven," one journalist concluded.[14]

In other words, had his sickness not defeated him, Sharon would have brought us to the Promised Land—"peace with the Arabs and clear and recognized borders." The thwarted hope, or illusion, intensified the sense of loss. Not their own acts and foibles, but "the angel of death, sharpening his scythe," had robbed Israelis of the chance for peace. After sixty years of struggle, fate denied Sharon his deepest aspiration: to eliminate the Palestinian demographic threat.

While Sharon lay in deep coma in Hadassah Hospital, general elections took place in the Palestinian territories, and the Islamist party, Hamas, won a landslide victory and formed a cabinet, which won a vote of confidence at the end of March 2006. The corrupt Fatah regime collapsed, and Israel had to face reality: the triumphant "terror organization" Hamas would not play the role of docile collector of leftovers after disengagement that had been assigned the PA. There were different opinions about the strategy that Israel should adopt vis-à-vis Hamas, but most observers agreed that the prospects of progress in the peace process were now very slim, because Hamas advocates the destruction of Israel and refuses to abide by the PA's international commitments.

In fact, "peace" vanished from the Israeli election discourse. "Since there is no partner for peace," most Israeli politicians stated in their election campaign, "unilateral steps, based exclusively on Israel's needs" were the only option. What lurked beneath the "convergence" strategy that replaced "disengagement" (but meant the same thing) was one sole ambition: to get rid of the Palestinians, one way or another. Transfer or wall, "disengagement" or "convergence"—let them get out of our sight.

Some viewed this as a clear expression of racism; others, as proof that the settlers and the Right had lost the political battle, and that the majority of Israelis now wanted "separation in peace," albeit unilaterally.

It seems that there is a consensus uniting the majority of the Israeli public, with the exception of the right-wing and left-wing fringes: after 120 years of Zionism, Israelis have finally recognized that there are millions of Palestinians who can be neither ignored nor exiled. Hence, they have decided to confine them to cantons, placing them beyond the pale by means of the barrier wall, on the one hand, and turning them into virtual prisoners by retaining total control of their borders with the outside world, on the other.

SHARON'S SUCCESSORS

Ehud Olmert, who became acting prime minister after Sharon's illness, and Kadima's candidate for prime minister, stated in a major speech:

> [T]here is no doubt that the most dramatic and important step we face is shaping the permanent borders of the State of Israel, in order to ensure a Jewish majority in this country.
>
> . . . In order to ensure the existence of a Jewish national home, we will not be able to continue ruling over the territories in which the majority of the Palestinian population lives. We must create a clear boundary as soon as possible, one which will reflect the demographic reality on the ground. Israel will maintain the security zones, the Jewish settlement blocs, and those places which have supreme national importance to the Jewish people, headed by a united Jerusalem under Israeli sovereignty. There can be no Jewish state without the capital of Jerusalem at its center.[15]

The Israeli general elections, hailed as "a referendum on the future of the territories," were held in an atmosphere of apathy, manifested in the lowest voter turnout (63%) in the history of Israel and a protest vote that gave an obscure list of old age pensioners seven seats in the Knesset, thanks to massive voting by the yuppie Tel Aviv crowd. Sharon's goal of accruing decisive political power that would enable the Kadima party to control the country unequivocally was not attained. But the results could be seen as a blessing in disguise. Kadima needed a major partner, and that partner, the Labour party, headed by the "leftist" Amir Peretz—helped to blur the distinction between Left and Right and increased support for the disengagement/cantonization plan. The basic guidelines of Olmert's government included the following: "The Government will strive to shape the permanent borders of the State of Israel as a Jewish state, with a Jewish majority. . . . Israel's territory, the borders of which will be determined by the Government, will entail the reduction of Israeli settlement in Judea and Samaria."[16] Peretz, a supporter of the Geneva Accords, would oversee the construction of the separation wall, the checkpoint regime, the fragmentation, the starvation of the Gaza Strip, and the targeted assassinations. Labour party ministers—so unsuccessful at preventing the creation of illegal West Bank outposts in the past—will now be unable to hold back construction in the rather elastic "settlement blocs."

The Hamas government continued to declare its refusal to recognize Israel and fulfill the obligations of the Palestinian Authority. There could not have been a better excuse for unilateralism than the Hamas takeover of the PA. It seemed that a path had been cleared for a stable Israeli coalition that would waste its early years in a stubborn struggle against the legitimization of Hamas and continue the construction of settlement blocks, while quietly postponing the "convergence" plan year after year. But in July 2006, the scheme collapsed dramatically in the blaze of the worst wave of violence in years.

Palestinian violence, and especially constant launching of homemade rockets from the Gaza Strip at bordering Israeli settlements, brought about an intense Israeli reaction, including artillery bombardment, army incursions, and closure of border crossings. The deteriorating security situation—which peaked when an Israeli soldier was kidnapped in early July 2006 by armed Palestinians, precipitating harsh reprisals—dealt a serious blow to public support for the disengagement/convergence plan. The widespread feeling was that if unilateral withdrawal produced a Hamas regime and unremitting violence, what was the point in continuing with the same policy on the West Bank, where exposure to missiles threatens the very heart of Israel?

A sudden, ferocious conflagration in Lebanon opened a new act in the tragedy. After Hezbollah forces in south Lebanon attacked an Israeli patrol on 12 July 2006, killing three soldiers and taking two hostages, the Israel government retaliated with a massive multi-casualty aerial and ground pounding that caused extensive destruction in Lebanon. "We're skipping the stage of threats and going straight to action," Israel's Defense Minister, Amir Peretz, declared.[17] A million Lebanese refugees escaped to safer regions, and Hezbollah fired thousands of rockets at Israeli towns, causing major dislocation. The Israeli Air Force's bombardment of residential neighborhoods in Beirut and elsewhere caused hundreds of civilian casualties, among them many children. This outrage caused a wave of indignation against Israel in Europe, while violent expressions of hatred even in moderate Arab countries were reminiscent of the pan-Arab, anti-peace atmosphere of the late 1960s.

The war began with patriotic solidarity in Israel, but soon profound debates about its conduct and aims began to break the consensus. The debate as to who won and who lost the war—or perhaps it was a tie—was only marginally influenced by the real outcome. But the war itself has had a profound influence on what happens in the region and in Israel in particular—an influence such that, had the war's perpetrators been aware of it, they would have thought twice about turning a border incident into a campaign involving millions of people.

Again, with tragic consistency, when the public discourse has been open to discussion of a new Israeli agenda, violent events have restored the concept of "the existential threat," suffocating these efforts. A commitment to social welfare was central to the Israeli election campaign, and a new coalition government was taking its first steps on the path of repairing the damage caused by the neoliberal policy of the former finance minister Benjamin Netanyahu, but now the war has come along and reinstated the security agenda for many years to come. The slow, rickety process of improving relations between Israel and the moderate Arab states has been interrupted and replaced by a process of radicalization, which has first and foremost frightened the leaders of the moderate countries who signed peace treaties with Israel. And under the aegis of the war in Lebanon, the IDF has killed hundreds of Palestinians in Gaza and imprisoned dozens of Palestinian Authority parliament members and ministers. Israel, by its disproportionate reaction and failure of restraint, has reaffirmed its position as a foreign element in the region, as the neighborhood bully, the object of impotent hatred.

Restoring "deterrence capability" has been the goal of the war that most closely approached rationality. But this was an internal Israeli matter that bore no relation to the enemy's perceptions. After all, every time Israel has gone to war with the slogan of creating "deterrence capability" (at least three times), it has actually spurred the enemy to prepare for a more serious confrontation. The last time, it was called "searing the Palestinians' consciousness," and its results were the victory of Hamas and a bleeding blind alley in the West Bank and Gaza Strip.

There is no better proof of the subjectivity of the Israeli approach than the arbitrary description of the enemy: "the Arab world," which must be "deterred." What threatening Arab world remains after the peace with Egypt and Jordan and the occupation of Iraq? Qatar? Or was the Israeli operation in Lebanon a self-fulfilling prophecy that in itself has recreated the threatening "Arab world," enabling Israelis once again to wallow in hatred of the old familiar demon? Admittedly, this demon is somewhat shopworn, and Israelis have therefore had to add Iran. But deterring Iran is already another matter, unless Israel turns the local Hezbollah incident into a kind of "Sarajevo, 1914" in the "clash of civilizations." In that case, IDF soldiers will have died on the altar of a global "proxy war" that Israel has volunteered to spearhead.

The war and the atmosphere that has prevailed in its wake have caused Israel to regress by a generation. It is no wonder that Israelis see history as a cyclical process, and that the war (like its predecessors) has been seen as the "last lap of Israel's War of Independence." And those who did not rush to fill the heroic role being forced on them, and instead countered with a desire for normalcy, were treated with fury. Those who began this unrestrained war wanted to inflate its importance in order to justify the terrible—and steadily increasing—price that has been paid in what amounts to a gamble for an impossible jackpot. They are conducting a 1950s strategy in a twenty-first-century society and culture: it can't work.

Prime Minister Olmert's comments suggesting that the war in Lebanon might serve as a catalyst for reviving the convergence plan enraged settlers and Israeli right-wingers, forcing Olmert to apologize. Despite his assertions, it seems that the war has wrecked the convergence plan, which is viewed as divisive and damaging to the newfound national unity. Hezbollah's success in terrorizing northern Israel has served as an argument against withdrawal from the West Bank.

In August 2006, it was leaked that a "convergence committee" set up to evaluate the idea of a unilateral withdrawal from most of the West Bank had submitted a report to the foreign minister in which it raised legal, security, and economic difficulties that are likely to inhibit the plan's implementation. The report's main conclusion was that Israel has no security solution to the threat of rockets launched from the West Bank against population centers. Another conclusion was that Israel will not gain international recognition for an end to the occupation if it continues to hold significant portions of the West Bank. Indeed, the report stated that it is doubtful whether such recognition would be forthcoming even if Israel unilaterally withdrew to the Green Line.[18]

The Israeli-Palestinian conflict, temporarily eclipsed by the Lebanon tragedy, has reemerged and resumed its unstable status quo. Lip service is paid to "separation," but all that remains of "convergence" are coercive closures, fences, armed incursions, and a constant effort at fragmentation.

EXTERNALIZING THE PALESTINIANS

The declared strategy of "unilateral determination of permanent borders of the state of Israel" has one paramount purpose: to externalize the Palestinians. It is fascinating to follow Israelis' oscillations between their perception of the Palestinians as an external and an internal element throughout the history of the conflict. It was convenient for classical Zionism to view the Palestinians as a dependent, noncohesive "Arab population of Eretz Israel," whose affinity is with the "Arab world," an external constraint and objective obstacle on the road to Jewish statehood. For Israelis, the 1948 war confirmed the externalization of the Palestinians: they left areas under Israeli control and became "refugees"; Palestinian territories were annexed to neighboring Arab states; and the conflict became an "Israeli-Arab conflict" between sovereign states, that is, an externally generated conflict.

The 1967 war and its aftermath opened a new phase in Israeli perceptions. The ruling Likud party perceived the takeover of the West Bank and Gaza as a fulfillment of the Zionist dream, and the perpetuation of an internal communal conflict between Jews and Arabs as an acceptable consequence. Menachem Begin's "Autonomy for the inhabitants, not the territory" and ruthless coercive measures were Likud's solution to the internal conflict. The opposition Labour party continued to toy with an external, Jordanian option until King Hussein severed Jordan's link with the West Bank and thus closed the lid on the internal Israeli-Palestinian cauldron. As we have seen, extreme violence brought about a longing for "separation" and physical externalization of the Palestinians. The erection of the barrier wall between the West Bank and Israel ostensibly transformed the Israeli-Palestinian conflict into a border dispute pure and simple—"us here and you there"—thereby externalizing the Palestinians and eliminating the threat of a binational state.

The problem has been that there was no Palestinian ready to pick the leftovers that Israel was ready to discard, and there could therefore be no further unilateral disengagement. The de facto binational state is, by default, approaching its penultimate stage, despite misleading signs that provide a false sense that its creation has been successfully prevented.

The factors laying the foundations for a binational reality and destroying the option of "two states for two peoples" are in fact precisely the measures aimed at furthering unilateral disengagement, partitioning Israel/Palestine, and warding off the Israeli nightmare of a binational state: withdrawal from the Gaza Strip, the barrier wall, and the separate road system, as well as the aftermath of the second Lebanon war of 2006. The acceptance by countries and organizations throughout the world (with the United States in the lead) of the legitimacy of unilateral moves being made by Israel without regard to Palestinian interests, U.S. positions supportive of the fragmentation strategy being pursued by Israel, the deterioration in the functioning of the Palestinian Authority, and the victory of Hamas—all of these combined have intensified the perception, shared by many Palestinians, that there is no longer any chance of establishing a viable independent Palestinian state, and that it is therefore necessary to return to a "one-state" stratagem and to rely on their growing demographic advantage to achieve this.

Of course, given that I postulated the institutionalization of a de facto binational regime as far back as the early 1980s, you might suspect me of interpreting things in such a way as to prove and reinforce my original thesis. To this I would reply simply that for over twenty years, I have maintained that partition of Israel/Palestine into two states has already become impossible and impracticable and would create insurmountable problems, and that the existing binational condition will therefore continue by default—and for the time being, it does not seem that I was mistaken.

CHAPTER 7

Descriptions and Prescriptions

In the early 1980s, I formulated a theory that gained notoriety under the title of "the irreversibility thesis" and came under frequent attack in the ensuing twenty years and more. In an article in the *New York Review of Books*, I wrote in October 1983:

> The Likud government has implemented a settlement policy completely different from that of Labor. The difference does not lie only in the policy of building settlements in areas heavily populated by Arabs, which is an abomination to Labor; the major innovation has been aimed at creating internal political facts, not geostrategic facts. The Likud estimated correctly that the decision about the future of the territories would result from domestic political struggles within the state of Israel rather than from direct external military or political pressure.

"When the settlers have crossed the critical threshold—consisting of convenient access roads, physical infrastructure, and the minimal number of housing units needed in order to have a functioning community," I added, "it will be difficult to halt the spontaneous and diffuse forces that are unleashed."[1]

This critical threshold was actually crossed as far back as the late 1980s, and even at that early stage, I did not hesitate to state that the situation had already become irreversible. The sums poured into the construction of settlement suburbs of cities just over the Green Line in Israel proper—as well as into more remote settlements—by successive

Israeli governments (Labour, Likud, and "national unity" alike) have reached mythic proportions, an estimated U.S.$40 billion by 2004. Demographic, political, and economic "facts" have been created that make the hard core of ideological and political settlers a force to be reckoned with.

This far from large collection of activists—imbued with a right-wing, theocratic, and messianic worldview—took full advantage of the executive power vested in it by the authorities (as well as economic resources accumulated thanks to canny investment) and became one of the most formidable power bases on the Israeli political scene. Propelled by enormous self-confidence, these activists progressed from forming themselves into marginal groups on the far Right to attempting to take over the Likud itself, a party with a massive popular base and control of the government. Right-wing forces—of which the settler leaders were the ideological nucleus—brought down the rightist government led by Yitzhak Shamir in 1992 because he had agreed to participate in the peace process following the Madrid Conference of October 1991. They subsequently also made a decisive contribution to the downfall of Benjamin Netanyahu in 1999. Moreover, in 2004, their part in the fight against Ariel Sharon and his "disengagement plan" was executed openly and ruthlessly: the settler leadership provided the logistical and financial wherewithal required for organizing the political opposition to the withdrawal from Gaza and repeated attempts to unseat Sharon. The irony of this was lost on no one. The man the settlers had in their gun sights was the very person who had directed the settlement enterprise and had placed in their hands the weapons they were training on him. Sharon eventually prevailed, but when further withdrawals had been planned, it was too late to change the map of the West Bank to allow the creation of a viable Palestinian state.

My "irreversibility thesis" was based on conclusions drawn from the findings of the West Bank (and Gaza Strip) Database Project, which I had directed for a full decade, beginning in 1981. This research project gathered and analyzed the physical, demographic, economic, and legal changes that had taken place in the occupied territories since 1967, paying particular attention to monitoring the development of the settlements. The project's conclusions had a huge impact, becoming the axis around which the political discourse concerning the Israeli takeover of the territories revolved. The findings, published in Israel and abroad, received enthusiastic reviews, but also a barrage of contempt and ridicule.

PRAISE AND ABUSE

"It is not often that a piece of social science research becomes the symbol of a fateful national debate," Anthony Lewis wrote in the *New York Times Magazine*.[2] The prominent Palestinian scholar Walid Khalidi commented: "This is the most thorough study to date by an Israeli on Israel's colonization policies—one might disagree with the author's pessimism regarding the future of these territories, but can only admire his painstaking research and the depth of his concern."[3]

On the other hand, I vividly recall the insults that were heaped upon me during the 1980s by some Israelis. "[The author of] such seditious nonsense deserves therapeutic treatment, with all possible patience and concern," Abba Eban said of the irreversibility thesis. "I find it rather hard to speak calmly about that thesis."[4] Amos Oz could not disguise his fury: "He wants to be a prophet, or maybe a messiah. Jerusalem is filled with angry prophets," he scoffed.[5] Shimon Peres, an erstwhile supporter of the settlements who had become their sworn opponent, said scornfully: "He doesn't interest me. This is like an argument between two children over whether there is a G-d. If there's no G-d, there just isn't. If there is, we're in deep shit. If this fellow is right—we're in real trouble."[6]

A typical hate pamphlet, distributed at a lecture I gave in Seattle, Washington, in 1990 and signed by a group calling itself Americans for a Safe Israel, contained the following diatribe:

> As soon as it was announced that some Seattle area Jewish organizations were bringing Meron Benvenisti to town to lecture, we were bombarded with aggressive questions. "Isn't this the fellow whose Israeli-Nazi equation (he has called Israel 'the master-race democracy') is regularly invoked by local Arab propagandists?" "Didn't Benvenisti come to the defense of Yassir Arafat in a November 1988 debate on TV with the Arab scholar Fouad Ajami, when the latter called Arafat a rogue and a scoundrel?" "Isn't Benvenisti the person who told the world press that Israel's confiscation of the archives of the PLO's intelligence center in west Beirut in September 1982 was an attempt 'to take from [Palestinian Arabs] their history'?" "Isn't it Benvenisti who keeps assuring Anthony Lewis and Thomas Friedman, and other Israel-bashers that Israel is the devil's own experiment station, a place of 'rampant chauvinism, xenophobic, ethnic and national discrimination, clerical influence, political malaise, economic and social instability'?" "Hasn't Benvenisti admitted to looking upon Israelis who are religious or, worse yet, non-socialist, as 'lower forms of human life'?"
>
> . . . Those who lend themselves to this obscene anti-Zionist campaign, even though they claim to own the purest Zionist pedigree, deserve only your Contempt [*sic*].

This dispute continued into the early 1990s. Yossi Sarid, a long-standing leader of the Zionist Left, wrote an article enumerating the Left's accusations against me:

> There are people who have angered and disgusted me more, but no one has caused me more frustration than has Meron Benvenisti, author of the theory of the irreversible situation in the occupied territories. No theory has caused more harm than has this one. Despite its groundlessness and absurdity, for many years we were powerless before it. This theory was known to carry unique force because of the attributes of the man who postulated it: a man of peace and a good friend, an intellectual, a specialist well-versed in his field like no other—and he authoritatively states that what has been done in the territories cannot be undone, that it is a fait accompli. . . .
>
> Benvenisti and his followers simply did not understand that the claim that a world has behaved in a certain way for twenty years proves just one—extremely trivial—thing: that it is not necessarily how it will be in another twenty years, in another year, or even in another day.
>
> . . . . To speak of an irreversible situation whilst everything is being shaken to the foundations is a real joke. But for Dr. Meron Benvenisti, the situation continues to be irreversible. The time for public confessions has also passed, never to return. Therefore, Meron my friend, neither remorseful confession nor—heaven forbid—beating one's breast while enumerating one's sins is what is required. But a small amendment to your theory would, in fact, be appreciated.[7]

Thomas Friedman had a different view:

> The question of the day was this: Had years of Israeli settlement building in the occupied territories gone so far as to inextricably knit Israel, Gaza, and the West Bank together, or could one still speak of Israel giving back these areas one day, despite the degree to which they had been integrated into the economic and political life of the Jewish state?
>
> One of the remarkable things about that debate, though, was that for all its centrality in Israeli political life and for all of the attention it got in the international media, very little hard data had been assembled to inform the arguments of either side. Wishful thinking was the currency of this debate.
>
> That was what led me to Meron's door. Working out of a small apartment, with a computer and a few researchers, he combed through Israeli government budgets, official abstracts, agricultural and water data, and brought them all together in something called "The West Bank Data Project," which painted a statistical picture of developments in the occupied territories. On a per capita basis (number of times quoted divided by the number of researchers involved), the West Bank Data Project, founded in 1982, was without question the most influential think tank in the debate about the occupied territories. Meron's conclusions alternately drove each

side in that debate crazy and provided them with the statistical resources for their best arguments. . . .

Meron was probably the most oft-quoted and oft-damned analyst in Israel in my day—Jeremiah and Jonah wrapped into one.[8]

Since Sarid's pronouncement that "the settlements' best days were behind them," the number of settlers has exceeded a quarter of a million (400,000, if one includes the Jerusalem neighborhoods constructed to the east of the 1949 Armistice line), and they hold the keys to the fate of millions of Israelis and Palestinians.

WHERE DID I GO WRONG?

The most difficult test of the "irreversibility thesis" came at the time of the signing in 1993 of the Oslo Accords, which purportedly brought about an absolute change in the political and territorial status quo, while at the same time supposedly fulfilling the principle of the partition of Eretz Israel / Palestine and the creation of "two states for the two peoples" living there, amid widespread euphoria. I became the target of ridicule by several highly influential columnists, since my "prophecy" had apparently been disproved. I myself lost my self-confidence and published an apology entitled "Where Did I go Wrong?"

I have long suspected my political positions—and especially the rational conceptual universe that I developed in order to hone my "scientific" analytical skills—of having been excessively molded by the influences of the household where I was raised, my education, and my personal life experience. Overly nostalgic, and attached to anachronistic ideas, I had failed to attribute proper weight to historical processes and political exigencies, which might force the implementation of crucial decisions with the ability to transform the "irreversible" to "reversible." I gravitated to and identified with the tragedy, failing to perceive how drawn people are to catharsis. Yet I concluded:

> The future will demonstrate that intercommunal reconciliation is a complex and lengthy process—one that never really ends—where everything depends on the sincerity of the two sides' intention to cooperate in the ongoing management of what is essentially an endemic crisis, albeit of variable intensity. In this matter I am not convinced that I was in error: intercommunal conflicts have no absolute and conclusive solutions, and those who equate talks—or even rapprochement—between the elites of neighboring and interdependent communities with the process of entering into a peace treaty with a foreign state know not whereof they speak. . . .

> The territory of the West Bank will remain a twilight zone where Jews and Arabs go about their lives subject to parallel and overlapping governing authorities.[9]

This conclusion of mine encountered numerous antagonistic responses. In addition, opposing theories were elaborated by scholars in the field, the best-known of which was that of Ian Lustick, who spoke in terms of "state building and state contraction" and challenged my theory, greatly underestimating the import of the "physical facts on the ground" and denying their irreversibility.[10] Writing in 2004, Dr. Gary Susman summed up our opposing positions:

> The critical question we return to with regard to the Israeli settlement effort is whether there exists a "point of no-return," beyond which Israel would create so many "facts on the ground" that it would be impossible for it to disengage. Proponents of this argument, identified with Meron Benvenisti, have argued that Israel has created the geography of a single state, which obviates separation along ethnic lines. Ian Lustick, on the other hand, eloquently rejects this thesis. Harnessing Antonio Gramsci's writings, and the precedents of Algeria, Northern Ireland and Israel–West Bank, Lustick argues instead that it is rather "facts" or "constructs in the mind" that determine whether processes of territorial incorporation are reversible. In terms that Ariel Sharon has defined, Lustick's basic contention is that disengagement is only unlikely when Israelis considered [sic] the destiny of Netzarim [an isolated settlement in the Gaza Strip] to be the same as [that of] Tel Aviv. Ian Lustick, as Ariel Sharon has recently confirmed, was right. Tel Aviv and Netzarim are not equivalent, and the process of Israeli incorporation of the Palestinian territories is far from complete.
>
> Meron Benvenisti was, however, correct in a more fundamental way. Most Israelis would agree that Israel can indeed roll back the settlement effort. But, they also recognize that its continued expansion means that Israel will be less likely to go back to the starting point, the Green Line. There are at present (2004) over 230,000 settlers on the West Bank and in the Gaza Strip, excluding the 190,000 settlers who live in neighborhoods in the greater Jerusalem area. Moreover, the settlers and their communities control . . . 50 percent of the West Bank. So, whereas the settlers may have failed to preclude a full Israeli withdrawal, they have succeeded to alter [sic] Israel's future borders in her favor. Hence, the settlements have undermined the prospects for a viable Palestinian state and make the eventual failure of partition more likely. They, ultimately, ensconce Israel's binational condition.[11]

When the number of settlers topped a quarter of a million, when more than 100 ("illegal") outposts had been established on the West Bank, when the barrier wall had been built deep in Palestinian territory, and when "border crossings" had been set up near Nablus, Bethlehem, and Ramallah, the number of voices finally trying to relate to the reality created by the settlements—and the shattering of the occupied territories into isolated cantons—started to grow. President George W. Bush's letter to Ariel Sharon recognizing the new reality "that includes large concentrations of Israeli population" appeared to ratify the theory of irreversibility, as well as proving that "facts on the ground" do indeed become "constructs in the mind."

It is no surprise that the evacuation of the settlements in the Gaza Strip and northern Samaria has been conceived of as earth-shattering, the demise of irreversibility. Now it was clear, after all, it seemed, that everything is reversible, and the destruction of the Gaza settlements is a precedent. Yet almost nobody pondered the impact of the withdrawal from Gaza on the "facts" that have been created on the West Bank. Still, my theory needed refinement, for there had been a change of attitude concerning territory. The al-Aqsa Intifada has compelled the Israelis to recognize the invincibility of the Palestinians, forcing the former, for the first time in their history, to fence the borders of their territorial expansion and to give up those territories that could undermine the Jewish demographic majority. The remainder, a fragmented area that Israel has no wish to retain, may become, if the Palestinians so desire, a Palestinian state. But as we have seen, the isolated cantons lack the power to sustain themselves, and the Palestinians will therefore refuse to grace them with the status of a state. So the status quo will probably endure and in the not-too-distant future, once again, the shattering of the theory of irreversibility will be declared by the same pundits who declared its falseness so many times in the past.

The argument over the primacy of the settlements has become, as I have mentioned, moot. Moreover, Lustick's theory makes the assumption that only the "hegemonic party" is involved in the process of "state building and contraction." He completely ignores the consequences of the physical and political changes for the dominated population. In other words, according to Lustick, the Israelis alone determine the boundaries of the state and any changes to them, whereas the Palestinians are absolutely passive. It is, however, safe to assume that it is precisely the Palestinians—who bear the brunt of the measures undertaken by the regime and who are sensitive to political changes that worsen their situation—who would react more strongly to the creation of "facts on the ground" than the Israelis and who would more readily draw the logical political conclusions.

And, indeed, voices calling for abandonment of the "two states for two peoples" option and its replacement by efforts to achieve a unitary state in Israel/Palestine are increasingly being heard in Palestinian circles. Of course, all of those who make their living within the institutional framework of the Palestinian Authority, not to mention those employed in its ramified apparatus, reject such talk, since the establishment of a Palestinian state is, after all, their raison d'être. It is also true that the PA, even in its wretched condition, symbolizes the demand of self-determination, and its activity in civil matters, no matter how limited, is important to the process of building the Palestinian nation. The Palestinian people, no doubt, need national institutions. At the same time, the "one state" slogan makes a handy threat for Palestinians to hold over the Israelis; and that is how most Israelis, in fact, relate to it. Spokespersons from both the Right and Left and, notably, even Jewish intellectuals abroad, view the binational state as a real danger, "which inherently threatens to bring an end to the Jewish state." Palestinians take this so seriously that some threaten to trade their struggle for national independence for a struggle for civil rights in a binational state, provoking Israeli diplomats to respond angrily that this is further proof of the Palestinians' unwillingness to reach a peace agreement, since a binational state means the destruction of the state of Israel. Other Israelis express apprehension that a Palestinian demand that Israel annex the territories and grant civil rights to their inhabitants constitutes a greater danger than does the demand for an independent state, because equal rights for all citizens is the universal norm and has across-the-board support in the West, and any regime that does not observe it is stigmatized as being racist, apartheid-South-Africa-style.

BINATIONALISM DENOUNCED

No wonder the establishment of a Palestinian state is perceived as immeasurably preferable to the alternative of a binational state even by the ideological Right in Israel, and anyone who dares entertain thoughts of the binational option is denounced as anti-Zionist. In a critical article that typifies this attitude, Yosef Gorni, who specializes in Zionist history, writes: "This [the binational option] is an absurd approach, not only from the political point of view, as Benvenisti knows, but also in the substantive and ethical sense. . . . Benvenisti's vision is undoubtedly a sublime utopia, but it necessitates a wrong-headed policy liable to lead to never-ending warfare between the two peoples, two religions, two cultures, two standards of living, and so on and so forth."[12]

An interview in which I supported the idea of a binational state garnered a torrent of reactions, most of them hostile: "Escapist romanticism . . . a dangerous idea . . . the idea of a binational state—meaning yet another Arab nation-state—is a pathetic attempt to destroy the Jewish state."[13] Uri Avnery, who believes in the inevitability of the Palestinian state, was outspoken in his criticism: "The principle of two states for two peoples has gone from triumph to triumph—in both the national and international arenas—it now enjoys worldwide consensus." Avnery went on to rail against the "irreversibility theory," which provides the basis for the "dangerous idea" of binationalism, on the grounds that "no condition is irreversible or inevitable."[14] But he himself is convinced that the process leading to "two states for two peoples" is indeed irreversible, and that the success of this project is inevitable. Ran Halévi wrote,

> It is not difficult to enumerate the reasons for which this project appears eminently unrealistic. If the cohabitation of two states is truly doomed, how can one believe that a "cantonal federation" would be more viable? If hatred and mutual distrust have indeed attained such depths, the binational solution seems still more chimerical than any other project of separation. As to the question of whether the situation in the Territories should be considered irreversible, a subject of endless debate in Israel, it is by definition an unresolvable question and will remain so until the day when a peace treaty is concluded between the two sides—or a unilateral decision to leave the Territories is taken—impelling the Israeli government to face the obviously formidable challenge of evacuating some of the settlements. . . . To dissolve the state of Israel into a vague binational project on the uncertain premise that nothing can be done about the settlements is to confuse the problem with the solution—at an unfathomable price.
>
> But there exists an ultimate reason, in fact the very first one that makes such an outcome illusory: No one, or almost no one, wants it, either on one side or the other. Those Palestinians who continue to advocate for dialogue with Israel remain committed to the two-state solution, and the most radical who refuse it do not need any arguments besides their radicalism in order to reject any binational idea. In Israel itself, hostility to this approach is one of the rare subjects of national consensus.
>
> A proposition that provokes such a universal rejection is, by definition, politically unrealistic, even assuming it could be viewed as desirable. If, however, Meron Benvenisti continues to brandish it and to explore its premises, it is not because of some sort of academic doggedness, but because he considers it, wrongly in my view, to be a lesser evil—and an inevitable lesser evil.[15]

A survey published in *Ha'aretz* in 2004 showed that two-thirds of Israelis "are strongly or moderately fearful" at the prospect of Israel's finding itself in a binational scenario. Hostility to the notion of binationalism grew in direct proportion to the prevailing urge to get rid of the Palestinians, one way or another through transfer or barrier wall, "disengagement" or "convergence" (see chapter 6 above), as expressed in the 2006 general elections.

Outside the country, reactions to statements in support of binationalism have been unprecedented in their vitriol. Tony Judt, a Jewish American academic, stated, in an article that appeared in the *New York Review of Books:* "The time has come to think the unthinkable, the two state solution—the core of the Oslo process . . . is probably already doomed. . . . The true alternative *[sic]* facing the Middle East in coming years will be between the ethnically cleansed greater Israel and a single, integrated, binational state of Jews and Arabs, Israelis and Palestinians." Judt put forth several arguments in favor of a binational state, one of which was that "the behavior of a self-described Jewish state affects the way everyone else looks at Jews. . . . The depressing truth is that Israel's current behavior is not just bad for America . . . the depressing truth is that Israel today is bad for the Jews."[16]

And indeed, it is not the chances or dangers of binationalism for Israel and Palestine that have been uppermost in the minds of Jewish American intellectuals, but the implications of the continued existence of the Jewish nation-state versus the creation of a binational state for their image and identity in their homes far from the Middle East, and the influence these alternatives might have on their peaceful lives there. Thus, an alarmed Leon Weiseltier attempts to shoot down Judt's binational state argument. "Judt and his editors have crossed the line from criticism of Israel's policy to the criticism of Israel's existence . . . they have taken the heroic step of calling for the dissolution of the Jewish state."[17] In other words, in Weiseltier's eyes, a binational state is nothing less than "Jewish homelessness"; indeed, not a political alternative for Israel but "a recipe for its destruction."

The debate has exited the realm of the political, or even the ideological, and is being conducted on an emotional level. Furthermore, some advocates of binationalism (all non-Israelis) use it to delegitimize Zionism and "to put an end to the anachronism of the Israeli nation-state." So, unlike me, they view binationalism not as a lamentable consequence of the protracted conflict but as a project that should replace the Israeli state. Ian Lustick displays a greater degree of equanimity in his approach to the matter. He writes: "I do believe binationalism is an important idea and that it deserves serious attention—not because it can replace the separate state idea as a target for diplomacy, but because we may never see a negotiated settlement, and thinking about how binationalism might arise as an unintended consequence of failed negotiations might make that failure less likely."[18]

DESCRIPTION, NOT PRESCRIPTION

My position has always been that binationalism is an unintended and lamentable consequence. My preference, as a Zionist, is for a Jewish nation-state, but I fear that the historical process that began in the aftermath of the 1967 war has brought about the gradual abrogation of this option. Hence, binationalism is not a political or ideological program so much as a de facto reality masquerading as a temporary state of affairs. It is a description of the current condition, not a prescription. Binationalism can even take the form of a fictitious "partition," allegedly fashioned in accordance with the Oslo Accords or as a result of "convergence," that will create an ostensibly separate entity called the Palestinian Authority or a Palestinian state.

The binationalism debate is taking place in the context of the perceived Palestinian "demographic threat" to the Jewish state and of fears for the cultural, or even physical, survival of the Jewish entity in Israel/Palestine. That is to say, all of the problems are being projected into the future and are not being dealt with in the immediate context, in the present. Thus, a de facto binational structure is, willy-nilly, becoming increasingly entrenched, based on direct and indirect control by the Jewish ethnic group over fragmented subgroups: Gazans, West Bankers, Jerusalemites, and Palestinian Israelis.

Debate on the issue of binationalism versus partition into two states is being conducted on an ideological and ethical plane, and its very existence is being presented to the Israeli public as constituting a threat—and the absolute negation—of the accepted and desired solution of partition ("the two-state solution"). For this reason, the precise definition of terms is regarded as unimportant. On the contrary, the arguments pro and con are presented in dichotomous terms, as being diametrically opposed—as if this were a genuine metapolitical, moral, and ethical dilemma. However, an examination of the two concepts (binationalism and partition) from a theoretical perspective and from the point of view of political attitudes toward them reveals that each has multiple variants incorporating diverse political structures. Moreover, a comparison of these models shows that the two concepts are not as dichotomous as they seem. Rather, they form a continuum, with some variants of each concept actually overlapping to a degree.

"Two states for two peoples" is generally perceived as implying the assumption that the state of Israel (in its 1948 borders) will continue to be "the state of the Jewish people," constructed on the model of "a tyranny of the majority," as it is today, where the Arab minority is denied collective political rights. Theoretically, of course, a model also exists for "a state of all its citizens," essentially a de facto binational state within the 1948 borders of Israel. As to the "Palestinian state," its innumerable variants make that designation ambiguous at best and at worst farcical. First, there is the Palestinian variant: a fully sovereign state within the borders as they stood on 4 June 1967 (i.e., the eve of the 1967 war)—or, according to others, the boundaries as laid out in the 1947 UN General Assembly Partition Resolution (# 181)—with free access to the outside world by land, sea, and air; total control of all its natural resources; sovereignty over the Old City of Jerusalem, including the Temple Mount / Haram al-Sharif and the whole area to the east of the 1949 armistice line; the dismantling of the settlements; and implementation of the Palestinian refugees' "right of return," with some flexibility of interpretation (but without losing sight of the principle).

Similar, although not identical, to this variant is the unofficial Geneva Accord model (of December 2003), under the terms of which several limitations (some of them temporary) would apply to the Palestinian state's sovereignty: 4 June 1967 borders—with "mutual" adjustments on a one-for-one basis in terms of land area; partition of Jerusalem (including the Old City); settlement blocks close to the border to remain under Israeli sovereignty. Another model, which was proposed at Camp David in July 2000 and subsequently at Taba, failed to receive the support required for its implementation. The then U.S. president, Bill Clinton, summarized that model as follows (7 January 2001): "Palestinian sovereignty over Gaza [and] the vast majority of the West Bank, the incorporation into Israel of settlement blocks. . . . For Palestine to be viable, it must be a geographically contiguous area . . . a non-militarized Palestine. [In Jerusalem] what is Arab should be Palestinian—what is Jewish should be Israeli. . . . [Jerusalem] should encompass the internationally recognized capitals of the two states—Israel and Palestine."[19] The borders of the Palestinian state were supposed, according to Clinton, to incorporate the whole of the Gaza Strip and between 94 and 96 percent of the West Bank, with territorial exchanges totaling no more than 3 percent.

Ariel Sharon—sworn opponent of the idea of a Palestinian state west of the Jordan River and the architect of the "Jordan is Palestine" scheme—surprised observers after he came to power by expressing support for a Palestinian state. Many saw this as a victory for the Left and as proof of the inevitability of a partition-based solution. In actuality, however, Sharon had been thinking in terms of a Palestinian state modeled on the South African "homelands" (or Bantustans) since the late 1970s. On the partition-binationalism continuum, Sharon's plan stands at the junction of the two alternatives. On the one hand, the Palestinian cantons fulfill the minimum requirements for being considered "a state"; on the other, these territories—cut off from the outside world, with no independent means of becoming economically viable and no physical infrastructure—are no more than semi-autonomous provinces, such as one might see in a decentralized binational structure.

All of the models that I have enumerated (and I have only listed the principal ones) supposedly come under the heading of "partition into two states." What is required in each case is, of course, agreement by both sides to the proposed partition; and so it remains an ideal and a slogan that it is convenient to bandy about, but that need not be put into practice, "since the other side is being inflexible."

And thus, a fluid, violent status quo persists—itself, as previously mentioned, a kind of undeclared de facto binationalism—where an Israeli government effectively controls the whole of what used to be Mandatory Palestine, either by sovereign rule within the boundaries of the state of Israel, through its military regime in the occupied territories, or indirectly through military and economic control of the boundaries. The Palestinian Authority, the establishment of which was mandated by the Oslo Accords, theoretically continues to function, but lacks the means to enforce its rule; and without massive monetary aid from the "donor nations," it would not be capable of carrying out even the limited civil functions (provision of education, health, municipal services) that it does. This de facto binational condition has endured in its present form for over twenty years. It became quasi-permanent in the wake of the signing of the peace agreement with Jordan (in 1994), which completed the final demarcation of the external perimeter of Eretz Israel / Palestine, following the international boundaries (excepting that of Syria) of Mandatory Palestine. This put the kibosh on the "Jordanian option," ending attempts to turn the occupied territories into a border area that could be annexed to a foreign country and thereby be prevented from becoming a national entity able to stand on its own feet.

"THE DEMOGRAPHIC THREAT"

The danger of a binational state is portrayed by its detractors, not in terms of the racist and discriminatory practices that are becoming a reality of everyday life in Israel, but by holding up the bogey of the "demographic threat." According to most forecasts, by the end of the first decade of this century, there will be more Arabs than Jews living in Eretz Israel / Mandatory Palestine. Continuation of this demographic trend, some Israeli pundits claim, will destroy the Jewish state and turn Israel into a country with a Jewish minority, just as in the Diaspora. A variety of ways to forestall this threat have been proposed, all of them difficult to implement, since they run counter to powerful interests. Israelis have therefore simply continued the practice of not collecting official data on the total number of non-Jewish inhabitants in the occupied territories, even while the numbers of Jews in Israel and in the settlements of the occupied territories are minutely monitored and presented together as belonging to "the population of the state of Israel." As in Lebanon, manipulation of population statistics can conveniently be used to show whatever demographic "balance" suits the ethnic group in power. It is precisely to "prove" that the demographic threat is indeed a bogey that frightens only the gullible that the some right-wing Israelis claim the statistics showing an Arab majority are fabricated by the Palestinian Statistics Bureau, which purportedly publishes tendentious data.

The argument over the question of when exactly there will be demographic parity between Jews and Arabs in the area west of the Jordan River shows no signs of abating. On the contrary, the disengagement from Gaza has made it a hot issue, whose character is clear: it is not about numbers, but ostensibly serves to provide scientific support for ideological positions. This debate, which has gone on since the beginning of the Zionist movement, has taken many forms. At times, it has served as a mobilizing tool for the moderate Left, and sometimes it has served the same purpose in the hands of the extreme Right. In its present form, it was used by opponents of disengagement who wanted to undermine one of the central arguments of those who supported the pullout from Gaza—that disengagement would remove more than one and a half million Palestinians from the demographic balance, ensuring a Jewish majority in the rest of Eretz Israel. There was no need for disengagement, its opponents argued, because the numbers released by the central bureaus of statistics—Israeli and Palestinian alike—are inflated, and demographic parity is a long way off, if it ever becomes a reality.

The supporters of disengagement and the proponents of separation have been sounding the alarm, claiming that demographic parity had already been reached in 2005, and that even if non-Jewish immigrants from the former Soviet Union are counted on the Jewish side of the balance, the decisive moment will arrive in a few years' time. But in the heat of the argument, the following questions are forgotten: What is so dramatic about demographic parity? What is the terrible significance of the loss of Jewish majority?

The answer, according to Zionists of every stripe, is obvious: A non-Jewish majority in the Land of Israel turns the Jewish community into a minority in its homeland. This argument, as understandable as it may be, has only been heard since what was a Jewish minority during the years of the British Mandate became the majority in the wake of the expulsion of hundreds of thousands of indigenous Palestinians in 1948 and the partitioning of the country. During the Mandate, the leaders of the Yishuv were not bothered by the fact that they represented a minority—some one-third of the population—in their demand for independence and self-determination. Nor did they see it as a slap in the face of democratic values when they rejected the demand of the majority—the Arab majority—for the establishment of a state that would accurately reflect demographic-ethnic ratios.

DEMOGRAPHY AND DEMOCRACY

The current fear of demographic parity is significant only if it is seen as evidence of adherence to democratic values; that is to say, if the Palestinians become a majority in Israel/Palestine, the Jewish community would lose its right to govern the state, which would thus lose its Jewish character. This approach carries a hidden assumption—that the Palestinians will obtain political rights that will allow them to translate their demographic strength into electoral power. But no one, in any Israeli political camp, is considering granting the Palestinians (even the Israeli-Arab minority) voting rights that could affect the character of the Jewish state, and at present only few Palestinians are interested in converting their struggle for self-determination into a struggle for civil rights.

The demographic bogey has meaning only when presented in relation to one specific binational model, that of "one man, one vote." This is the model of a centralized, unitary state where the civil rights of the individual citizen are respected but the collective rights of ethnic groups are not grounded in constitutional law—the model adopted in post-apartheid South Africa, for example. It works there both for historical reasons and because of the nature of the balance of demographic and economic power in that country, and also because the alternative is less attractive or is not achievable. The unitary binational model is wholly inappropriate for Israel/Palestine, for the simple reason that its presentation would result in perpetuating the supremacy of the Jewish ethnic group, securing its rule by undemocratic legislative measures and other means. A liberal democracy cannot function in a milieu such as Israel's, where ethnic polarization—political, economic, and cultural—runs deep. Here the problem is not one of individual rights but is focused on mutually incompatible collective rights, and the political system (elections, separation of powers) lacks the means for channeling the interethnic frictions.

One has a sneaking suspicion that Israeli public discourse concerns itself solely with the unitary binational model precisely because this is a truly unworkable option, thereby delegitimizing the whole concept of binationalism. There are, of course, other, more appealing binational models, whose implementation might be more efficient and practical than that of the partition option. Alternatively, preservation of the binational territory's integrity might prove to be simpler and less costly than "partition." There is also the possibility that the binational option might become unavoidable. That might be the case if, for instance, the Palestinians were to relinquish their claim to self-determination and demand in its place "civil equality"—or, in other words, if they were to agree to the annexation of the occupied territories to Israel on condition that they be granted individual and collective rights.

BINATIONAL MODELS

In this context, it should be pointed out that nearly all the intercommunal peace processes launched between 1989 and 2004 were based upon binational or multinational models. This fact flies in the face of the conventional wisdom that the binational model has failed everywhere in the world with the exception of Switzerland, Belgium, and Canada. One of the reasons binational models are used in the resolution of interethnic conflicts is that a partition solution—which requires the alteration of international borders—disturbs the existing geopolitical balance and gives rise to tensions in nearby countries. For example, resolution of the Kurdish problem via the partition of Iraq (or even by creating a federation) would send dangerous political shock waves throughout the three neighboring states, Iran, Turkey, and Syria, with their large Kurdish minorities. It is therefore preferable to retain the recognized international borders—which are like a mosaic, in that every little change distorts the picture and causes problems—and to aim, if possible, for *"soft" internal boundaries,* as in federated or confederated states.

Northern Ireland

Another example of a situation where partition is not an option is Northern Ireland, where it is impossible to draw internal ethnic boundaries, because the populations are intermingled. Hence the Good Friday Agreement outlines a framework for shared rule ("power-sharing"), the principal points of which are: a 108-member elected assembly with institutions to be set up "in proportion to the strengths of the [respective] parties"; decisions to be taken on a cross-community basis in one of two ways: decision by a majority of the members representing each community (Protestant Unionists and Catholic Nationalists) or by 60 percent of the members of the assembly, including at least 40 percent of the voting participants from each of the two communities; the government—consisting of prime minister and deputy prime minister—to be chosen by the assembly as decided by representatives of the two communities as described above; and the European Convention on Human Rights and the Northern Ireland Bill of Rights to serve as "safeguards ensuring that all sectors of the population will be able to participate and to work together successfully in the operation of these democratic institutions." The agreement enumerates steps to be taken to ensure ethnic parity in administration, the economy, urban planning, the financing of community institutions, and particularly in education, recruitment to the police force, housing, and the like. An Equality Commission was established to deal with complaints of default on the above conditions.

Bosnia

On 21 November 1995, in Dayton, Ohio, a peace agreement was signed that brought an end to the bloody intercommunal war in Bosnia-Herzegovina. The three communities—Serb, Bosniac (Muslim), and Croat—agreed (with mediation, encouragement, and pressure from many members of the international community) to preserve the existing borders of the state. Excerpts of the agreement:

> [Bosnia and Herzegovina] shall continue its legal existence under international law as a state with its internal structure modified as provided herein and with its present internationally recognized borders.
>
> Composition: Bosnia and Herzegovina shall consist of the two Entities, the Federation of Bosnia and Herzegovina and the Republika Srpska.
>
> International Standards: The rights and freedoms set forth in the European Convention for the Protection of Human Rights and Fundamental Freedoms and its Protocols shall apply directly in Bosnia and Herzegovina. These shall have priority over all other law.
>
> Citizenship: There shall be a citizenship of Bosnia and Herzegovina, to be regulated by the Parliamentary Assembly, and a citizenship of each Entity, to be regulated by each Entity, provided that: All citizens of either Entity are thereby citizens of Bosnia and Herzegovina.
>
> Parliamentary Assembly: The Parliamentary Assembly shall have two chambers: the House of Peoples and the House of Representatives.
>
> 1. House of Peoples: The House of Peoples shall comprise 15 Delegates, two-thirds from the Federation (including five Croats and five Bosniacs) and one-third from the Republika Srpska (five Serbs).
>
> 2. House of Representatives: The House of Representatives shall comprise 42 Members, two-thirds elected from the territory of the Federation, one-third from the territory of the Republika Srpska. . . .
>
> Presidency: The presidency of Bosnia and Herzegovina shall consist of three Members: one Bosniac and one Croat, each directly elected from the territory of the Federation, and one Serb directly elected from the territory of the Republika Srpska.[20]

The relatively satisfactory operation of this combination of federal-territorial components and power sharing is possible only because Bosnia-Herzegovina is essentially a NATO protectorate. A High Representative appointed by NATO has the final say, and policing powers are effectively international. The country, which was left in an economic shambles by the civil war, is able to function solely by dint of massive infusions of foreign aid. What is most important for our purposes, however, is the fact that the international community understood the advantages of preserving Bosnia's territorial integrity, preferring "soft" internal boundaries to rigid dividing lines, which would have made it difficult to travel freely and would have hindered economic recovery.

Cyprus

UN Secretary General Kofi Annan's program for the reunification of Cyprus was supposed to form the basis for that country's acceptance by the European Union. The plan did not earn the necessary majority in the plebiscite held in the Greek sector of the island and has therefore not been implemented as yet. Nonetheless, the components of the plan exemplify the principles that the UN would like to see play a fundamental role in the resolution of this and other intercommunal conflicts. The proposed arrangements are based on a united Cyprus and not a perpetuation of its division.

The plan is for a "bizonal" federation, which its supporters say has a better chance of managing relations between the two communities than squaring off behind the concrete walls that slice across the land and the capital. And even if this is still only a fond desire, there are some exciting formulations in the draft agreement (known as the "Annan Plan"): "Cyprus is our common home . . . we resolve that the tragic events of the past shall never be repeated . . . acknowledging each other's distinct identity and that our relationship is not one of majority and minority but of political equality . . . deciding to renew our partnership on that basis and determined that this new bizonal partnership shall ensure a common future in friendship, peace, security and prosperity in an independent Cyprus."[21]

The Annan plan describes a federated "bizonal" republic "modeled on the status and relationship of Switzerland," made up of two states, each of which "sovereignly exercises all powers not vested by the constitution in the federal government, organizing themselves freely under their own constitutions." The key word here is "bizonal," with the borders between the Turkish and Greek zones (after certain minor changes) left open, and all fences, walls, and obstacles removed.

The comparison between Cyprus and the situation in Israel/Palestine almost begs to be made: What is the difference between the physical and geopolitical separation here and the two-nation federation in Cyprus? How is it that international peace seekers have mobilized the prospect of membership in the European Union to achieve *unification* in Cyprus, whereas conversely they offer EU membership to Israel as an incentive for *dividing* the land into two states? Are not the values in the Annan plan of a common home, recognition of separate identities and the obligation to prevent the tragic past from ever repeating itself, applicable in Israel/Palestine?

Of course, I could cite Belgium, Canada, and Switzerland as models of successfully functioning multicommunal states. It is also worthy of note that—contrary to the popular view of Lebanon as an example of the failure of multicommunalism (or power-sharing)—in fact, ratification of the Taif Accord of 1989 brought an end to the civil war, thereby reaffirming the preexisting multicommunal Lebanese method of governance (with added guarantees of equality between Muslims and Christians).

Binationalism in Historical Perspective

Both the Zionist and Palestinian national movements have in the past entertained the idea of one state for the two peoples, whether as a unitary or a binational state. In the late 1960s, left-wing factions in the PLO proposed the model of a "secular democratic state," which was approved (with certain changes) at the PLO convention in 1969. In this "secular state," Jews and Arabs—including all the Palestinian refugees who might choose to return—would live together in one state that would be ruled by the Palestinian majority in coalition with Mizrahi Jews. This idea was rejected by most Palestinian groups, since it envisioned equal status for Jews "who had immigrated to Palestine and grabbed Palestinians' homes" and was, for that reason, regarded as "rewarding aggression." The Islamist factions opposed the establishment of a secular state on the grounds that this was not in accordance with Islamic law. To Israelis, the secular state seemed like a plot to destroy the Jewish-Zionist nation-state.

By 1974, the PLO had changed its strategic goals, replacing the ideal of the secular democratic state with the "strategy of stages" ("the establishment of a Palestinian state in any part of the country that becomes available, if necessary through a negotiated process" culminating in the eventual "liberation of all of historical Palestine"). This strategy, in turn, was replaced in 1988, this time, by willingness to agree to a permanent arrangement that would grant the Palestinians a state in the territory originally allotted to them in 1947 by the UN partition plan, later amended to acceptance of the lines set down in the armistice agreements concluded between February and July of 1949, which remained in place through 4 June 1967. Under this arrangement, the Palestinian state was to consist of the West Bank and Gaza Strip, with East Jerusalem as its capital, and the Palestinian "right of return" was to be implemented. The Palestinian imprimatur on "two states [as delineated by the Green Line] for two peoples" has thus been of relatively brief duration—less than two decades.

Every national liberation movement has as its objective the establishment of a sovereign state. The Zionist movement refrained from unequivocally defining its nationalist objectives until the mid 1940s. Its aim of establishing a sovereign Jewish state in Eretz Israel was implicit in its self-definition as a movement of national liberation, although throughout the years of the Yishuv, there was an ongoing debate over the advantages of making this aim explicit; this was the principal bone of contention between the followers of Revisionist Party leader Ze'ev Jabotinsky and the majority of the Zionist movement. The Zionist movement chose to formulate the goal of Zionism as follows: to turn Eretz Israel into an independent entity with a Jewish majority. The Zionist movement—for reasons that I shall not dwell on here—long contented itself with setting interim political objectives, which were modified in accordance with changing conditions. In chronological order, these were: a national home; unlimited immigration and the creation of a Jewish majority; "organic Zionism" (unrestricted settlement and the establishment of an independent Jewish economic sector); equal division of rule between Jews and Arabs ("parity"); a binational state; a federation of Jewish and Arab cantons; partition; and a Jewish "commonwealth." It was only in the early 1940s that an official demand was made for the establishment of a sovereign Jewish state. Even then, the territorial aspirations of the Zionist movement remained undefined. Many Zionists regarded agreement to proposals for the partitioning of Eretz Israel (by the Peel Commission in July 1937 and the UN in November 1947) merely as a stage along the way to the realization of the movement's full territorial aspirations, whereas others viewed partition as a fundamental compromise between the Zionist and Palestinian national movements. Subsequently, the absence of a clear definition of Zionism's goals proved to be the decisive factor in generating the intellectual confusion that prevailed when the West Bank and Gaza Strip were first occupied.

In the early stages of the Zionist enterprise—during the British Mandate—the idea of a binational state was accepted by the official Zionist establishment, including such prominent public figures as Chaim Weitzman and David Ben-Gurion. It should be recalled, however, that during that period, the Jewish Yishuv constituted less that 30 percent of the population of Eretz Israel / Palestine, and it was considered presumptuous to contemplate demanding a Jewish state; arrangements providing for Arab-Jewish parity in power-sharing seemed preferable. Even a federation of Jewish, Christian, and Muslim cantons might have mitigated the influence of the huge demographic disparity favoring the Arabs, which caused the Jewish Yishuv to oppose any British attempt to grant even a minimal degree of self-rule that would have placed the Jews in the position of a powerless minority. Luckily for the Jews, the Arabs opposed all efforts by the British to set up an advisory council alongside the government. The Arabs, though they would have held a majority of seats on such a council, opposed its establishment on principle because they absolutely denied the legitimacy of the British Mandate in Palestine, which included a commitment by Britain to implement the Balfour Declaration. For their part, the leadership of the Jewish community viewed the British government's plans regarding the establishment of a Palestinian state with an Arab majority (the White Paper of 1939) as a betrayal of its promise to the Yishuv and as reason for rebellion against the authorities.

A group of respected, though only marginally influential, Jewish intellectuals—foremost among whom were Martin Buber and the president of the Hebrew University, Yehuda Magnes—regarded a binational state as the embodiment of lofty ethical values and as the sole means of preventing a never-ending blood feud between Arabs and Jews. They championed the establishment in Eretz Israel / Palestine of a binational state based upon the Swiss model, though they placed greater emphasis on the principle of parity than on specifics. Indeed, they had no need for such details, since both the Palestinians and the Zionists rejected the binational concept, and many Jews viewed the mere proposing of such a plan as anti-Zionist treachery. The socialist Zionist Hashomer Hatza'ir movement adopted certain components of this program, but the founding of the state of Israel put an end to that initiative. The view that the only true realization of Zionism was a Jewish nation-state prevailed, and anyone whose support for this article of faith faltered was labeled a traitor.

The choice between a binational Eretz Israel / Palestine and partition was made twice. In 1937, the Peel Commission rejected the cantonization plan proposed by the Jewish Agency and opted for partition. In 1947, the UN General Assembly approved the partition Plan calling for the establishment of two states—as proposed by the majority faction of the Special Committee on Palestine—and rejected the minority proposal of a federal state. Following the 1967 war, it was the Israeli Right, of all people, who began to show enthusiasm for the binational model; of course, in a form suited to their ideology. The Labour party and groups associated with it advocated "territorial compromise," either by unilateral disengagement or by handing over parts of the occupied territories to Jordan ("the Jordanian option") or transferring them to the Palestinians (the Oslo Accords). Their ideological stance enabled them to define Israel's control of the territories as "temporary," and they elected "to decide not to decide" about their permanent status and also not to define the permanent territorial boundaries of Israel. They were thus able to entrench Israeli rule there without needing to concern themselves with the consequences that long-term control of the territories might have for the structure of the regime inside Israel.

The ideology of the Likud (the former Herut party), on the other hand, required it to adopt a stance of denying the temporary nature of Israeli control and rejecting its characterization as military rule. But the "Greater Israel" position itself collided with demographic reality and confronted the liberal-democratic faction of the Likud with the oft-repeated question, Did they want a Jewish state or a democratic one? Menachem Begin's reply to this conundrum derived from the reality he was familiar with from post–World War I eastern Europe: cultural—not territorial—autonomy for national minorities, as set out in the minorities' treaties that the states granted independence by the Treaty of Versailles in the aftermath of that war had signed. Begin's autonomy plan, as modified at Camp David (the 1978 Camp David Accord) added a territorial component, forming the basis upon which (with substantial adjustments) the concept that led to the Oslo Accords took shape. The Oslo Accords, too, can be thought of as de facto binational arrangements, since the Palestinian Authority's areas of jurisdiction—both geographical and legal—were deliberately left unclear, and the outer perimeter (the borders of Mandatory Palestine) remained in Israel's hands, as did control of the economy. Moreover, the whole series of convoluted agreements that came out of Oslo required tight coordination with the Israeli government; and considering the vast imbalance in Israel's favor, it was clear that the Palestinian Authority would be granted inferior powers—essentially giving it the status of a glorified provincial, or even municipal, ruling body.

The settlers—whose efforts to gain control over the land on the West Bank and to colonize it had played such a significant role in the creation of the de facto binational condition—proposed that the Palestinians content themselves with what Menachem Begin had offered them; that is, cultural and local autonomy. Others strove to revive the Jordanian option, wherein the Palestinians would vote for representatives to the Jordanian parliament.

Ariel Sharon and Ehud Olmert's unilateral "disengagement/convergence" plan and the ensuing cantonization of the West Bank fitted well into the Likud's version of binationalism, which had gone through numerous permutations, but remained as it had been, a mix of direct and indirect control over the entire territory of what had been Mandatory Palestine without any clear definition of the character of the overall regime. The prevailing Israeli solution of calling the "disengaged" Gaza Strip and the cantons of the West Bank a state is a distorted variation that combines the worst aspects of the two ends of the spectrum, partition and a unitary state.

ISOLATED PHENOMENA MISUNDERSTOOD

The fact that the existing binational reality is not perceived as such, and that in liberal circles, people have the impression that the majority of the Israeli public supports the establishment of a Palestinian state—and that, therefore, "all the options are open"—makes it possible to treat measures such as the construction of the barrier wall and "disengagement" as isolated phenomena, without taking in the overall picture. Warnings—and, of course, binational plans—are received with scorn by these liberal spokespersons, who up to only a few years ago reserved their scorn, or outright revulsion, for the idea of a Palestinian state.

The continuing violence, Israel's oppressive measures in the occupied territories, and the disarray in the Palestinian Authority have caused those who speak on behalf of the Palestinians, and their supporters in the Western world, to become increasingly interested in the option of a binational state. The number of articles, meetings, and conferences dealing with binationalism has grown dramatically in recent years. In Israel, too, this has begun to be discussed, albeit on the margins of intellectual discourse—although even the Zionist Left dismisses the idea as "anti-Zionist," impractical and dangerous, not to mention as "a plot to spoil the chances of the establishment of a Palestinian state." The following are excerpts from an interview with me conducted by the Israeli-Palestinian e-zine *Bitterlemons* (19 January 2004):

> *Bitterlemons:* Is a viable two-state solution no longer feasible?
>
> *Benvenisti:* We have a problem of definition. What two states? Viable solution or viable states? This needs a lot of clarification. By now the chances for two completely separate sovereign states, say resembling Israel and Jordan, are impossible. To make that surgical partition and create boundaries that leave both states independent and sovereign in all respects is impossible. . . .
>
> *Bitterlemons:* Is a single-state solution good for Israelis?

Benvenisti: A single state can be a model for [a] "soft" partition, as opposed to a surgical partition with finite borders that separates two distinct political entities. You can come up with a model of power sharing on the federal level and sharing the territory. The boundaries of the provinces will be softer than the rigid borders of two political entities, and this can resolve some of the problems that surgical partition exacerbates. . . .

Bitterlemons: Is the Palestine Liberation Organization (PLO) capable of making the switch? . . .

Benvenisti: Now, absolutely not—nor is the Zionist establishment in Israel. The PLO thrives on the two-state solution; the Palestinian National Authority [PNA] cannot survive without it. It is only when [Palestinians] face the total bankruptcy of the PNA and its failure that they will understand that not only did [the PNA] not do anything, it ruined the chances of the Palestinians to get anything out of the Israelis. The notion that there is a PNA is what allows the ongoing occupation.

Bitterlemons: Are there Palestinians who advocate your point of view?

Benvenisti: There are a lot of them, but others cherish the pipe dream that they'll win the battle of the womb. A system that allows the automatic victory of those that breed [i.e., most rapidly] is impossible. I don't suggest that Israel commit suicide. My system can be made to work with the Palestinians. This is a Siamese twins situation of Israel and Palestine living in one ecosystem in which only close binational cooperation will work. If there's no close cooperation nothing will happen, and Israeli domination and superior power will be the case forever.

Bitterlemons: So matters will get worse before they get better?

Benvenisti: Things are already bad enough. The only thing not clear to people is where they are. Once the illusions are dispelled, people on both sides will have to turn to interim agreements as steps toward the creation of new conditions and a new level of cooperation.[22]

A SAMPLE OF THE DEBATE

In November 2003, a seminar was held at the Palestinian Academic Society for the Study of International Affairs (PASSIA), a research institute in East Jerusalem headed by Dr. Mahdi Abdul Hadi, some of the notes from which I have chosen to present below as an illustration of the substance of this debate. Equal numbers of Israelis and Palestinians participated in the deliberations; several weeks later, a similar event was held at the Van Leer Institute in West Jerusalem.

THE CONCEPT OF "BINATIONALISM" —
A SUMMARY OF MERON BENVENISTI'S POSITION

The first key point to be stressed is that binationalism is not a plan for the future or a proposed solution, but a currently existing condition. It is a description of the current conflict not a prescription. It is important to stress this point and make sure a distinction is drawn between the two. The model of the "binational condition" is meant to provide a framework in which a viable solution can be developed.

Some further points:

* The term "binational condition" is preferable to the occupier/occupied model because it captures the mutual interdependence of the two societies and their physical, economic, etc., interconnection.

* When a two-state model is proposed, it is presumably the case that an extensive degree of co-operation between the two entities will be envisaged (e.g., on water, security, etc.). It is only a small step from there to seeing how really there is only one state in operation on this model.

* There is a huge disparity of power between the two communities and this must be acknowledged in any peace negotiations. Israel has used this disparity to its advantage in the past (as the more powerful entity) during peace talks to push for agreements that work in its favor. An equitable agreement must seek to redress this imbalance if it is to be durable.

Attempts to apply a two-state model will simply result in "cantonization." A Palestinian "state" would be too weak to be an equal partner to Israel and would end up simply being an appendage to Israel, reliant on that state, especially economically. A two-state approach only succeeds in postponing the hard questions to a future stage.
Discussion:

Several individuals at the seminar expressed dissatisfaction with this model. The following points were raised:

* A common viewpoint was that two separate states are highly desirable in the short term at least, in order to achieve some kind of separation between the two communities. This is something which majority opinion on both sides is in favor of.

* A one-state model is unworkable and would lead to civil war or major internal strife of some kind (Lebanon is cited as an example). The only possibility of peace is via a separation of the two nations into their own polities.

* A two-state solution is the best approach; it has failed in the past because it has not been attempted properly, not because it is fundamentally unworkable. "Oslo" was flawed because it lacked an end-

stage, and all substantive issues were left to some unspecified future date.

- The kind of model advocated by individuals such as Meron Benvenisti is likely to prove particularly unpopular in Israel. The whole Zionist project is based on the notion of a sovereign state that is exclusively for the Jewish people. Any kind of one-state agreement would place that in jeopardy.

In general, opponents of binationalism focused on the unworkability of a one-state model, either because it was undesirable to one or both communities, or because it would be unstable (like Lebanon). Given sufficient political will and proper leadership, a two-state model can be made to work. Just as Israeli Prime Minister Begin went against public opinion with regards to dismantling settlements in the Sinai, so it will be possible to implement the kinds of changes that will make a Palestinian state possible.

Responses to these points:

The speaker, along with other participants partly or wholly sympathetic to his viewpoint, addressed these criticisms at length.

- The idea that "separation" is achievable is illusory. The two communities are too intertwined for any kind of division to be possible. Attempts to remove the settlers, to take one example, are likely to be unsuccessful as they are too firmly rooted on the West Bank.

- Although it is fair to say that some of the attempts at one-state, power-sharing models have failed elsewhere (e.g., in Lebanon), it is also true that all recent peace deals in ethnic/intercommunal disputes have been based on some form of power-sharing model. Partition has not been seen as a viable option.

- Several people pointed out that two-state models have been pursued for decades without success. What reason is there to think that future attempts will prove to be more successful? Oslo failed, not because it was not properly formulated, but because it was based on the false premise that a two-state solution was possible.

The key argument is that opponents of the binational model are ignoring the high degree of interconnection between the two nations. A two-state model would only be possible if there was at least some degree of equality between the two communities, but given the relative powerlessness of the Palestinians such an approach would only generate future problems.

Conclusion:

There was little agreement on the Israeli side with Meron's position. Most felt that a binational unitary state model would be unworkable, either because it would lead to serious internal conflict, as in the case of neighboring Lebanon, or because it would be unacceptable to Israelis (because it would fatally compromise the Zionist project; i.e., the notion of an exclusively Jewish state). On the Palestinian side there was much more sympathy with the idea of some kind of one-state solution, but a belief that in the short term at least it would be unpopular among ordinary Palestinians because of a strong desire for separation from the Israelis. In addition, it is likely that PNA would perceive any attempt to move to a one-state model as a threat to their position.[23]

DEBATE AS ESCAPE FROM REALITY

The intensification of Israeli enmity toward Palestinians and of expressions of ethnic estrangement—amounting to the commencement of a descent into a morass of racism—accompanied by almost complete indifference to the day-to-day lot of more than three and a half million Palestinians who are routinely being subjected to the plundering of their land and resources and the trampling of their honor and are experiencing the collapse their education, health-care, and welfare systems—all of this has transformed the debate over "the solution" into one more escape from reality. Inherent in Israeli support for separation, partition, or a Palestinian state is the desire to externalize the Palestinian problem and to label it as a matter that touches Israeli society only insofar as it poses a military and political threat, but not as a subject requiring humanitarian or moral consideration. The Gaza Strip, for example, ceased to be an Israeli problem the moment the IDF pulled out and became, in Israeli eyes, "a foreign country." Israelis have as little concern for the fates of the Palestinians in Gaza as they do for those of the impoverished millions in India or Egypt.

Israelis reject out of hand the claim that they created the problem of the Palestinian refugees (who make up the majority of the Gaza Strip's population), since "the Arabs started the war." Just as Israelis (and, notably, the liberals among them: those sensitive to injustice) salve their consciences and atone for past mistakes and misdeeds by supporting the concept of a Palestinian state, they project their fears for the future onto the "binational state"—the incarnation of all the hypothetical dilemmas that will never (they hope) become real problems. In the prevailing circumstances, what does it matter whether one supports "two states for two peoples" or a federal state, power-sharing in the context of a "consociational democracy," cantonization, or other models, some of which have been elaborated above?

In the current situation, all it is possible to do is to deal with the immediate problems that are the result of the oppression and the violation of basic rights and human dignity, and to attempt to redress historic injustices and remedy ethnically based discrimination—and the rest of the problems that are the outcome of a state of war that has dragged on for more than a century. Above all, we are obligated to do battle with prejudices and stereotypes, with propaganda that portrays Palestinians as subhuman and Israelis as brutal taskmasters.

The bottom line is this: The coexistence of the two national communities is a destiny that cannot be avoided. This coexistence must be based upon communal equality and ethical principles, human dignity, and freedom; otherwise, it will not endure, but will again descend into violence. The nature of the constitutional framework for this coexistence is secondary. In any case, productive discussion of this topic will only be possible when the people of this region have taken psychological ownership of the binational condition that has been thrust upon them and have begun to strive together to pave a road to reconciliation.

Epilogue

Some years ago, before it became fashionable to bash the sons of the founding fathers, I participated in a conference on "Israeli Identity." When asked, "What, to you, defines being Israeli?" I replied, quite arrogantly, "My youth."

In my opinion, this response contained a modicum of truth, or at least subjective truth: in essence, I was heir to a stereotypical Israeli identity; and one can—by using my family's CV and my own—construct a composite picture of what is customarily, perhaps somewhat anachronistically, described as "the Israeli identity." Note the images that I invoke and the elements of my identity that I am able to list in support of my claim to membership in the select company of "authentic Israelis": I am the son of a man who arrived in Palestine with the Second Aliya, and my mother is from the Third Aliya; on my father's side I have roots in Jerusalem that go as far back as the sixteenth century; on one side, I am the grandson of a graduate of the renowned Volozhyn Yeshiva in Lithuania, and on the other, the great-grandson of the head of the rabbinical court of the Salonika Jewish community. Thus I am a Sephardi-Ashkenazi hybrid, and my late aunts had names like Sonia, Frieda, and Gita, as well as Lucia, Donna, and Luna. In my parents' home, I could hear firsthand accounts of my father's exploits in the Jewish Legion during World War I and my mother's experiences as a nurse in the Jewish Quarter of Hebron during the disturbances of 1929.

I come from a home where no language but Hebrew was spoken: with a Sephardi father and an Ashkenazi mother, the only common language was Hebrew. The family I come from was dedicated to the principal ethos of Israeliness, "Knowing the Land."

My personal journey was no less stereotypical: the youth movement and its trademark blue shirt, the kibbutz, hiking, and archeology. And later on: involvement in the political establishment, Jewish-Arab relations, Israeli-Palestinian dialogue, confrontations between doves and hawks. Have I left out anything?

I can identify with each and every one of the almost sacrosanct elements that together constitute the collective Israeli identity. I hardly need list them: Zionism, Jewishness and the ingathering of exiles, Sephardi-Ashkenazi unity, and homeland and defense and peace. These are all documented in my family album—and for me they are real. This is neither a rented identity nor a purchased one; these are my personal experiences and those of my parents. Of course, I am not unique. I belong to "the first generation of redemption," itself a Zionist myth. We were the first to spring from this soil and can take pride in authentic Israeliness, in the sense of being the first modern Jewish natives of this land. I will therefore not allow anyone to call me a traitor, and I will not allow anyone to say that I am not from here; not even the Palestinians will I allow to say I am not from here. I am as much a part of this land as its stones.

I am exactly what my father wanted me to be, a native. He wanted me to grow like a tree from the soil, to be a natural part of the landscape. And he may have succeeded: I am a son of this land. But this is a land that has always had Arabs in it; it is a land where the Arabs are the human landscape, the natives. Hence, I do not fear them. I cannot see myself living here without them. To me, Eretz Israel without Arabs is a barren land.

This is a bizarre statement when the prevailing mood—and the political agenda—in my land are focused on getting rid of the Palestinians, one way or another. It is probably derived from my anachronistic and nostalgic infatuation with the distant past, when one viewed the Arabs as either neighbors or intimate enemies, but omnipresent. Now, when one can hide behind a concrete wall, proto-racist attitudes, or "separation" schemes, it is possible to externalize them. The vanishing Palestinians are not a unique Israeli phenomenon. Amerindians were taken for granted as members of the white neighborhoods in the United States until the early decades of the nineteenth century, but they later disappeared from the lives of the whites and became "rare curios and exotic specimen[s]."[1] I guess that my political views are based on the anachronistic intimate relation with my Arab neighbors, and the antagonism toward binationalism originates in the attempt to evaporate the Arabs.

The Israeli identity of a man like myself is supposedly so deeply engrained that he has no doubts about it, and this should evidently make me immune to all bewilderment and all obsessive preoccupation with the question of Israeli identity. What I have observed in myself is precisely the opposite. As socialization to the values that I listed earlier has come to be the cornerstone of Jewish education and the defining of personal identity (not only for those living here in Israel, but essentially for the entire Jewish world), so I could see myself moving in exactly the opposite direction, stripping off these values one by one. For what had happened—it seemed to me—was that many artists had taken this composite picture of "the Israeli" and, by emphasizing certain of its aspects and inflating them out of all proportion, ended up with a monster. Everything is still there in the new version, but it is all exaggerated, synthetic, inflated—in a word, kitsch. What I perceived in my youth as a balanced and harmonious set of values has become a collection of empty symbols serving merely as a means of justification for a self-serving policy of force; for a self-righteous rolling of eyes—in the advancement personal and collective interests—all in the name of the sacred values with which I supposedly identify.

These values remain sacrosanct simply because they have been successfully realized. People continue to revere them, not understanding that every value is a double-edged sword—that for every moral stance there exists an immoral alternative. This, in my opinion, is the reason that I began to shed all these values, one by one—including those that are regarded as being inescapable, such as the importance of one's ethnic identity. I am grateful to my parents, not for imbuing me with collective values, but rather for teaching me to live with the contradictions that were the outcome of their own conflicted identities.

Yes, you can tell me that I am a walking mass of internal contradictions and have become marginalized, a person espousing strange, heretical ideas. You can tell me that my prescriptions are in error. Yet my diagnosis is correct: even within the boundaries of 1967, Israel is well on the way to becoming a binational state. In another decade, when Arab citizens of Israel proper (excluding the occupied territories) constitute 25 percent of the Israeli population, it will be a binational state. The attempt to fight the "demographic threat" by dragging more and more new immigrants from every remote corner on earth has been carried to absurd extremes. These new immigrants are liable to cause the implosion of Israeli society. So I think the time has come to declare that the Zionist revolution is over. The paradigm of multiculturalism and binationalism should be the conceptual universe we reconcile ourselves to.

Could things have worked out differently? Not necessarily. The Zionist idea was wrongheaded from the outset. It did not take into account the presence here of another national group. Therefore, from the moment the Zionist movement decided that it was not going to get rid of the Arabs, its dream became unattainable. This land cannot accommodate two sovereignties, so the options are terribly simple: either one nation will not be or the other nation will not be, or one nation will subjugate the other and condemn itself to perpetual enmity, or both nations will forgo their demand for full sovereignty. That is what I am now proposing to both the Jews and the Palestinians on an equal basis.

In 1948, Zionism was truly victorious. It succeeded in consolidating itself in 78 percent of historic Palestine. But in 1967, Zionism won one victory too many; and in the twenty years that followed, it sealed its fate by implementing the settlements project and undertaking the de facto annexation of the West Bank. Paradoxically, the peace treaties with Egypt and Jordan only exacerbated the situation, because they determined the outer limit of the borders of western Palestine. They sealed us into the binational reality of a territory that cannot be divided. The result is that now Zionism has become the victim of its victories, the victim of a terrible history of missed opportunities.

I am not happy about what I am proposing. I know that what I am struggling to express here is not truly a solution, because even if some sort of federal structure is established here, it won't bring peace. There will not be peace here. Even if there is some sort of binational arrangement, it will do no more than contain the crisis. Violence will always be waiting in the wings.

The problem is that the whole situation that has evolved in our society is one of antagonisms and contradictions and the absence of solutions. And because of that, I am today a sad and pessimistic person, beset by a profound sense of brokenness. It has not been easy for me to bid farewell to my father's dream of a Jewish nation-state. For most of my life, it was my dream, too. But now I really fear for my grandchildren. Every time I look around me, I fear for my grandchildren. How will they live here? What am I leaving them?

Because I know that there is neither a Jewish nation-state nor two states for two peoples here, I seize on this faint hope that maybe, after all, something shared will evolve instead. That maybe, despite every-thing, we shall learn to live together. Maybe we shall come to under-stand that the Others are not demonic, that they, too, are part of this place.

I was born in the old Rothschild Hospital on Prophets Street, and my burial plot is ready beside those of my ancestors in the old Sephardic sec-tion of the cemetery on the Mount of Olives—the section called al-Buraq, the Arabic name for the Western Wall. The distance between these two sites is about a kilometer as the crow flies. In this space, my identity is rooted. I do not need to depict it in complex and sophisticated terms. Indeed, in my opinion, the whole game of identity definition reflects the immigrant's lack of connection. Natives don't question their identity.

It seems that one issue has been settled for me. I did not know where to begin the story, but I know where to end it. Is that not the ultimate victory of Zionism and the fulfillment of my parents' aspirations? I am rooted here like these cypresses. Like these orchards. What the land brings forth.

Notes

CHAPTER 1. A FOUNDING FATHER

Unless otherwise specified, all quotations are from David Benvenisti's archives in the author's possession.

1. *Jewish Community Book: Suwalk and Vicinity* (in Hebrew) (Tel Aviv: Yair Publishing House, 1989), 83.

2. David Benvenisti and Pinchas Cohen, *Guide to Eretz Israel* (in Hebrew) (Jerusalem: self-published, 1937).

3. Meron Benvenisti, *Sacred Landscape: The Buried History of the Holy Land since 1948*, trans. Maxine Kaufman-Lacusta (Berkeley: University of California Press, 2000).

4. Daniel Pipes, *Middle East Quarterly,* March 2000; www.danielpipes .org/article/847 (accessed 2 July 2006).

CHAPTER 2. DELAYED FILIAL REBELLION

1. Meron Benvenisti, *The Sling and the Club* (in Hebrew) (Jerusalem: Keter, 1988), 58–59.

2. Meron Benvenisti, *Ha'aretz,* 16 March 1995.

3. Benvenisti, *The Sling and the Club,* 149.

4. Israel Bartal, *Cathedra 100* (in Hebrew) (Jerusalem: Yad Ben Zvi, 2001), 26.

5. Benvenisti, *The Sling and the Club,* 20.

6. Ibid.

7. Ibid.

8. James Morris, *Heaven's Command: An Imperial Progress* (New York: Harcourt Brace, 1973), 457.

9. Erez Tzfadia in Meron Benvenisti, ed., *The Morning After* (Jerusalem: Carmel Publishing and Hebrew University, 2002), 257–322.

10. Baruch Kimmerling, *The End of Ashkenazi Hegemony* (in Hebrew) (Jerusalem: Keter, 2001), 11–12.

11. Yossi Yonah, *Ha'aretz,* book section, 7 November 2001.

12. Amos Oz, *But There Are Two Different Wars* (in Hebrew) (Jerusalem: Keter, 2002), 90–91.

13. Ben-Dror Yemini, *Kav Hashesa* (in Hebrew) (Tel Aviv: Yediot, 2001), 44.

CHAPTER 3. JERUSALEMITES

1. Amos Oz, interviewed by Ari Shavit, *Ha'aretz,* supplement, 1 March 2002. And see also Amos Oz, *A Tale of Love and Darkness* (in Hebrew) (Jerusalem: Keter, 2002), trans. Nicholas de Lange (Orlando, Fla.: Harcourt, 2004).

2. Oz, interviewed by Shavit, *Ha'aretz,* supplement, 1 March 2002.

3. Avirama Golan, *Ha'aretz Books,* 2 September 2005

4. Amos Oz, quoted in *Ha'aretz,* 1 March 2002.

5. Ibid.

6. Ibid.

7. Edward Said, *Out of Place: A Memoir* (New York: Knopf, 1999), 111.

8. Ibid., 109.

9. Meron Benvenisti in *Ha'aretz,* 25 August 2000.

10. Edward Said in *Ha'aretz,* 30 August 2000.

11. Zeev Sternhell, *The Founding Myths of Israel, Nationalism, Socialism, and the Making of the Jewish State* (in Hebrew) (Tel Aviv: Am Oved, 1999), quoted here from David Maisel's translation of the French original (Princeton, N.J.: Princeton University Press, 1998), 177.

12. Amos Oz, *But There Are Two Different Wars* (in Hebrew) (Jerusalem: Keter, 2002), 92.

13. Muki Tsur, "The Lost Generation" (1989 Israeli television Channel 1 documentary).

14. Meron Benvenisti, "Crusaders and Zionists," in "Israelis Reply," *Bulletin of Tel Aviv University Students of Middle East Affairs,* no. 28 (June 1973).

15. Meron Benvenisti, *Jerusalem, the Torn City* (Minneapolis: University of Minnesota Press, 1976).

16. Meron Benvenisti, *Conflicts and Contradictions* (New York: Villard Books, 1986).

17. Meron Benvenisti, *The Sling and the Club* (in Hebrew) (Jerusalem: Keter, 1988), 127–29.

18. *Jerusalem Post International Edition,* 19 September 1978.

19. Interview by Yaron London, *Monitin Magazine,* Summer 1979.

20. Eric A. Nordlinger, *Conflict Regulation in Divided Societies* (Cambridge, Mass.: Center for International Affairs, Harvard University, 1972), 9.

21. Meron Benvenisti in *Ha'aretz,* 10 January 2002.

22. See www.fmep.org/documents/clinton_parameters12–23–00.html (accessed 10 August 2006).

23. Meron Benvenisti in *Ha'aretz,* 28 December 2000.

24. Dan Pagis, *Kol Hashirim* (All Poems) (in Hebrew) (Tel Aviv: Hakibbutz Hameuchad, 1991), trans. Maxine Kaufman-Lacusta.

CHAPTER 4. "THE CEREMONY OF INNOCENCE IS DROWNED . . ."

1. Meron Benvenisti in *Ha'aretz,* 7 June 2001.

2. Meron Benvenisti in *Ha'aretz,* 25 February 2002.

3. S. Yizhar, *Hirbat Hizaa [sic]* (in Hebrew) (Tel Aviv: Zmora-Bitan, 1989), 33. Yizhar was probably the most prominent Israeli writer of the postindependence period.

4. Meron Benvenisti in *Ha'aretz,* 30 May 2004.

5. www.mzv.cz/servis/soubor.asp?id=1873 (accessed 29 June 2006).

6. *Ha'aretz,* 7 October 1999.

7. "An Urgent Statement to the Israeli Public," www.fiz.huji.ac.il/~damita/sito_pol/ISR_PAL/Pal_int_stat.html (accessed 13 August 2006).

8. Elis Zureik, *Palestine Refugees and the Peace Process* (Washington, D.C.: Institute of Palestine Studies, 1996), 47–48.

9. David Grossman in *Yediot Aharonot* (in Hebrew), 28 March 1997.

CHAPTER 5. THE MORNING AFTER

1. Meron Benvenisti, ed., *The Morning After* (in Hebrew) (Jerusalem: Carmel Publishing and Hebrew University, 2002), 54.

2. Proceedings of the opening session of the Morning After Project (internal papers), 8 February 2001, 70–80.

3. Sarah Helman in Majd al-Haj and Uri Ben-Eliezer, eds., *In the Name of Security* (in Hebrew) (Haifa: Haifa University, 2003).

4. Zeev Sternhell in *Ha'aretz,* 7 November 2003.

5. Michael Feige in Benvenisti, ed., *Morning After,* 521.

6. Ilan Saban, ibid., 65.

7. Ibid., 79

8. Daniel Levin, ibid., 19.

9. Sufian Kabaha, ibid., 129.

10. Erez Tzfadia, ibid., 257.

11. Sigal Ben-Porat, in ibid., 407.

12. Moshe Ya'alon, interview by Ari Shavit, *Ha'aretz,* 30 August 2002.

13. Ben-Porat in Benvenisti, ed., *Morning After,* 411.

14. Ya'alon, interview by Shavit, *Ha'aretz,* 30 August 2002.

15. Tzfadia in Benvenisti, ed., *Morning After,* 278–82.

16. David Benvenisti, *Israel Arzennu* (Israel Our Land) (in Hebrew) (Jerusalem: Kiriyt Sepher, 1946), 46.

17. Tamar Achiron-Frumkin in Benvenisti, ed., *Morning After,* 203.

18. Quotations in the related text here are all from Dirk Sadovsky, ed., *Israel 2025: Scenarios for Israeli Society* (in Hebrew) (Herzliya, Israel: Friedrich Ebert Foundation, 2001).

CHAPTER 6. SEPARATION AND DISENGAGEMENT

1. See Meron Benvenisti, *Intimate Enemies: Jews and Arabs in a Shared Land* (Berkeley: University of California Press, 1995), 184–96.

2. Meron Benvenisti, "Birds and Moles," *Ha'aretz,* 1 July 1999.

3. Michael Waltzer, *The Company of Critics* (New York: Basic Books, 2002), chap. 8, "Albert Camus and the Algerian War," 139.

4. See Heribert Adam and Kogila Moodley, *Seeking Mandela: Peacemaking between Israelis and Palestinians* (Philadelphia: Temple University Press, 2005).

5. Dov Weisglass, interview with Ari Shavit, *Ha'aretz,* 7 October 2004.

6. U.S. Department of State, Office of the Spokesman, "A Performance-Based Roadmap to a Permanent Two-State Solution to the Israeli-Palestinian Conflict" (press statement, Washington, D.C., 30 April 2003), www.state.gov/r/pa/prs/ps/2003/20062.htm (accessed 13 June 2006).

7. "President Welcomes Palestinian President Abbas to the White House," www.whitehouse.gov/news/releases/2005/10/20051020.html (accessed 13 June 2006).

8. Weisglass cited in n. 5 above.

9. *Ha'aretz,* 5 and 13 April 2004.

10. Weisglass cited in n. 5 above.

11. David Ben-Gurion, *From the Diary: The War of Independence,* ed. Gershon Rivlin and Elhanan Oren (in Hebrew) (Tel Aviv: Ministry of Defense, 1986), 444.

12. Motti Golan, *Wars Don't Just Happen* (in Hebrew) (Ben Shemen, Israel: Modan 2002), 168–85.

13. *Yediot Aharonot,* 14 January 2006.

14. *Maariv,* 14 January 2006.

15. www.standwithus.com/news_post.asp?NPI=625 (accessed 14 August 2006).

16. See Geoffrey Aronson, "Disengagement's Uncertain Fate," *Foundation for Middle East Peace Settlement Report* 16, no. 4 (July–August 2006), www.fmep.org/reports/vol16/no4/01-disengagements_uncertain_fate.html (accessed 14 August 2006).

17. Amir Peretz quoted in *Ha'aretz,* 13 July 2006.

18. *Ha'aretz,* 15 August 2006.

CHAPTER 7. DESCRIPTIONS AND PRESCRIPTIONS

1. Meron Benvenisti, "The Turning Point in Israel," *New York Review of Books,* 13 October 1983.

2. Anthony Lewis, "Israel's Bitter West Bank Harvest," *New York Times Magazine,* 22 July 1984.

3. Meron Benvenisti, *The West Bank Data Project* (Washington, D.C.: AEI, 1984), back cover.

4. Abba Eban, "The Central Question," *Tikkun* 1 (1986): 22.

5. Amos Oz quoted in Roger Friedland and Richard Hecht, *To Rule Jerusalem* (New York: Cambridge University Press, 1996), 179.

6. Shimon Peres quoted in Yigal Sarne, *Hadashot,* 3 January 1986.

7. Yossi Sarid, *Ha'aretz,* 22 September 1990.

8. Thomas L. Friedman in Meron Benvenisti, *Intimate Enemies: Jews and Arabs in a Shared Land* (Berkeley: University of California Press, 1995), "Foreword: Jeremiah and Jonah," viii–ix.

9. *Ha'aretz,* 15 September 1993.

10. Ian Lustick, *Unsettled States, Disputed Lands: Britain and Ireland, France and Algeria, Israel and the West Bank* (Ithaca, N.Y.: Cornell University Press, 1993), 11–37.

11. Gary Sussman, "Is the Road to Bi-nationalism Paved with Unilateral Intentions?" (draft for discussion, early 2004; by permission of the author).

12. Yosef Gorni, *Ha'aretz,* 12 December 2003.

13. Ari Shavit, "Cry the Beloved Two-State Solution," *Ha'aretz Weekend Supplement,* 8 August 2003; id., 15 August 2003, letters to the editor.

14. Uri Avnery, "One State Solution Ploy Too Dangerous," *Palestine Chronicle,* 2 October 2003.

15. Ran Halévi, "Israel and the Question of the National State," *Policy Review* (Hoover Institution), no. 124 (April–May 2004). Translation by Robert Howse of an article that originally appeared in French in *Le Debat* (Gallimard).

16. Tony Judt, "Israel, the Alternative," *New York Review of Books,* 23 October 2003.

17. Leon Weiseltier, "Israel, Palestine, and the Return of the Bi-national Fantasy: What Is to Be Done," *New Republic,* 27 October 2003.

18. Ian S. Lustick, "The Cunning of History," *Boston Review,* December 2001–January 2002, http://bostonreview.net/BR26.6/lustick.html (accessed 12 August 2006)

19. www.bitterlemons.org/docs/clinton.html (accessed 14 August 2006).

20. www.mtholyoke.edu/acad/interel/bostalk.htm (accessed 18 July 2006).

21. www.hri.org/docs/annan_plan_april2004.pdf (accessed 18 July 2006).

22. www.bitterlemons.org/previous/bl190104ed3.html#pal2 (accessed 14 August 2006).

23. www.passia.org/meetings/2003/Nov12-Text.htm (accessed 14 August 2006).

EPILOGUE

1. Gordon S. Wood, "The Divided Ground," *New York Review of Books,* 6 April 2006, 50–51.

Index

Text: 10/13 Sabon
Display: Sabon
Compositor, printer, and binder: Sheridan Books, Inc.
Indexer: Roberta Engleman